# A MENNONITE WOMAN IN TWO WORLDS

## Janet Runion Patton

### Illustrated by Charles A. Patton

*For Kathie, Blessings*

*Janet RPatton*

Xulon Press
www.XulonPress.com

Xulon Press books are available in bookstores everywhere, and on the Web at www.XulonPress.com.

❧

*For*
*our mothers,*
*Mildred Elizabeth Runion*
*and*
*Rosemary Elizabeth Patton*

# Contents

# Prologue

When I met Charles Patton at the University of Pittsburgh in the summer of 1964 I was a member of East Hanover Mennonite Church, a Lancaster Conference congregation in central Pennsylvania. He was an active member of the Church of Christ, but having grown up just south of Los Angeles he knew nothing about Mennonites.

"If you aren't dating anyone," he said a few days after we met, "I'd like to spend some time with you. But only if you're also serious about this."

"There's nobody else," I said. "But I honor my church's standards. I will never date a guy who smokes or drinks."

"Oh, no. I've never done either," he assured me.

"Also I want to go overseas as a missionary. I'm getting my college debts paid off and then I want to go abroad and teach. Have you ever considered anything like that?"

"Not really. In my church only pastors go abroad – to evangelize. I've never heard of teachers as missionaries."

"We have evangelist missionaries," I said. "But our churches also support Mennonite Central Committee, our relief and service agency. We make quilts and kits for needy people. You know, newborn kits, school kits, refugee kits, all sent 'In the Name of Christ.' MCC also sends doctors, nurses, farmers, teachers, and other volunteers to work in deprived countries."

We spent the next six weeks studying French and getting to know each other. Most of our discussions revolved around our religious beliefs. To him the round white covering I wore was just a cute little cap; to me it indicated my submission to God and the church. He believed a Christian should be immersed; I'd been baptized by pouring and didn't think mode of baptism was important. He had a teacher deferment from his I-A military status; I believed Christians should be conscientious objectors and do alternate service in lieu of the compulsory two years in our US military.

When our summer classes ended Charles came home with me and we spent four weeks with my parents. And then he returned to his teaching position in California. For the next ten months our discussions continued in daily letters and weekly phone calls. Eventually we decided our love could transcend religious differences if we respected each other's beliefs.

Two years after we married in 1965, we signed on as volunteers with Mennonite Central Committee. They sent us to teach in a secondary school in Congo since we already had a working knowledge of French. We became comfortable in our African setting and at the end of our three-year term with MCC we decided to stay. Year-by-year we renewed our contracts with the Congolese government, remaining a total of six years before returning to the States in 1973 with our ten-month-old baby.

People often ask why I gave up a comfortable home and job to work as a volunteer in a third-world country. Growing up, I was taught to be a doer of the word, as the apostle James said, and not just a hearer. I've never wavered from my belief that as a Christian I have a duty to help those in spiritual or physical need.

In the essays that follow it is my intent to reconstruct

and maintain the integrity of what I experienced in two worlds: growing up Mennonite in Pennsylvania and working as a volunteer teacher with MCC in Africa. I've chosen parallel experiences from each of these segments of my life to illustrate not only the differences but also the links in my own spiritual growth as a Mennonite woman.

# Beginnings

You have put off the old man with his deeds
and you have put on the new.
Colossians 3:9-10

# My First Mennonite Christmas
# December 1948

We'd seen a lot of changes in our home after Mom and Daddy became Mennonites, but when Mom said there'd be no Christmas tree in our house that year I was devastated. She insisted that having a tree and all the paraphernalia that went with it was pagan. "Now that we're Christians we're going to act like it," she said.

"What about presents?" I asked.

"I'll give you some presents," Mom said. "But we're not going to wrap them or put them under a tree anymore." She explained that Santa was just a made-up character, and Mennonites didn't tell their children he brought gifts because that wasn't the truth.

"May I be in the Christmas program at church? And get a new dress?"

"Mennonites don't have pageants. They're just for show. We go to church to listen to the minister preach the Word. I will see if I can find some material and make you girls each a new Sunday dress."

"What about cookies?" I asked. "And pies. Can we have pies?"

"Don't be silly," Mom told me. "Of course we can have

cookies and pies and a big Christmas dinner."

At Christmas the aroma of baking permeated our house. Heaps of fat sour cream cookies, gingerbread men, chocolate drops with black walnuts, jumbo Grandma's Molasses cakes made with thick buttermilk, vanilla wafers spread with butter frosting, and sparkling sugar cookies shaped like festive Christmas ornaments tempted us from their gallon glass jars.

But this year, after rolling out the dough, Mom told me to put the tree, Santa, and his sleigh tin cookie cutters back in their box. "We're going to make cookies that tell the true story of Christmas," she said, handing me a star, an angel, and a bell to press into the cookie dough. I was sure my Sunday school teacher would agree, but as long as I had crunchy cookies to dip into half a cup of hot milky coffee, I didn't mind about the shape.

I was relieved to find out Mennonites loved pies. When Mom made pies it was an all-day affair. She loved to bake. And at Christmas she made everybody's favorite pie. She needed several baskets of goodies to take to Grandma's house too because my nine aunts and uncles loved Mom's pies and cookies as much as we did.

I always hung over the sink or climbed up on a stool beside her and observed. I liked to watch her turn the little handle to sift flour down from the tin bin in her ivory and oak Hoosier kitchen cabinet. "Anita, run down to the cellar and fill this pan with lard from the big crock at the bottom of the steps," Mom said to my older sister.

"Can Janet come with me?"

"Yes, just be careful not to fall down the steps. And don't forget to take the flashlight along."

Unlatching the side door we went out on the porch of our summer kitchen to the cellar door. I was afraid of the dark gaping stairwell closed with a huge ancient door, five feet wide and eight feet long, that lay flat on the floor over the stairs, hinged at the back. A heavy rope, tied to a pull-handle at the front of it, was threaded through a pulley fastened to the ceiling. On the other end of the rope a steel counterweight was suspended below the pulley, swinging high above our heads when the door was shut. When Anita tugged on the handle, the weight dropped, helping her lift the front of the heavy door and then holding it suspended at a sixty degree angle high up in the air. We climbed down the six wide deep concrete steps into the small ground cellar, a ray of light seeping through the grungy window at the far end, all the time fearful the door would somehow come crashing down on our heads.

"Oh, and bring up a couple of jars of peaches and raspberries too," Mom hollered down the steps as Anita scooped lard into her pan from the crock where it was stored after Daddy had butchered our pigs in November. Shining the flashlight on the rows of canned fruit, vegetables, and meat lined up in jars on the shelves, I picked out the ones Mom wanted. Damp spider webs hung in the corner above the potato bin.

"May I bring up a jar of sausage for supper?" I yelled up the steps, my mouth watering at the thought of Mom's canned sausage with mashed potatoes.

"And some sauerkraut?" Anita called out. She loved our homemade sauerkraut with sausage. We'd helped Mom chop up cabbage and put it in brine in the crocks next to the lard.

"Okay," Mom said, "but hurry up with the fruit. I need to get these pies made." We had to make several trips up and down those deep high steps, placing the jars on the step above before climbing to the next level.

Mom darted around the kitchen, cutting lard into the flour, sprinkling in a dash of salt, a bit of milk, mixing it just long enough to make a tender crust. She floured the enamel top of the cabinet, grabbed her rolling pin, and shaped circles of dough the size of her pie tins. In between, she heated the peaches, adding cornstarch to thicken the juice and cinnamon for flavor. "Stir the raspberries till they boil," she said to me, adding a stick of wood to the fire in the cookstove. "And don't burn yourself."

On the back of our yellow enamel kitchen range raisins simmering in a bit of water were getting plump. Mom loved raisin pie. I hoped I wouldn't have to eat any. Or mincemeat pie. Yuk. Mr. Burkholder had brought two packages of mincemeat when he came in his truck with his weekly delivery. I wondered how I'd get out of eating it: ground beef and pork sweetened and flavored with rum. She'd heat it up for supper. It was worse than raisin pie.

The day before we'd brought a big crookneck pumpkin from the haystack in the barn. Mom had peeled, boiled, drained, and mashed it. Now she added canned milk, brown sugar, eggs, and cinnamon to make the best pumpkin pie I could imagine.

"Anita, get the molasses out of the cupboard," Mom said. "Just remember, the secret to good pumpkin pie is a couple of tablespoons of Grandma's Molasses."

"Pull your raspberries back from the fire before they boil over!" Mom shouted over my shoulder. I pulled the pan away from the firebox side and let it simmer by the raisins.

Mom was lining pie pans with circles of dough and trimming the edges with her peeling knife. After flipping a top crust on her pie and crimping the edges, she'd use a fork to jag holes in the top to let out steam as it baked, and to write the first letter of the filling: R for raspberry, P for peach. Or if she had a bit of dough left over she'd roll it up and shape it in the form of the letter and place it in the middle of the pie. Mom didn't worry about making pretty pies. She made pies that tasted good.

Not having a Christmas tree made me gloomy. But Daddy agreed with Mom. "It was a shame to cut down that beautiful white pine last year," he said, "just to hang stuff on it here in the house for a few days. It's not natural. We need to celebrate Jesus' birth and not do all those worldly things that have nothing to do with the story in the Bible."

I knew Daddy was right. Even at Fishburn Church we'd learned the story of Jesus and how he was born in a stable and slept in a manger. But I loved to look at shiny Christmas trees and dangling ornaments and tinsel.

The previous Christmas, just before Mom and Daddy became Mennonites, Anita and I had followed Mom up the steep stairs to the attic where the decorations were stored in dusty boxes on a back shelf. I watched wide-eyed as she opened and checked each one.

"Can you carry the wreaths downstairs?" she asked me.

"Oh, yes," I whispered, elated that she'd decided I was old enough that year to help her and my sister put each shiny decoration in its proper place. On the front door we hung Mom's tinkling silver bells dangling snow-spattered pinecones on red ribbons. Anita fastened two small store-bought wreaths in the living room windows. "Mom, may we set candles in the windows this year?" I asked.

"Absolutely not. They're too dangerous. I don't want the house burned down on Christmas Eve." And that was final. I knew better than to beg. Anita filled the little square brown handmade basket with evergreens, tied a bright red bow at the top of its tall handle, and set it on the back room windowsill.

I couldn't wait to play pretend with the tiny sparkling cardboard church and village houses surrounded by snow-covered bottlebrush trees that we would set up on the buffet under our Christmas tree. Anita and I would get out our paper dolls and pretend they were going shopping for new dresses, hats, and shoes in the little cardboard stores.

Daddy and the boys had bundled up in their plaid Mackinaws, toboggan hats pulled down over their ears, and black rubber boots buckled to the top with a row of metal clasps. Walking back into the woods behind the meadow, they chose a perfectly formed white pine from a stand of medium sized evergreens. Daddy cut it down with his double-bladed axe, and the boys dragged it home through the snow. On the porch they helped him secure it to a base he'd built from scrap wood. Shaking the flakes of snow from its fragrant branches, he brought our Christmas tree into the house and hoisted it up onto the oak dining room buffet against the back wall, turning it round and round until he was satisfied that its best side was showing.

"Mom, the boys said Santa won't be able to come this year because you have a fire in the cookstove and he'll get burned up coming down the chimney," I whined to my mother.

"That's ridiculous," she said. "He came last year, didn't he?"

"Yes, but how did he get in? He can't get out through the stove lids."

"When you don't have a fireplace he comes through the front door."

Satisfied, I watched Mom standing on a chair stringing the frayed set of multi-colored lights on our little tree. "Plug it in, Anita," she said. The painted bulbs glowed softly amid the pine needles.

My sister and I then began the delicate task of opening the boxes with individual compartments full of fragile shiny silver, pink, green, red, and blue glass Christmas balls. We gently handed them up to Mom who hung them on the furry branches.

From another box we pulled out tiny ornaments depicting wonderful Victorian images printed on stiff paper, examining the old fashioned Santas, flower bouquets, ladies with parasols, and happy babies in their cradles before fastening them to the branches with a little string.

The smell of fresh pine permeated the room as we draped our tree with red and gold garlands and streams of silvery swishing tinsel and white icicles. Mom climbed up on the buffet and fastened the shiny gold star to the top branches near the ceiling. Finally we crinkled red tissue paper around the base and arranged our glittering village in front.

I stood back and gazed in awe at the twinkling lights knowing Santa would be coming by that night and leaving wonderful presents for us under our dazzling tree.

That was all changed. From now on our Christmases would focus on the birth of Jesus. We'd still have a big dinner at Grandma's and delicious desserts. Mom would make me a new Sunday dress and we'd sing carols at church. I really didn't mind if my gifts weren't wrapped as long as I got a new doll. Maybe Christmas wouldn't be too different after all.

Mom and the cookstove she used for more than 60 years.

# Christmas in Africa
## December 1968

My husband Charles and I were teaching at Ngombe Lutete Secondary School on a British Baptist Post out in the bush in Congo, 100 miles from the capital, Kinshasa. It was 1968 and we were celebrating our fifth Christmas together, the first away from our families on the other side of the world.

After morning classes on Friday, December 20, huge beat-up transport trucks, similar to those used for carrying army troops, arrived at the school. Our boarding students and Congolese teachers shouted, "Joyeux Noël, Monsieur," and "Happy Holidays, Madame," as they climbed on the back of a truck for the grueling trip home, standing hanging on to the metal framework overhead, their suitcase between their feet.

Then silence reigned. Besides the eight British, Belgian, and American staff members left on the station, our director, Ian Secrett, was expecting a British family with four children for the Christmas holiday. And Charles and I were anticipating the arrival of an American couple, teachers who'd come out to Africa in the Teacher Abroad Program with us less than a year before.

After months of hearing only British English or Belgian

French, Phyllis's and Dave's California accents were like a whisper of home as we exchanged stories, visited empty classrooms, biked over the hills, and played board games all weekend.

"One of the British missionaries went home to England this summer and left me a little silver tree," I told Phyllis. "I grew up in Pennsylvania without Christmas trees, but I think Charles would like having one."

"Do you have any decorations?" she asked.

"No, but that won't stop us. We'll make some."

By Monday evening Phyllis and I had transformed our little dining/living room into Christmas land. Snowflakes we had cut from white paper were twirling in front of the windows and dangling from the electric light bulb overhead. We set the silvery tree on the sideboard on a bright red Christmas cloth I'd embroidered. In between, we made macaroni and cheese and baked chocolate chip, peanut butter, and molasses cookies. The aroma of Christmas wafted through the house.

"How about some popcorn, Dave?" my husband asked, frustrated with his latest move in one of their endless games of chess.

"Popcorn? Where would you get it out here?" Dave wanted to know.

"Ah, my mother mailed me eight pounds in August and it just arrived last week. And she says there's more on the way."

"Do you have a popper?"

"Why do I need a popper? I have a big iron frying pan, a lid, and a propane gas stove. Dave, let me show you how to pop corn in Africa."

Phyllis and I sneaked into the kitchen and confiscated some of the biggest fluffiest puffs of corn and shook them in a paper bag with drops of food coloring. After stringing them on thread we draped the lovely red and green garlands over the two windows, above the door, and around the shiny branches of our tree. Then we added balls, bells, and stars we'd cut from paper and sprinkled with glue and colored sugar.

"Let's decorate the wall with Christmas cards," I said. "I've had seven so far this year."

"But that won't be enough, will it?"

"No, but I have a collection of old ones." We picked out the prettiest cards and hung them on the wall in the shape of an evergreen. By the time the guys looked up from their chessboard, we'd wrapped their presents and had them scattered around our festive tree.

When Mpanzu, my houseboy, came by with buckets of water, his eyes were popping as he took in the decorations and the food preparation. "Madame, I know why the Americans celebrate so many holidays," he said. "It's because you like to eat."

"You know, he's not too far off," Phyllis and I both agreed.

"Now we need to wrap presents for the British and Belgians," I said to Phyllis. "They're having a gift exchange at tea on Christmas afternoon." We had fun choosing gifts from the cache I'd been hording over the year. I'd made a rag doll for the little girl from England, embroidering the face, fastening brown yarn on her head, stuffing her with dried grass, and fashioning a blue print dress and white pinafore from sewing scraps. I had quilted pillows for the British ladies, books for the men, and matchbox cars for the boys.

Christmas Eve dawned hot and humid. "Let's go to the waterfall and have a picnic," Charles suggested.

"Good idea," I said. "You won't believe the difference in temperature below the falls." We packed a picnic basket with cheese and pâté sandwiches, cookies, and chunks of fresh pineapple and papayas. Ian lent us the mission's VW Bug for the hot four-mile trek over dusty ruts in the dirt road to Ngombe Matadi. Skirting the small village, we bumped through some fields and came to rest under a grove of tall tropical trees.

The stream flowed gently through fields on a high plateau and then suddenly dropped off a steep cliff into a gorge below. Boulders, strewn throughout the ravine, made wonderful seats from which we could watch the continual cascade and feel the gentle cooling mist. We spread my red and white-checkered tablecloth on a rock and thought we were enjoying a private lunch until we saw brown faces peering through the bushes. The village kids shyly accepted the cookies we offered them and then disappeared deeper into the tall grass.

After lunch we read and napped on the rocks, our bare feet dangling in the cool ripples. Suddenly, the billowy white clouds began to thicken and darken, readying for a typical rainy season afternoon downpour. "It's going to rain. Let's go before the road gets wet," Charles shouted. We grabbed the picnic basket and ran for the car, knowing well how dangerous these dirt roads became when they turned to a mud that was like greasy glass.

On Christmas Eve I rounded up a group of Americans, Belgians, and several Congolese neighbors to go caroling, a tradition I'd always enjoyed back home in Pennsylvania. Armed with flashlights and papers with the words of favorite carols in French, we walked along the pitch black trails past tall swaying palms and majestic mango trees, stars twinkling overhead. First we serenaded Ian and his guests, then the local pastor's family, and finally the people in their thatched mud huts in the nearby village of Kivianga. They came and stood at their doors with kerosene lanterns, a bit unsure of what this was all about. Then when they realized it was the "Americani," they laughed and waved and shouted "Joyeux Noël, Madames et Monsieurs."

As we walked back home, I said, "Okay guys, we leave for Ngombe Matadi at 11:30 sharp. We'll come by your houses and pick you up in the jeep. Be ready." I loved going to midnight mass and didn't want to be late for this one being sung in French and Kikongo, the local language, in a big brick cathedral out in the bush in Central Africa.

We weren't disappointed. The Catholic school students performed the pageantry complete with Mary, Joseph, shepherds, and wise men in full regalia, and their clear voices formed a mighty chorus for the carols.

On Christmas morning we got up early and had a leisurely typical African breakfast of sweet hot tea and locally-baked breakfast rolls with peanut butter and jam. Afterwards, we opened the presents scattered under our little tree on the sideboard.

At 8:30 we walked over to the Baptist Christmas service in the campus church. Dave and Phyllis remarked that the old building, made of corrugated tin fastened to a metal frame and painted blue and green, had only openings for windows. We explained that the veranda running the whole way around kept out the rain, and it was always so warm that windows weren't needed. The entire service was done in Kikongo, except for the song pages, which were given out in French. We followed along as best we could, enjoying the women's choir accompanied by tambourines and whistles, their way of welcoming the Christ Child. We were thankful for our health and strength and for friends when we were so far from our families.

Phyllis and I decided the Europeans needed to learn to appreciate some American foods, so along with stuffed roasted chicken and American style thickened gravy, we opened several cans of corn, and had baked two pumpkin pies to take along to the shared Christmas dinner at Ian's house.

A Belgian lady provided the most wonderful mashed potatoes we'd ever eaten. The British ladies brought vegetables, breads, and chicken seasoned with sage and rosemary. Seventeen of us sat down to the ample meal, which was followed by a typical British dessert: Christmas pudding, a mixture of nuts, bread, raisins, currants, spices and sugar which are boiled together until it becomes dark and thick. Everyone got a slice and then poured over it a thin liquid-like vanilla custard they called hard sauce. "Oh, isn't the Christmas pudding lovely?" the British ladies exclaimed to each other. "What do you Americans think of it?"

"It was tasty, especially with lots of custard," I agreed.

"And the pumpkin pie?" Phyllis asked.

"Oh, yes, 'tis lovely," they cried.

Everyone went home to rest while some of the house-boys cleaned up. They'd wanted to come and do this chore because, besides a nice tip, they each got a plateful of Christmas dinner, desserts, and the leftovers to take home.

"Dave, we hate to tell you, but you've been volunteered to play Father Christmas at the tea this afternoon," Charles said when we got home, showing him the short-sleeved European-style Santa suit Ian had pulled out of his storeroom.

"Come on, Dave, you're perfect for the job," I begged. "And it's your size." We padded him with pillows, tightened the black belt, pulled the funny-looking red cap over his hair, and fluffed the white beard.

Before we were twenty yards down the path to Ian's house, a crowd of spindly village children, who'd been play-ing with their homemade cars, trucks, and even a helicopter, started following us. "Where'd they get those toys?" Dave asked, stopping to get a closer look.

"They make them from a soft wood like balsa," Charles said. "They cut it in the forest with their machetes and use pocketknives to fashion all those intricate parts. The wheels are coke bottle tops! Pretty incredible, aren't they?"

"Why's he dressed like that?" the kids asked, pointing to Dave.

"He's Father Christmas," I said.

"C'est le Père Noël," they called to each other, giggling

and dancing along beside us, as he handed them each several pieces of hard candy.

We sneaked Dave into Ian's outside kitchen, off the back veranda, and hid him in a dark corner until time for his entrance. The houseboys grinned as Dave reached into his large white sack and pulled out candy for them.

The rest of us gathered in Ian's living room just before 4:00 to hear the Queen's message. Everyone sat silently crowded around the radio during the ten-minute speech. Elizabeth II spoke about the past year and then wished all her subjects at home and abroad an enjoyable day and a wonderful year ahead.

As the Queen's message ended, one of the adults said, "Time for presents."

"But we aren't at home. Father Christmas won't know where we are," one little boy said.

"Oh, no, Father Christmas can always see you. He knows where we are," his older brother said. "Isn't that right, Papa?"

And then to their astonishment, who should appear at the front door but a jolly fat old Saint Nick, who looked and sounded a bit American. "He's not real," the boys shouted. "It's Uncle Ian dressed up." But Ian was standing behind him. They looked around trying to decide who was missing; Uncle Gordon was there too. Convinced Father Christmas hadn't forgotten them, even out here in the bush, their eyes danced as Dave pulled wonderful gifts out of his sack and handed them round. And the children fared well; all of us had remembered them. The little girl got three dolls. There was a gift for each adult as well. And then as quickly as he had appeared, Santa was gone. Dave sneaked around to the kitchen, pulled off his steaming suit and eventually rejoined us unobserved by the children. They never did figure it out.

Then it was time for Christmas cake and tea. One of the British ladies had baked a traditional English fruitcake several weeks in advance and covered it with marzipan, a thick hard icing. Exclamations of "Super quality," and "baked to perfection," delighted the cook. Our plate of American cookies, which they called biscuits, soon disappeared along with many cups of hot tea served in pretty china cups with a spot of milk and a lump of sugar.

After thanking our British hosts for an enjoyable tea, the four of us gathered up our gifts and headed back to our little brick house, ready to crash after a super-charged week. In spite of being half way around the world from our family and friends, this had turned out to be a most memorable Christmas.

Dave Nichols playing Father Christmas,
handing out candy on the way to the British party.

Congolese boy with his helicopter handmade from
a soft wood cut in the forest.

# "Words of Cheer"
# November 1949

Getting used to Stauffer Mennonite Church wasn't always easy for me as a child. The simple interior – white plastered walls, brown pull blinds at the windows, dark wood trim and furniture – was so different from the light airy church we'd attended before. I missed the organ and piano on the platform, the ornately carved railing along the balcony, colorful stained glass windows, and the bell tower rising high above the front entry.

Our Mennonite church, still surrounded by sheds from horse and buggy days, had a stern exterior. Two small attic windows in the gabled end peered down its stark brick face. A tall rectangular window with eighteen clear panes hung on each side of double-entry solid doors that swung beneath a wide transom. No porch or foyer, only half a dozen steps leading to an uncovered stoop.

And the people and clothing were different, too. Inside, we stopped by hooks screwed into boards on the back wall. I found an empty low hook and hung up my jacket. While Mom unfastened the strap of her black outdoor bonnet and hung it over her sweater and Mary Anne's little coat, Anita held our baby sister. As usual, Mom had dressed her all in white from her snowy diaper, lawn dress, and sweater all the way down to her long cotton stockings and freshly polished high-topped shoes. Our baby looked like a doll, her dark eyes shining like black jade.

Mom straightened her cape and white covering, slung her diaper bag over her shoulder, took my little sister, and walked halfway down the aisle to the married women's section. She had to hold Mary Anne on her lap. Anita sat with the girls' youth class near the back. Daddy and the boys were on the men's side with their Sunday school classes.

I slid in beside the junior girls lined up on the bench behind our mothers. Mrs. Ebersole, my teacher, looked over at me and smiled. And then Earl Lepperd was walking to the front and announcing, "Take your *Life Songs* and turn to page one ninety-five, 'A Wonderful Saviour Is Jesus My Lord.' One hundred and ninety-five." Taking his tuning fork from a vest pocket, he shook it next to his ear.

Everyone liked Earl Lepperd. He was big and had a huge nose. But he always smiled and carried pink and white mints in his pockets that he handed out to any of the children who came around to talk to him after services. And he could sing. His deep bass kept the hymns moving and he was always on pitch. We pulled hymnbooks from the rack on the bench in front of us and found the page. Acappella four-part harmony was the best thing about Mennonites. When we sang the church became an awesome choir. I loved to hear the basses bring out the rich resonant tones, and I resolved to learn to sing alto.

Charles Brubaker, our Sunday school superintendent, walked to the small podium down front.

"Stay off the platform," Mom told us over and over.

"Why?" I asked, fascinated by the two steps on the men's side the ministers used each Sunday. The preacher sometimes reached down and pulled a pitcher from a shelf behind the big pulpit and poured a little water into his glass.

I was curious to know what else might be hidden back there. "Only ordained ministers or deacons may stand behind the pulpit," Mom said. "The Sunday school superintendent doesn't even go up there." But I didn't understand. At our other church my favorite thing had been getting dressed up and reciting a poem or verse in a Christmas program, standing on the platform behind the fancy carved rail.

Brother Brubaker was a farmer, the father of ten well-behaved children. Mom often held them up to us as examples of how to behave in church. But I didn't understand how they could sit so quietly. My legs were always swinging; I needed to write or read or look around. He didn't look like a farmer in his plain-cut dark blue suit and long-sleeved white shirt buttoned to the neck. He was a good reader, and Daddy said Brother Brubaker was his best Sunday school teacher. And his wife was Mom's.

"The verses for our devotions today are found in Genesis thirty-seven," Brother Brubaker said as we opened our King James Bibles and turned to the passage – background material for the lesson in our Sunday school quarterly. Mennonite Publishing House in Scottdale, Pennsylvania, printed our church materials. That day Mennonites everywhere were learning about Joseph in the Old Testament.

Brother Brubaker waited until the rustling of thin Bible paper hushed. "Follow after as I read," he said, his deep voice reaching to the farthest corners. When he finished he lifted his weather-beaten bronzed face and said, "May God bless the reading of His Word." He made a few comments about Joseph and how we should try to follow his example, and then, as usual, ended with, "Let us kneel in prayer." We stood, turned, faced our seats, dropped to our knees, bowed our heads in our hands, and listened to his prayer of thanksgiving and praise, concluding with a request that God would bless our service.

"Turn to page four forty-four if you need the music to

sing as the children go quietly to their classes," Brother
Brubaker said when we were seated again. The congregation joined in as Earl Lepperd softly led out,

> *Be silent, be silent a whisper is heard.*
> *Be silent and listen oh, treasure each word.*
> *Tread softly, Tread softly; The Master is here.*

The adults stayed in the sanctuary for their classes and
continued to sing. Children noiselessly filed out of the
benches a row at a time to the side aisle – we girls on one
side, the boys on the other – tiptoeing to the front of the
church and through an open door. In the anteroom we
passed the rockers where mothers nursed their babies and
hooks where the old women hung their long black coats and
big bonnets, and then headed down the stairs.

The primary class was mixed; boys and girls up to age
six sat on little benches in the men's anteroom. But we older
children had segregated classes in the musty basement. I
was glad for my navy blue wool sweater in our chilly classroom where we sat on backless benches along a trestle table.
Our teacher had a chair at one end. We could hear the little
children singing "This Little Light of Mine." We juniors
didn't sing. We just did our lesson.

Mrs. Ebersole was a kind lady, a good teacher. She
marked the attendance in the register and gave us each a blue
ticket for being present. We opened our quarterlies and read
the verses. I liked my teacher and listened as she talked about
the lesson. "Joseph was willing to let go of his bad feelings
against his dishonest brothers even though they'd wronged
him. After he became a ruler in Egypt they came to him for
food. He pardoned them in spite of his earlier mistreatment
at their hands. We must learn to let go and forgive," she said.

We practiced our memory verses and checked our
homework in the quarterly. Our teacher asked questions to

make sure we'd understood the meaning of the story. I jumped when the buzzer rang. That would be Brother Brubaker pushing the button on the side of the pulpit to warn us we had five minutes left. We recited our verse for Mrs. Ebersole and she gave us each a red ticket before the final bell. That'd make seventy-two tickets in my little box at home, almost enough to buy "The Lord's Prayer" glass motto I wanted for above my bed.

Mrs. Ebersole passed out copies of "Words of Cheer." I couldn't wait to read the stories and poems, and the letters from children wanting pen pals, but Daddy got annoyed if we looked at our Sunday school papers during preaching. So I folded mine and put it in my Bible.

Back upstairs Brother Brubaker made some comments about forgiveness and then asked our classes to stand one by one to say our memory verses. When he pointed to us we junior girls stood at our bench and recited in unison, "'For jealousy is the rage of a man: therefore He will not spare in the day of vengeance.' Proverbs 6:34."

We had about three minutes to change seats for preaching: children to their parents, Sunday school teachers to the adult sections. Mom let Anita stay with the teen-age girls but I was never allowed to sit with my class.

"Because I don't want you whispering and playing around during preaching," she'd answer whenever I asked why. Mom had her hands full keeping Mary Anne quiet. I got bored sitting on a hard bench for an hour and would try to entertain my baby sister, folding my hanky into the shape of a cradle with two babies and swinging it back and forth. She soon lost interest and fussed, and I was in trouble.

One Sunday Mom told me to go sit with the elderly women up front. I couldn't believe she'd actually make me do that. Nobody ever sat with the old ladies. But she gave me no choice. I crept down the outside aisle and slunk into a seat beside Jenny Lepperd, our song leader's wife. Before long I discovered a secret: the old ladies had deep pockets hidden in their pleated skirts where they kept stashes of mints and Lifesavers. And they willingly shared. Each time Jenny put a mint in her mouth she sneaked one to me. I soon figured out who brought the best candy and that was the lady I'd search out.

When Brother Oberholtzer preached, he preferred teaching Old Testament stories. Mom loved his sermons and told us how fortunate we were to have such a good preacher to explain the Bible. I'd slide down in my seat next to an old lady, my legs swinging. Lost in a maze of history and prophecy, I'd draw and write on the rainbow pad I carried in my little blue purse. When I couldn't stand it any longer I'd quietly pull out my "Words of Cheer," all the while sucking on whatever candy was handed my way. My brothers teased me for sitting with the old ladies, but I didn't pay any attention to them and continued Sunday after Sunday reading and enjoying my sweets. I didn't tell Mom, not sure what she'd say. She never did understand why I didn't rebel.

Stauffers Mennonite Church as it looked in the 1950s.

# Chickens, Kimbanguists, and Peanuts
# 1968 - 1970

January 21, 1968

Dear Mom and Daddy,

I thought you might like to hear about this morning's church service, the fourth we've attended since our arrival here at Ngombe Lutete last month. I never understand much of what's being said because the whole service is in Kikongo, although they sometimes call out the song pages in French. Otherwise I have to look over someone's shoulder. The village people and our students bring their own little blue hardback hymnal to church, so I bought one. Now whenever we sing I pencil in the English title if I recognize it. They seem to use a lot of the old hymns we grew up with, like "My Jesus I Love Thee," "What A Friend We Have In Jesus," "There's Power in the Blood." I check with a student when the scripture is announced so I can read it in English while it's being read in Kikongo. After that I'm totally lost. But I need to be in church to sit with my eighth grade girls.

This morning four dogs wandered in during the service. Usually they sleep on the cool flagstones beside their owner. But today two of them strolled down front, jumped up on the platform, circled, lay down, and slept through Tata Robert's entire sermon. (Tata means Mr. in Kikongo). Later a chicken ambled down the aisle clucking and pecking at the floor, eventually exiting through the men's side door. Nobody pays much attention to them, as though having animals roaming in and out of the sanctuary is perfectly normal. Sometimes the schoolboys are bored and pick at a dog, pulling his ears or tail. But they know better than to make it yelp!

Our church building is quite old, constructed with corrugated tin, including the roof, over a metal framework. Windows have never been installed in the openings, so we get plenty of fresh air. The roof overhangs the sides and back, forming a wrap-around porch with a brick floor. A glossy wood pulpit and a wheezy organ, probably brought out here by early missionaries before the turn of the century, stand on the circular brick platform. Every Sunday and every morning at "Prayers" I study the Kikongo words "Nzambi y Zola" arched on the front wall. Lesley told me it means God is Love. The beautifully polished communion table down front was made locally and is inscribed with "Muna Luyindulu Luame," which means In Remembrance of Him.

I think what surprised me most about this church is the men sit on the right and the women on the left. Families never sit together. I thought just Mennonites and Amish back in Pennsylvania do that anymore. Like Mennonites, Congolese women wear a covering! In Kikongo it's called a "kitambula" (a headscarf) although it doesn't appear to have any religious significance. Some of the more affluent ones, if you can call it that, wear an elaborate headdress, the material wrapped and puffed to resemble a beehive hairdo, and a matching skirt. Others tie on a thin scarf, and the poorest, just a rag.

Last Sunday a scraggly mother with a number of small children in tow came to me after the service, wanting to be introduced. She bowed, bending her knees, lowering her head, saying, "Kiambote, Nengua." That means, hello, Ma'am, but using a term reserved for VIPs. I find it horribly embarrassing when village women call me Nengua, so I stretched out my hands to her. She responded and shook my hand Congolese style, placing her left hand palm up under her right forearm. Ian said extending only one hand to someone in this society is terribly impolite. They always reach out with both hands to give or take anything.

"Kiambote, Mama," I replied. "Okelele?" (How are you?) Again she bowed saying, "Nkolele, Nengua. Ntondele beni." (Fine, Ma'am. Thank you so much).

Since that's all the Kikongo I know at the moment, I asked Yengo, one of my students, to translate from Kikongo into French. "This is my baby," Yengo translated, as a group of women began crowding around us. "She is my youngest child, my ninth." The lady held her hand to her mouth and giggled nervously. "Her name is Janet."

"Oh, she has my name," I said, reaching out and taking her baby. The mother was so proud. Janet is a cute little thing, about five months old. Most Congolese have an English or French name, a throwback to the Catholic influence. She probably knew a missionary by that name. I need to find a gift for my "namesake." I'll probably make her a little dress.

Ian asked Charles to play the old-fashioned organ for services – the kind with foot pedals you need to keep pumping so it doesn't die. He's not real keen on playing it because he says it's hard to pedal and sounds like it's struggling with asthma. But I like to hear it. It reminds me of the old organ Grandma had in the cabin when we were growing up. The Africans enjoy singing with it and since Pastor Ntela also asked him, he obliges them.

Most of the locals have given us the warmest welcome you can imagine. They're fond of Americans, and not having ever seen any before, they're curious and want to meet us and shake our hands. Several women came by our house after church one Sunday bringing a gift of a little dish of dried beans and an avocado. These are kind and gentle people. We feel appreciated. Love, Janet

April 28, 1968

Dear Mom and Daddy,

Last week we had a nice surprise! Just as we got back from our Saturday morning classes, John Gaeddert, our Kinshasa MCC director, along with his PAX-man secretary, three MCC teachers in our Teacher Abroad Program, and a Bible translator pulled up in front of our house. I invited them in for a cup of tea and the last of some cookies I'd baked a few days earlier.

They said they were on their way to Nkamba to visit the Kimbanguists at their religious center about 20 miles north of us. After a bit of discussion they decided we could all squeeze into their Landrover, so Charles and I dropped everything, grabbed our camera, locked up the house, and were on an African safari. We sloshed through mud and waterholes, and climbed hills so steep and slippery even the Landrover had trouble maneuvering. But John prevailed.

The Kimbanguist church holds similar basic beliefs to most Protestant denominations, the main difference being they revere Simon Kimbangu, like the Mormons have Joseph Smith. Kimbangu said he was visited by God in 1921 and told to preach against polygamy, liquor, fetishes, and the Belgians. They teach faith healing and have priests and priestesses who are called by God to heal. The Belgians feared them and, hoping to stop the growing movement, banished their leader to a Belgian prison in Katanga Province in eastern Congo. In 1951 Kimbangu died there, a martyr and a Congolese hero.

When we arrived at the center and John identified us as teachers with MCC, we were given a grand welcome and taken to their church headquarters on top of the highest hill – a truly beautiful spot with a grand view for miles around. Since Simon Kimbangu was born and is buried there, the site has been consecrated as holy ground, like in the story of Moses and the burning bush, when he had to take off his sandals. Nobody may wear shoes inside the gate. I've run barefoot all my life, so I had no problem. Poor Charles, who rarely removes his shoes, suffered as we made our way along stony, rough clay paths.

I asked permission to take a photo of Kimbangu's grave, but our guides refused "because," they said, "this is a holy place." They assured me the picture wouldn't come out anyway because of it being holy, but that we could take photos of anything else. We visited the church and the grave of Kimbangu's wife Mama Mwilu Marie before descending, still barefoot, to the holy river, which they call the River Jordan, where people come for healing.

Once outside the gate they gave back our shoes and then took us to see their secondary school. By then the damage had been done and Charles was barely able to walk even in his shoes. The Kimbanguists were kind, having us stop to rest from time to time and serving us room-temperature bottles of coke. When we left they gave us gifts: two huge pineapples and about four dozen eggs.

The guides begged John to send them American teachers. Charles and I are quite happily settled in our organized British-run school. We both cringe at the thought of coming back here in the mountains to run barefoot and teach without substantial leadership. But I'm sure John will find some daring young teachers willing to undertake such an adventure. Love, Janet

October 26, 1968

Dear Mom and Daddy,

Sunday school here is quite different from our traditional

classes back in Pennsylvania where we discussed the lesson in our quarterly for an hour before the morning church service. Here we, along with our students, attend the local village worship service which lasts anywhere from forty-five minutes to two hours depending on who's leading and preaching. Sometimes when it gets too long the boys shuffle their feet and cough. There are no rooms for Sunday school, so we have only the preaching service in Kikongo.

Early British missionaries had established a French Bible class for the schoolgirls on Sunday afternoons. Lesley Fuller, a seasoned British Baptist missionary who's been quite helpful to me, asked if I'd take on this class since it's conducted in French. Besides a full teaching load, she's a deacon and has a lot of responsibility in our campus church, which we can't help with since everything there is done in Kikongo.

British Baptists used to staff this whole mission post. But given the changes since independence, their missionary society is having trouble finding enough personnel to fill teaching positions, not to mention church related jobs. That's why they've been accepting outsiders like us Americans or Belgians who come out here to teach in lieu of military service. So the few British missionaries are finding themselves spread quite thin.

Lesley said the class is mandatory for our middle school girls. But I wasn't comfortable with forcing them to come to Sunday school by handing out punishments. In the end she agreed to make it voluntary, but warned me only two or three girls would show.

Well, you know me. I found a way to get them there without chasing them down – cookies and lemonade! At our first meeting we sat around, snacked, drank our juice, and talked informally. They have so many questions.

"Madame, look at the whirlwind," Malemba said, running to the window and pointing. I knew what she meant. Sometimes when I'm walking along the path suddenly out of nowhere a little swirling wind sucks leaves upward from the trail into a funnel shape. Children jump into these tiny tornados, swaying and twisting with them until they disappear. "That's Cain," she said.

"You know, from the story in Genesis," Kiabembo added. "Cain killed his brother. Ever since, he's been a fugitive and a vagabond tossed in the wind."

I knew it was useless to argue with them, so I smiled and said, "okay." There are so many other more important values that I feel compelled to teach them in the limited time we have together. In our school religion classes they learn events of the New Testament in seventh grade and the Old Testament in eighth grade. Since I'm teaching both of those, I needed a different format for Sunday school.

I asked for suggestions of problems they encounter in their daily life, topics we could discuss from a Biblical and Christian perspective, subjects not covered in our religion classes. When they shuffled and squirmed, I handed out paper, giving them the option to write. They came up with quite a list:

1.  What does a Christian do on a date?
2.  Is it wrong to date a non-Christian? Explain.
3.  Is sex before marriage *always* a sin?
4.  What is expected of a woman in a Christian marriage?
5.  What should a Christian woman do and not do?
6.  Christian families and raising children.
7.  How does a Christian woman control her temper?
8.  Is gossip a sin?
9.  Is it sometimes okay to tell a little lie?

They wanted to start with dating and relationships with boys. I went home and did some research. Fortunately, I had brought along several helpful books. I find verses dealing with each topic. Discussion has been animated and interesting.

They've told me things from their traditions and culture that I probably would never have learned otherwise. While discussing dating and relationships between Christian men and women, I told them I'd kept myself pure for my husband. They couldn't believe it.

"Here in our country everybody does it; even little kids. Nobody thinks it's wrong except here at school," one girl said.

"If an older guy invites a young girl to come visit him, she views it as an honor," another said.

"But aren't you afraid of venereal disease or getting pregnant?" I asked, trying to keep my eyes from bugging out.

They didn't know enough about VD to worry about it; as for getting pregnant, it wasn't that big a deal. "You just get married, or if he's already married your parents will find someone else," they said.

"But what about your education?" I asked.

"Madame, we'll never go further than eighth grade anyway," they said. Their attitude haunts me. I wonder how long it will take to change the plight and thinking of these women.

When the other girls heard we'd had cookies at Sunday school, they decided to come too. Didn't Jesus feed the people who came to hear him speak? Love, Janet

December 10, 1968

Dear Mom and Daddy,

A while back I wrote about our Sunday morning worship services, which are conducted in Kikongo. I told you that besides the hymns I recognize by their tune and the scripture I read in my English or French Bible, I don't understand what's being said. In light of that letter, I thought I should tell you about our Sunday evening services so you don't think we're deprived of religious worship.

Every Sunday evening the British Baptist missionaries on our post have traditionally conducted an English service, taking turns leading, meeting in the leader's home. It's not a formal service; they usually sing a couple of hymns, read something – a short book of the Bible, a selection from a Bible commentary, a religious story to discuss – and close with prayer.

When Charles and I arrived on campus they invited us to join their little group. After a few weeks they asked if we'd each take a turn leading. Someone suggested I talk about the Mennonites and explain our doctrine and traditions since they're not familiar with this denomination. They had lots of questions, especially about the peace issue. They'd known several conscientious objectors who served here in Congo in lieu of American military service. Our Belgian teachers don't come here for religious reasons. They simply don't want to do traditional military service and the pay is much better if they teach out here for a couple of years. They are generally non-practicing Catholics and not interested in our evening service, even though we've offered to conduct it in French.

Last week was my turn to lead again. We sat in a circle in our little living room, about seven of us. I'd borrowed a cassette tape from a missionary in Kimpese when we were down there at the internationally-staffed hospital several weeks ago – a sermon by a British pastor on what it means to be a Christian. The change was good and we all agreed Charles should take his turn leading next week and play the sermon on the other side, "Are You a Recognizable Christian?" Love, Janet

January 22, 1969

Dear Mom and Daddy,

The girls' Sunday school class has been going quite well. I'd often like to take a nap on hot Sunday afternoons, but their enthusiasm is inspiring. I'm truly grateful for the opportunity to share a bit of my Christian perspective and to learn from them.

As you well know, no situation is ever perfect much as we'd like it to be. As a matter of fact, I've been appalled at some of the moral dilemmas I've encountered in the past year. Growing up back in Pennsylvania I was taught that sexual activity outside of marriage is a sin. Here in Congo teen pregnancy is viewed differently. Let me try to explain.

Just before Christmas my seventh grade girls were putting the final touches on dresses they were making for themselves. That day in class they tried them on so I could pin hems and check for problems. Some had crooked darts or necklines, which I helped them repair.

Finally I'd finished all but Lusuki, a pretty little shy girl who rarely speaks out in class. Her dress was so tight I couldn't believe my eyes. I apologized and told her I must have used the wrong pattern, that we'd just have to cut another, and that I'd help her finish it.

The next day while reviewing for an up-coming anatomy test, I was standing in the back of the room having students go to the blackboard and write answers to my questions. When I asked Lusuki to take her turn up front, she mumbled and put her head down. I insisted and gave her no choice. She dragged herself up, draped an African print cloth over her school uniform and started down the aisle. I told her to leave the fabric on her seat; she hesitated, but finally dropped it on her chair.

After she'd written her answers she turned and waited for my response. When I saw her profile from that distance I finally understood what was wrong. This little 13-year-old girl was at least seven months pregnant. I held my tongue, got through class, and at lunchtime went to see Lesley. We took her to the clinic and the nurse said she was indeed with child.

Lesley sent a letter with someone on a transport truck to

the girl's village. The next day her parents turned up at school. Lusuki told them her sixth grade primary teacher had asked her to carry water to his house several times during the summer while his wife was working in her manioc field. Inside he caught her and took her to his bed. She hadn't told because she feared her father would be angry.

I thought the parents would be distraught. They weren't. Although they had wanted Lusuki to get another year or two of education, apparently, on the flip side, this was excellent news. Now that it was proven she could bear children, it would be easier to find a good husband for her. Unless they pressed charges, the teacher would not be prosecuted.

I'm thankful for the girls in my Sunday school group who try to live truly Christian lives. Several weeks ago Kiabembo suggested that perhaps I could train them how to teach primary school children. She said the little kids don't have Sunday school. As a result, our Sunday school is turning into a teacher training class. I bring materials – stories, pictures, a drawing to color – for them to teach to the little ones in their own language. We practice songs that have been translated from English into French and Kikongo. If you came by you'd hear us singing "Running Over," or "The B-I-B-L-E," or "Jesus Loves the Little Children." I know most of the songs in French and have been learning them in Kikongo as well. Being a phonetic language it's easy to read. And with the music I can figure out what I'm saying!

So now on Sunday mornings several secondary students take the children to a primary classroom and teach Sunday school during the morning worship service. Love, Janet

February 10, 1969

Dear Mom and Daddy,

Some time back Charles and I were asked to sponsor La League – a Bible reading club that seems to be quite popular with the British Baptists. As I've mentioned before, the number of missionaries on our post has dwindled to the point where they don't have enough to cover all the extra religious activities. That's how we've ended up with this added responsibility.

The League meets every Thursday afternoon. The officers plan the programs with us acting as advisors. When we suggested they do some service projects they decided to take turns helping with the primary Sunday school ministry. So now we're teaching them how to present a lesson and trying to provide materials. If you could send colored religious pictures, they would be most appreciative.

Several weeks ago the League was asked to be in charge of the Sunday morning worship service in French. We put our heads together and planned an interesting program about the importance of reading the Bible. Charles came up with the idea of having various people read a passage in as many different languages as we could find represented here on our post. They chose II Timothy 3:16-17. "All scripture is given by inspiration of God, and is profitable for doctrine, for reproof, for correction, for instruction in righteousness: That the man of God may be perfect, throughly furnished unto all good works."

Can you believe nine? Students read in three African languages: Kikongo, Lingala, and Swahili. Charles read in Spanish; Domingo, an Angolan refugee, in Portuguese; and two students in French and Latin. When we told Michel, our Latin teacher, about our project he said he'd come and read the verses in Greek. Nobody really believed he'd show up. But he did. Michel, an avowed atheist, not only showed up, he came into the sanctuary, sat on the platform throughout the entire service, and when it was his turn he stood at the pulpit to read his verses in Greek. We never understood why, but the important thing is he came to church. Love, Janet

April 20, 1969

Dear Mom and Daddy,

Nothing much besides the general round of school activities ever happens up here on our little plateau at Ngombe Lutete. So when somebody comes or something out of the ordinary like yesterday's excursion takes place, we make the most of it.

Someone yelling outside our bedroom window wakened us at six o'clock in the morning. Charles went to the door and opened to Margot Stockwell, one of our British missionaries. "I hate to bother you so early," she said, "but Marie-Louise Martin is at my house and needs a ride to the Kimbanguist center at Nkamba."

"Marie-Louise Martin?" I asked, buttoning my robe as I came into the living room. "We heard about her at our MCC retreat. She's an anthropologist and university professor with a specialty in Kimbanguisme. But they told us she was in South Africa."

"She left there this week under threat because of her close association with Africans," Margot said. "She came to Kinshasa to gather more information for her latest book on Kimbanguists. Since she was so near their headquarters, she decided to come and help commemorate the tenth anniversary of the death of Kimbangu's wife."

I remembered seeing Mama Mwilu Marie's grave when we were at Nkamba last year about this same time. "She came out yesterday in a Willis Jeep with a chauffer," Margot continued, "but heavy rains slowed them down and in the end mechanical failure forced them to abandon the vehicle and walk three miles to our post. They arrived here about midnight. We gave her a bed for the night, but now she's asking if someone would take her the last 20 miles to Nkamba. She's anxious to arrive in time for the service." Charles and I looked at each other, shrugged, and nodded. We knew the way, the lady needed a ride, and we were the most expendable in our own church service.

Half an hour later we were on our way, Charles inching the Jeep along a road paved with soft sticky mud as slippery as any black ice I've ever encountered back home. And while he drove, sliding sideways down hills, swimming through mud holes, crawling from side to side up the next incline, Miss Martin talked on and on about her work in Lesotho. She told us how upset she was to have to leave after 23 years of service, and of being told she could never return. Now she's wondering if maybe this was God's way of telling her to come and set up a theology school at Nkamba.

Even though we arrived late we were ushered up front to seats of honor. Our interpreter told us about Mama Mwilu Marie's wonderful work of giving strength to the weak, and keeping the Kimbanguist church together during those long years her husband had been in exile when many thought all was lost. Numerous impressive choirs performed throughout the service as well as a band with drums, rhythm instruments, flutes, and whistles.

After the service as the band played we marched with the women in parade to Mama Mwilu Marie's grave. There in front of the large white concrete monument, they held a short prayer service before whisking Miss Martin off with the VIPs. Mark Schomer, the sole foreign teacher at Nkamba Secondary School, took us to the house where he lives with two Congolese teachers. Their cook had prepared a tasty dinner of rice, potatoes, chiquanga – a local dish made from manioc, peas, and gravy. He told us MCC has promised them two more American teachers for next school year. We invited him to come by and visit and share a meal with us anytime.

The Kimbanguists were taking Miss Martin back to Kinshasa in a transport truck. We didn't linger; the rains were threatening again and we had lessons to prepare. Love, Janet

February 16, 1970

Dear Mom and Daddy,

All my years of Christian training and studying the Bible could never have prepared me for the events of the past two weeks. Tuesday afternoon several girls came to our house and asked to speak to me alone. I took them into my office and closed the door.

"We're afraid, Madame," Maleka said, staring at her feet.

"Why are you afraid?" I asked. "What frightens you?"

"It's Alphonsine," Nzusi said. "She's bleeding."

"Bleeding?"

"Yes. You know, because she tried to take out the blood."

My mind began racing. *Take out the blood. That means an abortion. An illegal procedure in Congo. Anyone having one, performing one, or having knowledge of one and not reporting it is considered a murderer and a criminal. That includes me, her counselor. This needs to be handled judiciously. But Alphonsine, the top student in the eighth grade? Alphonsine, with her beautiful smile, my best seamstress?*

"Where is she now?" I asked.

"In the dormitory, but she made us promise not to tell. We're afraid, Madame."

I made arrangements and the 16-year-old was taken to the clinic to see our school nurse. He verified that indeed she'd had an abortion and furthermore that she should have medical attention to stem the hemorrhage.

When pressed she named Kutubila, a muscular athletic young man with a pleasant personality, a teenage girl's dream, one of her teachers in our middle school. Even without the abortion, he could be jailed for having illicit relations with a student.

The chef du secteur was notified and a meeting called. The young man came in unsuspecting until he saw the police. When questioned he realized he was trapped. "I love her. She's my fiancée," he said.

"Then why didn't you just get married?" the chef asked.

"As you know, after I teach for one year I'll be eligible for a four-year university scholarship. That's the only way I can afford to go to university. Our idea was for Alphonsine to stay on here and finish her high school studies at the same time. Then we'd get married. All would be lost if we were found out. If she had a child."

"Did her parents know your plan?"

"I haven't spoken to them. I'm not a citizen of this country; I'm from French Congo, you know, across the river. When Alphonsine told me she was two months pregnant I panicked. I feared I would lose my chance to get an education. What would I ever be without a university degree?" he said, shaking his head, tears welling in his eyes.

"So you arranged to take her to Kimpese to the hospital?" the chef asked.

They were so sure no one would ever know. Alphonsine had asked for a pass on a long holiday weekend to visit her sister in a nearby village, and Kutubila had told his friends he was going to Mbanza Ngungu and would be back Sunday evening. Instead they got a ride to the hospital and found his friend, a last-year nursing student. He agreed to help, got the needed instruments from the hospital, and did the abortion in his dorm room.

The young man sat bent forward staring at the floor, his body shaking. "I didn't think anything could go wrong. I just wanted to make it all go away."

Charles drove Alphonsine, a woman to look after her, and a local policeman to the hospital at Kimpese where the borrowed instruments were found, still in the friend's room. A surgeon treated Alphonsine and sent her home. Her studies at our school are terminated; I don't know if she'll be able to get into another school.

Kutubila and his friend are imprisoned in the Ngombe

Matadi jail until they stand trial. The locals say they will most likely be incarcerated for five years, the maximum penalty.

Charles and I talked about this at length. I personally believe abortion is wrong. I know it's a hot issue in the States and will probably be legalized in the near future. In any case, we had no recourse. If we'd not reported it, *we* could have been imprisoned. And then we needed to consider the girl's condition; she might have hemorrhaged to death. If Kutubila had had some warning I'm sure he would have escaped across the river.

The irony of the situation is that the physician who attended Alphonsine in the hospital said if she'd waited a day or two the bleeding would have stopped on its own and she'd have been fine. The nursing student, using what he'd learned, had performed a tidy antiseptic procedure.

I've been so discouraged and disappointed that this happened in spite of my hard work to instill high moral standards in my girls. Like Kutubila said, I wish it would all go away, that it had never happened. My heart hurts for these two bright young people. Please pray for them. Love, Janet

Saturday, March 14, 1970

Dear Mom and Daddy,

Even though we were never involved in "Women's World Day of Prayer" back home, I know you'll be interested to hear about our goings-on here. Women from outlying villages came to our Thursday morning market excited and talkative this week. Their deaconesses had received letters telling them representatives from our post would be coming on Friday, March 13, to help conduct services in their little village churches - villages that rarely see a visiting pastor, not to mention a missionary.

Since I participated in this event for the past two years, I had a better idea of what to expect. Lesley gave me a copy of the brochure in French, which has been translated into Kikongo for the women in southern Congo. This year's theme is centered on "Courage." Women are advised to have courage in these days when many are forsaking Christ and leaving the church, when young people are losing respect for their elders. We're advised to have courage and depend on Jesus Christ; He will never abandon us.

Every year women from our mission post walk to outlying areas to encourage the faithful in villages, often without pastor or building. Many have nothing more than four poles holding up a low thatched roof over a six by eight area where they stoop to enter and sit on the bare ground to pray.

Our schoolgirls wanted to go. Some are genuinely interested in the religious part, but it also meant a day off from classes, and perhaps a chicken lunch or at least a snack. With state exams coming up in less than ten weeks we decided our eighth grade girls needed to be in class. So we organized the women to go out into the villages, each accompanied by two or three seventh grade girls. They had an early breakfast and left at seven o'clock, immediately after morning prayers, walking to the different villages, arriving in time for the services which would begin around eight-thirty or nine o'clock.

Because she knows a bit of French, Thérèse, the wife of our primary school secretary, was assigned to go with me. Since I hurt my foot last week and I'm still hobbling around, Lesley asked me to drive the school Volkswagen to the furthest village, about 15 miles from our station. Luengo and Nsimba, two schoolgirls, went with us. Can you imagine how excited they were to ride in the car while their classmates had to walk?

We arrived about nine o'clock, surprised to find eleven women, six men, and 20 children waiting for us. I could sense their excitement at having a white visitor, a "mundele" from America. I greeted them all in the Kikongo fashion, holding my forearm with my left hand as we shook hands and spoke the traditional greeting: "Kiambote, Mama." The women replied smiling with "Kiambote, Nengua." After three years here, that distinction still bothers me, but I try to accept it as part of their culture.

"Mwini osakidi," I said, knowing they'd giggle when I said the weather's hot in their language. They laughed and chattered, thinking I could understand. I regretted not being able to converse with them in Kikongo and vowed to make a greater effort to learn more of their language.

The ancient sun-dried brick building was covered with a corrugated tin roof that extended out on all four sides to large brick pillars, making a practical wrap-around porch to keep the church cooler on scorching days and give refuge during rainy season drenchers.

Inside, the villagers sat on handmade backless benches on a hard-packed dirt floor. The plastered walls hadn't been whitewashed in years. A chain suspended from the open rafters held a lantern that could be lit above the speaker who stood behind a simple table. A poster on the front wall admonished the congregation in French, "Lisez la Bible" – "Read the Bible." Plain wooden shutters on the side and back openings, where windows had never been installed, were thrown open to let in the morning light.

Thérèse was in charge of the service, so she asked me to hold her five-month-old son Charles. He'd been named after my Charles, as a souvenir they'd said, when he was born. He immediately proceeded to wet my skirt since he wore no diaper, just a little pair of shorts. Out here in Congo you don't worry about that; you just mop up baby and yourself and the rest will soon disappear in the heat!

Thérèse followed the stenciled program, letting our students and several local primary children read the verses from their Bible, and calling on several women to pray. A few members of the church choir were present so they decided to pick out a song and sing for us. They lined up along the west wall and sang acappella, in the African style, "What a Friend We Have in Jesus," clapping and swaying with the music. I'll write the words to the first verse here:

> *Yesu Nge u Nkundi eto,*
> *Nge okutuzolanga,*
> *Nge wanat'e tumbu yeto,*
> *Wau okutubanzanga.*
> *Nge olend'o van'o wete,*
> *Ntantu olend'o katula;*
> *Ovo se tunat'o mambu*
> *I kwa Nge tusambila.*

Half way through the service baby Charles started fussing. Thérèse came down the aisle, picked him up, and tied him on her back. Not missing a beat she returned to the front and continued her role as leader, a sleeping baby on her back.

The service ended with an offering (the equivalent of one dollar and two cents) and a closing prayer by a deacon. Then everyone went outside for the peanut offering on the porch, peanuts these women had labored over digging, planting, hoeing, and harvesting. They came one by one with peanuts they'd carried in an enamel dishpan, a bucket, or tied up in a cloth and poured them onto a mounded heap on the brick floor. One woman laid a bunch of bananas beside the pile. I thought of the widow in the New Testament and how Jesus said she gave more than anyone because she had given everything she had. Many of those women gave what they needed for themselves.

Luengo and Nsimba tied the peanuts in cloths and loaded them in the boot (as the British call the trunk) of our VWBug. Around four o'clock, when the lady deacons and students had returned from the villages, carrying buckets of peanuts on their heads, the local women gathered at our church and held a very nice service. My eighth grade girls had practiced and did a good job singing a couple of hymns with a tambourine.

Afterwards the deacon ladies sold the peanut offerings we'd all brought back. Lesley told me the money would be used for visitation and sewing classes in villages. I bought a big bucketful and sent it home with my houseboy's wife, Mama Louise. She dries, shells, and then rolls them with a bottle. When they're crushed into a paste she adds a bit of salt. This is the most excellent fresh peanut butter! If it's a bit dry Charles mixes in a little peanut oil. We're both looking forward to yummy crunchy peanut butter with our breakfast bread!

Our students reported good services and offerings in the surrounding villages. Several caught rides back to the station on transport trucks, but most returned on foot, each carrying a bucket of peanuts on her head. Poor Kiansansa arrived with her school uniform in ruins. Someone in the village she visited gave a stem of bananas, which she carried back on her head. Unfortunately, when the hot sun beat down on the stalk, the sap began to flow and dripped over her white blouse and blue pleated skirt. Banana sap stains are worse than blackberries – impossible to remove. So tomorrow I'll measure her and make a new uniform.

In spite of the long hot day, I'm glad I participated in this day of prayer. Things have been especially difficult in the girls' school recently. I've tried so hard to instill good morals in my students. Then out of the clear blue two weeks ago 15-year-old Marie-José, our local pastor's daughter turned up five months pregnant – again.

Her first, a baby boy, was born at the end of summer vacation. She's a big girl and had been able to hide her pregnancy last spring and finish seventh grade. At the beginning of this school year the pastor begged us to take her back, saying she'd made a confession to him. Marie-José pleaded with us to let her attend classes, said she was sorry and that she'd live with her parents in their home just across from the church. So under pressure from the pastor, but against my better judgment, we took her back.

Several girls had told me they didn't believe Marie-José was sorry or staying pure because she's been bottle-feeding her baby since he was born.

"What do you mean?" I asked.

They raised their eyebrows amazed at my ignorance and said, "Because she still wants to be with the guys!" Then I recalled a missionary telling me that as long as a Congolese woman is breastfeeding her child she's considered unclean and her husband won't touch her. The girls weren't a bit surprised when Marie-José admitted to a second pregnancy. The father is a handsome young Angolan refugee with no means to support her.

So just at a time when I needed it most, I received great encouragement from this special day of prayer, observing first-hand, Christians who, in spite of their difficult lives, remain faithful and courageous. Your loving daughter, Janet

Schoolgirls carrying buckets of peanuts from outlying villages on Women's World Day of Prayer.

## Women's World Day Of Prayer
## Friday, March 13, 1970

**Opening Prayer:**

*Our Father God, on this day set aside by the women of the world to come to you in prayer, we thank you for your abiding love and care for us, poor and weak though we be. Give us courage and strength to face our daily tasks, to live a life pleasing to you, to help our neighbors, to forgive those who've wronged us. Give us courage, Lord, to trust in you. Amen*

**Singing of Two Hymns:**

*"Pass Me Not O Gentle Savior" "Stand up, Stand up for Jesus"*

**Reading of the Scripture:**

*Psalm 27:1 The Lord is my light and my salvation; whom shall I fear? The Lord is the strength of my life; of whom shall I be afraid?*

*Psalm 27:14 Wait on the Lord: be of good courage, and he shall strengthen thine heart.*

*Proverbs 14:26 In the fear of the Lord is strong confidence: and His children shall have a place of refuge.*

*Isaiah 12:2 Behold, God is my salvation: I will trust and not be afraid.*

*John 14:27 Peace I leave with you, my grace I give unto you: not as the world giveth, give I unto you. Let not your heart be troubled, neither let it be afraid.*

**Remarks by the Leader.**
**Prayers for Courage.**
**Other Music.**
**Offering.**
**Closing Prayer.**

# A Horning Mennonite Funeral
# September 1951

"Nancy Smith's mother died," Daddy said as he sat down at the supper table one evening in early September. Mom looked up from fastening my baby sister Mary Anne into the old wooden high chair.

"Nancy's been worried about her," Mom said. "She had a stroke last week."

"Died at home in her sleep. Peter told me when I went out to rake the last of his hay."

"I want to go to that funeral. Peter's been so good to us and he *is* our deacon."

"It'll be later in the week. He said he'd let us know. I think we can all go," Daddy said, looking around the table at the five of us children."

"They know how to behave in church. But in this one you can't talk at all. Not even a whisper," Mom said, eyeing me.

My mother worried for the next two days. She said women in the Horning church all wear black for a funeral. But Mom didn't have a black dress. She hated black. She said she guessed she'd just have to wear her navy blue communion dress. It'd be all right because after all she'd be a visitor. Anita could wear the dark blue dress Mom had made her when she was baptized.

"What about me?" I asked. "What about me, Mom?"

"You can wear your charcoal dress," Mom said.

"But it's got pink lines in it," I protested.

"You're just a child. It doesn't matter."

But it did matter. I worried for two days about my dress. I could just see all the other eleven-year-old girls in their black dresses and there I'd be in a gray one with pink lines on it. I went back to my closet and paged through my dresses again and again, but couldn't find anything better.

Mom had starched the boys' long sleeved white shirts and told them to tuck them in good that morning, Carl in his blue Sunday pants and Dennis in his brown ones. After I'd pulled on my long brown cotton stockings and tied my oxfords, I went downstairs. "Janet, sit down here and let Anita put your hair up. Make it good and tight so it doesn't fall down," Mom added.

Anita parted my hair in the middle and combed it back, winding it into as tight a bun as she could. "Sit still," she whispered. I tried, but it was hard. I hated having my hair twisted. I could feel individual hairs pulling like a needle scratching across my scalp.

As Anita worked Mom set her dark blue crocheted handbag on the table next to me. "I need to take some quiet things for Mary Anne to play with," she said, talking to herself. Besides several diapers and an extra pair of rubber pants she put in two little dog magnets, a couple of tiny plastic dolls no bigger than my little finger, several colorful handkerchiefs, her folding cup, two picture books, a bottle of juice, several crackers. I knew she was worried about keeping our two-year-old sister quiet.

"That looks all right I guess," Mom said as she slid a couple of bobby pins in on each side of my head and straightened my covering. "Wear your sweater," she said.

"It's a little breezy today.

"We need to go or we'll be late," Daddy said as he shrugged into his plain coat. "I'll go get the car started." Mom said the Black Bumpers wore their bonnets year round, not just in cold weather like at our church. So we put on our black bonnets over our white coverings.

"We're not taking that Ford," Mom had said. "It would be the only one in the parking lot that's not black. We'll just have to take a chance and go in the old '35 Chevy."

Daddy had recently bought a dark blue car from a friend of his and hadn't even thought about the color. It looked conservative to him. But Mennonites drove only *black* cars, especially Horning Mennonites. They even painted the bumpers black. Mom said that's why people often called them Black Bumper Mennonites.

So Daddy had tuned up the old Chevy and said it would make the 15-mile trip to Fairview Church. We climbed in the back, Anita and I in the middle. The boys always got the window seats. Mom held Mary Anne on her lap up front.

We breathed a sigh of relief when Daddy finally steered the old Chevy into a parking space beside the 1950s models all around us. "I don't care," Mom said. "The color matches."

We could see people standing in groups outside the church, men on one side, women on the other. Anita and I followed as Mom carried Mary Anne to where the coffin was resting on a low wooden stand. It looked kind of like a couple of wheelbarrows glued together. Two handles stuck out on each end, but it stood on four legs instead of a wheel. I was surprised how low it was. *Just the right height for me to easily look inside*, I thought.

This was different from my Pop Snavely's funeral when I was nine. I remembered going inside Fishburn Church and walking past my great-grandpa's big shiny casket with creamy satiny material around him. The lid had been propped open at the back. Huge bouquets of fragrant garden flowers had lined the edge of the platform, and soft organ music had floated through the sanctuary. Pop had been dressed in a suit and tie and looked so clean and peaceful. Anita and I had worn our prettiest Sunday dresses and so did all my cousins. An usher had taken us to special seats at the front where we sat with Grandma and all my aunts and uncles.

This funeral was nothing like Pop's. Nobody had brought flowers. No music was played. Everyone stood silently watching. The casket was different too. Mom had told us it would be a handmade pine coffin shaped like an Egyptian mummy. Wow! She was right. And the lid didn't open like Pop Snavely's. This one had a little door that slid open at the top so all we could see was the lady's head and shoulders. Mom told us later Mrs. Brubaker was dressed in a shroud. She said Hornings preferred for their members to be buried in a simple muslin white shroud because that's how Jesus and Lazarus in the Bible were buried. They even had the verses written about it in their rules and discipline book.

After we got in line and walked past the coffin we stood around under the trees with the other women. More people came by to look. Nobody talked. I stood there and watched, listening to the falling leaves crunching underfoot and birds chirping overhead. Most ladies were holding a baby, like Mom. Her blue handbag dangled from Anita's shoulder. The Horning women carried big black purses and wore all black, from their long full dresses with wide capes and aprons to their plain bonnets with fat bows tied under their chins. Even the little girls wore big bonnets. I knew Mom was glad we'd worn ours even though they were more modern.

I pulled on Mom's arm and whispered, "What are we waiting for?"

"The family is at their home with the preachers. We're waiting for them to arrive," she said in my ear, and then pointed toward the road.

A line of cars was pulling up to the front of the parking lot. An old man got out. *I bet that's her husband*, I thought. Nancy and Peter Smith got out of another car. And I guessed the others were Nancy's brothers and sisters. When they came toward the coffin the men took off their black hats and held them in their hands. "Out of respect," Daddy always said.

We watched as Mrs. Brubaker's family filed by the coffin. Her daughters looked so sad; some were crying. Then a man closed the lid above the lady's face. Four men picked up the coffin carrier, one holding each of the handles. It reminded me of a picture I'd seen in my geography book of Chinamen carrying a rich person in the streets of Peking. The family and friends followed as the pallbearers carried the coffin down to the end of the parking lot and through the gate to the little cemetery. Anita and I shuffled along with Mom at the edge of the crowd. I saw my brothers and Daddy on the other side with the men. Behind them barn swallows flitted in and out of the unused horse sheds.

When the coffin was set over the grave, the pallbearers stepped back and the song leader called out in a heavy Pennsylvania Dutch accent that at the family's request they would sing "Asleep in Jesus." Crowded around the open grave, filling the little cemetery, and overflowing into the parking lot, the congregation joined him in singing this slow sorrowful hymn.

> *Asleep in Jesus! Blessed sleep, From which*
> *none ever wakes to weep;*
> *A calm and undisturbed repose, Unbroken by*
> *the last of foes.*

The harmony was beautiful, but the mournful tune made me cry as they sang through all the verses. I didn't want my brothers to see my tears so I hid behind Mom. Then in his deep preacher voice the bishop began reading Bible verses from his small black funeral book. Looking around the little cemetery, I wondered who was buried in the other graves marked with simple gray speckled granite tombstones.

"'And God shall wipe away all tears from their eyes: and there shall be no more death, neither sorrow, nor crying, neither shall there be any more pain,'" the bishop intoned. I wanted to ask someone how God could take away sorrow and crying when everyone was so sad. I wondered what it was like to die.

"'In my Father's house are many mansions: if it were not so I would have told you: I go to prepare a place for you …. I will come again ….'" *Is Mrs. Brubaker somewhere up there in a mansion watching us?* I thought. *Where is heaven? Will I be ready if Jesus comes back?*

Mary Anne was quiet in Mom's arms, looking around at the harvested fields and the cows in the pasture next to the cemetery. And then I heard the bishop's voice change to a quieter tone as he read more from his little book. "'For as much as it pleased Almighty God in His wise providence to take out of this world the soul of the departed – we commit the body to the ground, and the soul has gone to God who gave it, looking for the general resurrection of the last day and the life of the world to come through Jesus Christ our Lord. Amen.'"

And then they were lowering the coffin into the ground with straps. Several men picked up shovels and filled the grave with the loose dirt piled around it. When they'd finished making a rounded mound at the top, another minister pronounced the benediction: "'The grace of our Lord Jesus Christ, the love of God the Father, and the fellowship of the Holy Spirit, be with us all evermore. Amen.'"

The people seemed to know what to do. They turned and walked to the church. Daddy and my brothers followed the men around back to their door and we girls followed Mom behind the women to the right.

Our door led into the ladies' cloakroom. The women hung their stiff black outdoor bonnets on the rows and rows of hooks covering the walls. We did the same thing in our church except our bonnets weren't as big and old-fashioned as these. And we used a thin band and closed it with a hook and eye instead of a big wide ribbon and bow. They all looked exactly alike. I wondered if they ever got them mixed up.

Three elderly ladies greeted us and shook our hands as we entered the anteroom. "Where should we sit?" Mom asked them, shifting Mary Anne to her other hip.

"Go to this section right inside the door with the mothers." Mom went to the third row behind some girls about my age. Anita and I sat with Mom on a hard straight-backed bench. The slanted board for a footrest was too far away for me, but Mom propped her foot on it as she settled Mary Anne on her lap and pulled off her sweater.

I wondered how I was going to sit for almost two hours with just a slat across the top of the back of my shoulders. These people would probably laugh and say, "Oh, we're used to it. We grew up this way."

The congregation was filing in silently behind the family. Nobody smiled or nodded or shook hands. They just took their seats. I turned around and looked at the people. There were two sections of benches filled with girls and women. The little girls my age were on the front two benches. Behind them the teenage girls. We were sitting with women with babies at the back.

On the other side of the church the little boys were up front and the teenagers behind them. Married men holding toddlers were behind and around them. The old people sat behind the family on benches facing the center aisle so their sides were to us, the men on their side, the women on ours. Even Mrs. Brubaker's family was separated by this tradition.

Eight men were sitting at the singer's table, four on each bench along the sides. I knew that's what they called it.

Mom had told us about some of the differences in our churches. They didn't have a raised platform either. They just used a table for their pulpit.

I was fascinated by the rows and rows of black hooks on the men's side, standing out from the white walls like soldiers. Starting behind the preachers' table, they marched across the front wall, down the side, and across the back.

Suddenly one of the men seated at the singers' table called out in a loud voice, "At the request of the family we'll make use of the song 'On Jordan's Stormy Banks.'" Everyone bent and pulled a tiny four-by-six-inch hymnal out of the slot under the bench in front, little books printed with only the words, no musical notes. The chorister's voice led out without even using a pitchpipe:

> *On Jordan's stormy banks I stand, And cast a*
> *    wishful eye*
> *To Canaan's fair and happy land, where my*
> *    possessions lie.*

By the second note the low-ceilinged room was flooded with exquisite acappella four-part harmony. The voices of the young people gave the music a full youthful quality, the basses bringing out the rich deep tones. The packed church had become an awesome choir, singing verse after verse about the joys of heaven.

While we were singing four elderly men and two younger ones solemnly filed in along the front wall from a side door. They were carrying broad-brimmed black hats and wearing white shirts buttoned to the neck and collarless black plain suits. They turned, hung their hats on hooks on the front wall above their bench, and sat down behind the unraised preachers' table facing the congregation. On the table a glass pitcher filled with water and a tumbler stood next to a stack of books.

After the music died away a minister stood and read from his Bible. "'As for man, his days are as grass: As a flower of the field, so he flourisheth, for the wind passeth over it, and it is gone; and the place thereof shall know it no more.'" He talked for about 15 minutes about the brevity of life and everyone was sad again. Suddenly lowering his voice he said, "Let us bow for silent prayer."

Immediately we stood, turned, and dropped to our knees facing our bench. Mom set Mary Anne on the bench as she knelt in front of her. After two or three minutes of silence, the preacher shouted, "Amen," and the congregation rose, turned, and sat.

Another minister stood and read: "'As the cloud is consumed and vanisheth away; so he that goeth down to the grave shall come up no more. He shall return no more to his house, neither shall his place know him any more.'" The preacher expounded on his text, talking about death and heaven, the great resurrection, and judgment in the last days. He warned of punishment to come if we did not believe as Mrs. Brubaker had. Everyone, even the young people, sat stone faced, not uttering a sound.

In the background babies gurgled and cooed. If one cried the mother breast-fed him using her cape to cover his face as he suckled. I watched a three-year-old girl in blond braids sitting beside her daddy across from us in the men's section. She quietly played with his cloth handkerchief the entire two hours. Another toddler amused herself with her pacifier throughout the service, never getting off the bench. Mom gave Mary Anne her juice and she fell asleep. My sister would wake up and cry if Mom laid her down, so she didn't take her out to one of the cribs in the anteroom.

A young minister stood and said one of Mrs. Brubaker's daughters had asked him to read a poem in memory of their mother. Putting on his glasses he read from a sheet of paper:

### Mother Has Fallen Asleep

*Mother was tired and weary,*
*Weary with toil and pain.*
*Put by her glasses and rocker*
*She will not need them again.*
*Into heaven's mansions she's entered*
*Never to sigh or to weep.*
*After long years with life's struggles,*
*Mother has fallen asleep.*
*Near other loved ones we laid her*
*Low in the churchyard to lie*
*And though our hearts are near broken,*
*Yet we would not question, "Why?"*
*She does not rest 'neath the grasses,*
*'Though o'er her dear grave they'll creep*
*She has gone into the kingdom,*
*Mother has fallen asleep.*
*Rest thy tired feet now forever,*
*Dear wrinkled hands are so still*
*Blasts of the Earth shall no longer*
*Throw o'er our loved one a chill,*
*Angels through heaven will guide her,*
*Jesus will still bless and keep;*
*Not for the world would we wake her,*
*Mother has fallen asleep.*

Everyone was crying by the time he'd finished reading. The women had pulled out their pretty lacy handkerchiefs and were using them to wipe their eyes. Tears were running down my cheeks and I didn't even know Mrs. Brubaker. I looked up at Mom and her eyes were watery. I didn't want to think about what would happen to me if my mother died.

Joseph Hostetter, a minister the family had invited to preach the sermon, stood and in a loud voice solemnly addressed us. Brother Hostetter had grown up in Maryland speaking English rather than German like his Pennsylvania brethren. He was confident and his words flowed. "If sister Leah could speak to us today she would say, 'Weep not for me but for yourselves and your children.' She was prepared and has gone to be with her heavenly Father. The apostle Paul said, 'For we must all appear before the judgment seat of Christ; that everyone may receive the things done in his body, according to that he hath done, whether it be good or bad.' What about you and your children? Are you ready to meet your Maker?" he asked.

Again we knelt for prayer. This time the preacher prayed out loud for our souls. He prayed that like Mrs. Brubaker we would be ready to meet God at the judgment seat when the time came. Then he recited the Lord's Prayer as the rest of us prayed it silently.

We sang two more hymns about death and going to heaven. Finally the bishop rose and announced that everyone was invited to a fellowship supper at the farmhouse. Then he asked us to stand for the benediction. "Dismiss us with thy blessing, Lord," he said, raising his arm straight in front of him, slightly above his head, palm down. Then quoting Jude 24 he continued, "'Now unto Him that is able to keep you from falling, and to present you faultless before the presence of his glory with exceeding joy, to the only wise God our Saviour, be glory and majesty, dominion and power, both now and ever. Amen.'"

The church emptied quickly. I put on my sweater and bonnet and followed Mom and Anita through the women's anteroom.

"Can we go to the dinner?" I asked Mom, envisioning the pies and cakes they would be serving.

"No, it's just for the family and relatives. I have a pot of stew at home to warm up for us," Mom said as we made our way past groups of women standing around outside talking. I saw Daddy and my brothers coming toward us past the iron water pump. A couple of kids were pushing the long handle up and down filling a tin cup they'd taken from a hook. Water gushed through the low slanted trough and out onto the drying grass.

As Daddy steered our old Chevy back onto the Macadam road, I felt good about that day. Mom shouldn't have worried so much that I would embarrass her. I had behaved. How could I have been silly at a funeral when everyone was so sad and serious? I had a lot of questions about what the preachers had said. I wanted to know what happened to the life – the part that makes people move and think – when someone died. How did it leave when a person stopped breathing? And where did it go? I wondered if my brothers felt the same way. They were awfully quiet. I decided to ask Mom later.

The singers' table, perpendicular to the preacher's table and bench, inside a Horning Mennonite church.

# Mukielo
# 1969

Ngombe Lutete, Congo
April 3, 1969

Dear Mom and Daddy,

I thought I should write and tell you about a sad state of affairs we experienced last week. Since we don't have afternoon classes on Saturdays, we'd finished teaching at twelve o'clock and were looking forward to catching up on grading papers and taking it easy the rest of the day. Charles had just leaned back in his chair, commenting how good the dried salt fish and saka-saka was that Mama Tuzolana had sent over, when John Russell, one of the British missionaries, knocked on our door. "A letter arrived from Mukielo's village about a half hour ago," he said. "His mother died in childbirth early this morning."

"Mukielo, in our seventh grade?" I asked.

"That's right," John said. "They're planning on the funeral this afternoon. The boy needs to be taken home in the Jeep. Would it be possible for you to drive him? If the weather holds you should be able to do it in an hour and be back before dark."

Charles and I looked at each other and nodded. "I can be ready in ten minutes," I said, reaching for a basket. I put in a few oatmeal cookies, a bottle of boiled water, an umbrella, and some reading material, in case the pick-up broke down, as it often does.

John told us Mukielo's village has no pastor, so we needed to take our own Tata Ntela and his wife with us. Their only spiritual leader was the hardworking mother who'd just died. "And," he said, "you probably should know that her husband is an alcoholic."

Domingo, our school mechanic, filled the tank with gasoline, checked the tires, and wished us well. We drove across campus past the generator to Tata Ntela's house. There we found Mukielo sitting on a backless bench behind the kitchen with a primary student from his village. I'm sure the enormity of his mother's death hadn't yet sunk in, but his grief was apparent.

Although Tata Ntela rode in the cab with Charles and me, we didn't converse much because his French is limited and we speak no Kikongo beyond hello and goodbye. His wife, the two boys, a couple of other students, and a primary teacher sat on wood benches in the back of the truck.

Domingo had given general directions to get us headed in the right direction further out into the bush. After what seemed like hours of bumping over potholes on a rutted dirt road through drizzling rain, we suddenly came out of the forest into a small clearing and a little village. Three small adobe-style brick houses with corrugated tin roofs and windows that opened and shut with wood shutters were probably the homes of the chief and his relatives. The rest were tiny rectangle-shaped thatched mud huts. There wasn't a blade of grass to be seen. The bare clay made it easier to spot snakes or rats and to discourage them from invading the houses and hiding in the thatch. Villagers were constantly on the lookout for vipers and black mambas.

Tata Ntela motioned for Charles to stop near a mud hut where a palm branch-covered lean-to had been erected at the front. According to custom, the body, wrapped in sheets, would lie there on a mat surrounded by women who would sing and pray until the coffin was completed. But the rain, now a downpour, had driven them inside.

Wading through streams of water, avoiding mud puddles, dodging chickens, pigs, and goats we reached the veranda intact. A shirtless man in the doorway was introduced to us as Mukielo's father, the husband of the lady who'd just died. He sat on the dirt floor, his head in his hands. Inside, his five children and a group of women kept a quiet vigil in the semi-darkness.

When the rain slackened, village people gathered around and we stood there with them, beside Mukielo and family members as Pastor Ntela read some verses of comfort. We sang several hymns in Kikongo. The pastor prayed. But the carpenter still hadn't finished the coffin so the burial was scheduled to take place the following morning. Tata Ntela explained that we were pressed to get back before dark; he had pastoral duties on campus the next morning. I felt regret that this devoted mother and church worker would be lowered into the ground without benefit of the clergy, but we'd made no provisions to stay overnight in a village.

"Could I see the baby before we leave?" I asked.

"Certainly," a neighbor answered. "He's with his aunt in her house." We followed the man across the way and as we stooped to enter, our eyes had to readjust to the deep shadows. Aunty was sitting on a grass woven mat in the middle of the floor surrounded by her own toddlers and holding her sister's newborn. She was feeding him undiluted evaporated milk from a baby bottle. But adding water that hadn't been boiled could have been even more disastrous.

"Is there no other new mother who could nurse him?" I asked.

"None," my translator said. "But relatives are coming from Kinshasa by morning and it's certain they will take the baby back with them to be cared for in a dispensary."

We offered our sympathies and said a prayer. And then followed by several goats we tramped back to the palm-branched veranda where we offered our last respects to the deceased, the husband, and Mukielo. He assured us he'd return to school the following week. Inside the women wept silently, except for one who cried out, "Mukielo's mother was a hard worker. She loved her children and provided for them. She was our spiritual leader. Why must she be taken when so many others do nothing?"

I've been haunted by that question for years. To have it flung at me out here in the African bush in the cradle of poverty is unsettling. I wish I had the answer. Love, Janet

# Death in a Village
# Wednesday, April 10, 1969

One of the saddest aspects of life here in Congo is living with death – especially of women in childbirth, babies, and young children – often due to the lack of modern health care. And they have more than their share of fatalities from malaria, snake or scorpion bites, and more recently from road accidents.

Tata Wete and Mama Zola and their extended family are wild with grief at the loss of their son who died in Kinshasa on Monday. Sukama Jean was born thirty-three years ago in the little village of Kivianga on the edge of our post. A bright child, he'd been educated in our mission schools, always an honors student, graduating first in his class.

His family of poor subsistence farmers put their hopes on him, managing to scrape together the money for his elementary and high school education and later to get him into the University in Kinshasa. Mama Zola's dream came true when Sukama won a scholarship to UCLA and finished his undergraduate work and earned a Masters Degree in America.

After settling into a government job in Kinshasa two years ago, he didn't forget his family here in the village. He regularly sent his parents money for the nieces' and nephews' educations in spite of having a wife and three children to support there in the capital. Then late Monday afternoon a truck sideswiped him while he was walking home along a busy street, killing him instantly. Yesterday his body was brought back to his home in the bush for burial.

The whole village is in an uproar today. Just as I was leaving for school this morning to teach my seven-thirty class, Mpanzu came by. His face was strained. "I can't work today, Madame," he said in his broken French. "I'm needed in the village. Tata Wete is filled with grief. I must go."

"I'm so sorry," I said. "Poor Mama Zola."

"Sukama was her first son. What will become of the family now that he's gone?"

"I don't know," I said, shaking my head. "I just don't know." I was ashamed to even ask him to carry in several buckets of water from the cistern.

Last evening, hearing the drums, the singing, and wailing, I begged Charles to walk over to the village with me to pay our respects at the wake. He felt we would be intruding since we'd never met Sukama although we'd often heard people refer to him. But I convinced him the family would be honored to have us come by. After all, their son had been educated in Charles' home state.

"I hope it doesn't rain," I said, looking out the kitchen window at the swaying palms and papaya trees in our back yard. In deference to the grieving women, I wrapped an African cloth over my short dress in the ankle-length-style skirt Congolese women favor. On the way out Charles picked up an umbrella.

Swinging our kerosene lantern between us, we scuffed along the dusty road in our flip-flops, past the old corrugated tin church, and down into the village to Tata Wete and Mama Zola's little thatched mud-brick home beneath a canopy of mango trees. According to custom the narrow homemade wood coffin had been set on a low table under a hastily erected palm branch-covered veranda. The sliding lid had to remain closed because Sukama had not been embalmed, but his face could be seen through a little window at the top. There he would lie until morning, surrounded by the villagers, grieving for what might have been.

Several men came forward and, greeting us in French, led us to the casket. Charles stepped aside, but I leaned forward to get a glimpse of the handsome dark face lying on a snowy white pillow. They'd dressed him in a navy blue three-piece suit, undoubtedly one he often wore to his job in Kinshasa. Tears welled up in my eyes for this young man, barely older than myself.

His mother, seated in the dust, flung herself across the coffin wailing for this her eldest son who just the day before had been the hope of his family. Her heart-rending moans sent cold chills down my back. One of the village leaders called for chairs and invited us to sit down, but we drew back, not wanting to impose at this time of deep sorrow and anguish.

A group of women I didn't recognize had formed a circle beside the house and with measured sensuous steps were dancing gracefully round and round. In unison they chanted, singing a lament, raising palm branches to the sky, turning, twisting, folding the branches around their shoulders, bending and sweeping them over the dusty ground and back.

"What are they doing?" I whispered to one of my Congolese colleagues.

"They're calling on the spirits to stop the rain."

I understood their anxiety. The village had no building large enough to house the crowds. And everyone had to be fed. Behind Mama Zola's house women had piled wood, a lot of it sent from our school, to feed the small campfires under black cooking pots of bubbling brown beans, rice, or saka-saka with dried saltfish. Huge dishpans of donated chiquanga, a staple in their diet made from manioc, and cases of bottled Orange Fanta were stacked under a thatched lean-to beside the house. Our schoolgirls had helped by carrying buckets of water from the spring at the foot of the hill, but the bulk of the work fell on the village women.

At ten o'clock this morning we released our students from their classes to follow the enormous procession to the village graveyard carved into the red clay about halfway down the hill to the river. The narrow rocky footpath, eroded on the steepest parts by heavy seasonal rains, is a difficult descent in the best of circumstances. Today I feared for the pallbearers, but they were surefooted and gently placed the casket on boards over the yawning grave that village men had dug overnight.

We were halfway down the trail before I realized what was different – the silence. Not a drum, not a whistle. Nobody sang. No one talked. Just the thud of bare feet hitting the earth and the swishing of long skirts.

I'd never seen such a large crowd at a funeral out here in the bush. Many of Sukama's friends from Kinshasa stood stony-faced in smart dark three-piece suits beside villagers clad in faded kakis and plaid shirts. The women attired in colorful African cloths huddled together on one side, and our solemn students in their blue and white school uniforms spread out behind them on the fringes.

Under a relentless burning sun, Pastor Kwama, his flowing black robe rippling in the breeze, stood by the grave and read from the scripture. "'The Lord gave, and the Lord hath taken away; blessed be the name of the Lord. All flesh shall perish together, and man shall turn again unto dust. Then shall the dust return to the earth as it was; and the spirit shall return unto God who gave it.'" He ended with a long prayer thanking God for the time Sukama had lived among us, asking the Lord to give strength to this mourning family and friends, begging Him for some understanding of this tragic event.

And there on that wind-swept hill covered with tropical grass and stunted trees, overlooking the river where Sukama had been baptized as a schoolboy, amid sobs and whimpers, the pallbearers, using ropes, lowered their friend's dusky casket into the gaping grave. Then handing a shovel to his mother they stepped back as, tears streaming down her cheeks, Mama Zola began the process of filling the open tomb, throwing the first shovelful of red clay onto the coffin. One by one, family members, then friends, and finally school children took the shovel and tossed scoop after scoop of dirt into the open grave until a rounded mound of red clay covered it.

Slowly the women, babies tied on their backs, turned and started the laborious ascent climbing back to their daily toils, facing life without the one who'd been their hope and sustenance.

Tata Kwama, pastor of the village church
at Ngombe Lutete.

# Choices

He that believeth and is baptized
shall be saved;
but he that believeth not shall be damned.
Mark 16:16

# Baptism by Pouring
# April 1952

"**Y**ou need a new cape dress for your baptism," Mom said when I got home from school one Friday afternoon in early spring. "We'll go to Marion and Ruth's tomorrow and get some material."

"I have to wear navy blue, don't I?"

"As young as you are I don't think you need a dark dress for baptism. But we'll make you one for communion. And I'll get you a couple of new coverings."

I treasured visits to Marion and Ruth's, a covering and piece goods shop in Mount Joy. Mennonites from all over our conference went there to buy material, snaps, thread, needles, thimbles, in fact anything they needed to make their clothes and quilts. Anita and I would look at gingham plaids, crinkle crepes, and even the more expensive chambray or powder puff muslin, hoping to find something pretty and that Mom would approve.

And of course we'd get coverings after trying on a dozen or so from the ready-made stacks lined up on shelves according to size and shape. When Mom figured out what kind she liked best, she started buying hers from the shelf as well, rather than having them made to order. She preferred a wide front and corners behind her ears. She said rounded ones were too liberal, but she didn't want her covering *too* big, coming *over* her ears like the old ladies.

In her sewing machine drawers Mom kept a spool of narrow black ribbon for herself and white for my sister Anita and me to fasten ties at the corners of our coverings. Anita and I wore white strings. That's what everyone called them, strings. Mom put black ones on hers, because they were more conservative. But she refused to tie them under her chin like the older women did. That was *too* conservative and besides she couldn't stand anything around her neck. Mom fastened a little safety pin to the ends to weight her strings and then stuffed them inside the back of her dress. Lots of women did that and *all* the young girls. But we did wear them. No strings was just too liberal. Nobody talked about what was conservative or not. Everyone just knew.

The spring before, when I was in fifth grade, we'd attended a weekend Bible conference at the Steelton Mennonite Mission. George Brunk was the main speaker. I didn't get bored during his sermons; he was loud and told lots of stories so you'd remember what he talked about. For his last sermon he preached on "The Highway to Hell." It was scary to think about burning forever in a lake of fire. I made my decision that night, and stood during the invitation to accept Christ as my Savior. I was sitting next to Elsie Risser, our bishop's wife, on the second row. She was shocked.

"You're so little I never thought about you being old enough for that," she said.

"I'm ten years old."

"Well, that's certainly old enough to know right from wrong."

Brother Brunk sent those of us who'd responded out to an anteroom where some ministers prayed with us. Isaac Baer asked me why I'd stood during the invitation and I told him I wanted to be saved and go to heaven.

My parents were surprised too, but happy. "Our desire is to see all of our children get converted and join the church," my mother said. And I knew that was true. I'd often heard her and Daddy pray that prayer.

I wanted Mennonite clothes right then, in fifth grade. But Mom had a different idea. "It's so close to the end of the school year," she said, "Let's just wait till summer to get you a covering and make cape dresses."

"I don't want to wait," I whined. "If women are supposed to wear a covering, then I need one *now*."

"Since there aren't any other Mennonites in your school it'll be a lot easier for you to start wearing a cape and covering when you start sixth grade in the fall. Besides, you'll grow over the summer and we'll have to make you new dresses for school anyway."

"All my friends at church started wearing a covering when they got converted. They'll think I didn't really mean it."

My mother must have felt guilty because we soon made a trip to Marion and Ruth's. She twisted my slippery fine hair into a bun and stuck in hairpins. It was uncomfortable and I was sure it would fall down. Mom said the covering would help hold it in place.

Marion and Ruth didn't have any conservative coverings in my small size in stock. "Little girls like you usually wear a flat covering over their braids hanging down their back," Marion said.

"Absolutely not," my mother said. "That would just lead to liberalism."

"I want to wear my hair up like the other girls at church," I said.

Finally Marion found two that fit me, but made of a material that would shrink. They would need to be dry-cleaned. Mom decided to buy them to use for the time being and ordered several made of washable nylon net.

Monday morning I got up, dressed, fastened my hair in a bun, put on my covering, and went down to breakfast. "It's pouring rain," my mother said. "If that covering gets wet it'll shrink. Maybe you'd better wait another day."

"No," I insisted, "I'm wearing it today."

"Then carry it inside your raincoat and don't crush it. If you wear it under your bandana it'll get wet and squashed."

So I sloshed out the lane to the bus, protecting my new covering under my coat. When I got to school I made a beeline to the cloakroom off the front of our room and hung up my coat. Then I took off my bandana and hung it over the hook. Kids started looking at my hair in a bun. When I pulled out the covering and put it on they got quiet. That's when I began to feel nervous and realized my mother'd been trying to shield me from this.

Suddenly, my friend Marlene Dressler was standing beside me squealing in a loud whisper, "You joined, didn't you?" I nodded and she continued, "That's wonderful. Were you baptized on Sunday?"

"No, not yet. I have to go to instruction meetings first."

"We don't wear coverings till after we're baptized. And we just wear them on Sundays."

"We wear ours all the time," I told her. I knew she went to Spring Creek Church of the Brethren. I'd heard they wore theirs only to church. Mennonites said the covering is a prayer veiling and since everyone should be in a constant attitude of prayer, we needed to wear it all the time.

"Hey guys, look! Janet is joining her church!" Everyone in the cloakroom gawked at me. The first bell rang and we moved into the classroom to our seats. Mrs. Edwards did a double take, turning around to look again.

Marlene was still telling kids I had joined and I could feel everyone staring at the back of my head. I hoped I'd gotten my covering on straight. My friend, Ruthie, leaned over and said, "That's wonderful you decided to join." But I could hear other kids snickering and wondered if it was because of me. I found it difficult to concentrate on my lessons, but I was still glad I'd made my decision.

One Sunday morning that fall, the bishop announced he would begin instruction meetings for candidates who'd made a confession of faith. Anyone wanting to be baptized and join the church had to attend these evening classes at the bishop's house.

Five cape dresses hung in my closet – plaid or flowered cotton dresses I'd helped my mother sew and that I'd been wearing to sixth grade. Although I looked the part, wearing the regulation clothes and covering, I was eager to attend instruction meetings so I could be baptized at spring communion and become a full-fledged member.

Daddy dropped off my brother Dennis and me for our first meeting at Bishop Noah Risser and his wife Elsie's big white frame farmhouse. We stepped softly into the shadowy parlor. Straight-back chairs had been set between stuffed ones to form a circle. Looking around to see who else was present, we found seats and waited. One by one others arrived and joined us until all nine chairs were taken.

The bishop took charge and began by explaining the necessity of attending every session to learn what would be required of us as members of the church. His wife Elsie handed round a thin pack of papers duplicated on a purple copy master. The course was divided into six lessons beginning with the Bible, God, Christ and the Holy Spirit. The bishop explained that each lesson would probably take several sessions so our classes would last well into the winter. In lesson two we would study Satan, the fall of man, and sin. Later we'd learn about salvation, faith, and obedience. I already knew a lot of this material. I'd read our conference's pamphlet of rules and regulations and the Mennonite Confession of Faith, a little booklet containing our denomination's history and beliefs.

All winter long we attended instruction meeting once a week or every two weeks, working through those lessons, looking up verses in the Bible, listening to the bishop explain self-denial, Christian service, the church ordinances. He told us God hated pride. It was the most abominable of sins. He said that even though we were far too young to be worrying about being drafted into the military, that's not all the doctrine of non-resistance was about. It was about turning the other cheek and not fighting back. Learning to live in peace with everyone, especially our families.

The bishop told us if we got insurance, life insurance in particular, we were telling God we didn't trust Him to take care of us. That's why our churches had started a program of car and health insurance, so Mennonites everywhere could help each other. I liked the idea of being part of a caring church family.

Finally, it was springtime and our instruction meetings finished. The bishop told us communion would be the third Sunday in April and we'd be baptized the day before, at preparatory service, so we could participate in communion.

Almost a year had passed since I'd made my decision to become a Christian and a Mennonite. Dennis and I were finally ready to be baptized. My brother was 14 and looked so grown-up in his new light brown plain suit Mom and Daddy had bought for him in Elizabethtown at Martin's store. The tailor had altered one of their worldly suits, re-cutting the lapels and making his new jacket into a Mennonite plain coat.

I found it hard to sit still in the back seat of our 1935 Chevy. We passed cows grazing in green meadows, munching tender shoots next to newly plowed fields ready for spring planting. Finally, Daddy turned into the parking lot beside the big brick church and found an empty spot near the cemetery.

We hurried inside and hung our sweaters and bonnets on hooks at the back. Before going to our seats Anita helped me straighten my covering and the cape of my new pink, gray, and white plaid dress. I wouldn't be sitting beside Jenny Lepperd today or sucking on mints. The bishop had told the nine of us to sit on the front bench. I walked down the left side aisle and stopped beside Jenny. She looked up and smiled and whispered, "You're getting baptized today, aren't you?" I nodded and she slipped a fat pink mint out of her pocket and put it in my hand. I continued down the aisle and took a seat on the front bench.

Preparatory service wasn't new to me. I'd always attended with my family on Saturday afternoon, the day before communion, so I knew what to expect. Besides, the bishop had explained this service in our instruction class. We needed to prepare and examine ourselves to make sure we didn't sin when we took communion.

Mom said you needed to fast and pray and think about your sins and confess them before taking communion, which was a very serious business. If you took communion and hadn't confessed your sins the Bible said you would be eating and drinking damnation to your soul. Mom worried about that. Twice a year Mom fasted and prayed the day before communion to make sure her sins were all forgiven.

I felt odd sitting there on the front bench with the other girls in our baptismal class. The bishop came and rearranged us so I was seated closest to the aisle on the women's side and my brother Dennis was closest on the men's. That way when it came time for us to be baptized I'd kneel beside my brother in the middle of the line.

We'd been together for ten weeks learning about the Christian life, and now we were here to answer the bishop's questions before the congregation and to receive baptism. *I'm so nervous. This is such a solemn moment. The Bishop told us we were making vows to God – a serious business.* Sylvan Myers, one of our ministers, read the account of Christ's baptism and then asked us to kneel for silent prayer. We turned around and faced our bench kneeling before our Maker. *Dear God, please help me behave myself and do what's right. I get in so much trouble at home. Help me not to fuss with my brothers. Forgive my sins. I want to go to heaven.*

"Amen," Sylvan said. We rose, turned from our kneeling position, and again sat facing the platform where the ministers were seated.

Bishop Risser came to the pulpit to preach our baptismal service, reminding us of the importance of this doctrine. "Christ's last commission to his disciples was to go, teach, and baptize in the name of the Father, Son and Holy Spirit. Our Lord said that whoever believes and is baptized will be saved, but whoever does not believe will be damned." He told the congregation we were presenting ourselves for baptism and to be received into the communion and fellowship of the Mennonite Church.

"They have been instructed in the doctrines of the Gospel and in the ordinances and requirements of the church," he continued, "and have given evidence that they are prompted in their purpose by the Spirit of God, that they are willing to forsake sin and the world, to consecrate themselves to the service of God and from henceforth to be disciples and followers of Christ. And as there is joy in heaven over one sinner that repenteth, so let our hearts rejoice that God has led these precious souls to turn from their former ways and come into the fold of Christ. As we thus rejoice let us likewise pray that God may lead yet many more to follow their good example. Amen."

The bishop came down in front of the pulpit and asked us to stand in a row at the head of the aisle. My brother and I met in the center and stood beside each other, the rest of the boys to his right, the girls to my left. The bishop then addressed the following questions to us: "Do you believe in one true, eternal, and almighty God, who is the Creator and Preserver of all visible and invisible things? Do you believe in Jesus Christ, as the only begotten Son of God, that He is the only Savior of mankind, that He died upon the cross, and gave Himself a ransom for our sins, that through Him we might have eternal life? Do you believe in the Holy Ghost which proceedeth from the Father and the Son; that He is an abiding Comforter, sanctifies the hearts of men, and guides them into all truth?"

And we answered one after the other down the row, "I do."

The bishop continued, "Are you truly sorry for your past sins, and are you willing to renounce Satan, the world, and all walks of darkness, and your own carnal will and sinful desires?"

We answered one after the other, "I am."

Then the bishop asked his final question, "Do you promise by the grace of God, and the aid of the Holy Spirit, to submit yourself to Christ and His Word, and faithfully to abide in the same until death?"

To this last question we again answered, "I do."

After announcing that two of the candidates, Helen and her brother Glenn Brubaker, would be baptized in the stream behind the church after the service, the bishop asked them to be seated on the front bench, the rest of us to kneel, and the congregation to rise. He knelt with us and prayed for God's blessing upon us and that we might have grace to remain steadfast and be faithful to the end in the promises we had made.

The bishop stood while we remained kneeling. Peter Smith, our deacon, came forward with a small white enamel basin of water. Starting with the boys the bishop laid his hands on the head of the first applicant and said, "Upon the confession of thy faith, which thou hast made before God and these witnesses, I baptize thee with water, in the name of the Father, and of the Son, and of the Holy Ghost." As he said each name of the Divinity, he reached into the basin with cupped hands, took some water, and let it flow out over the head of the kneeling applicant.

I watched as they approached Dennis. He sat back on his feet and as the bishop poured a handful of water on his head it ran down over his new brown suit. I worried that it would be ruined and desperately wanted to whisper to him to lean forward. But I watched silently. As the bishop approached me I knelt straight and tall, my head tilted forward, the water running from my head to the floor, my new dress remaining dry.

Later I asked my brother, "Why didn't you kneel front so the water wouldn't make your new suit wet?"

"Wasn't that the whole point of it?" he replied. Thinking about his answer suddenly I regretted not having leaned back so the water could have drenched my clothes. *I wonder if the Lord was displeased with my baptism. I wonder if it even counts.*

After we'd all been baptized, the bishop returned to the first boy, took him by the hand and said, "In the name of Christ and his Church I give you my hand. Arise. And as Christ was raised up by the glory of the Father, even so thou also shalt walk in newness of life, and as long as thou art faithful and abidest in the doctrine of His Word, thou art His disciple indeed, and shalt be acknowledged as a member of the body of Christ, and a brother in the Church." He then gave him the kiss of peace, and said, "The Lord bless thee and keep thee. Amen."

He moved down the line repeating the same words and the kiss until he came to us girls. After giving me his hand and having me stand, his wife came and kissed me and the other girls on the lips, saying, "God bless you," to each of us. Then all the ministers and deacons came and shook our hands and their wives lined up and kissed all of us girls.

We were now full-fledged members of Stauffers Mennonite Church and could participate in council meetings, communion, and feet washing. I felt so grown-up, yet worried I hadn't done enough.

The bishop began singing "Blest Be The Tie That Binds" and we all joined in, harmonizing in four parts this ancient hymn, which that day took on new meaning for me. When the last notes died away, the bishop said, "We'll conclude our service down by the stream," and excused the two candidates to go and change into other clothes. Reverently we stopped by the coat hooks and put on our sweaters and bonnets, nodding to our friends as we quietly filed down the road to the little stream at the bottom of the hill where the deacon had had a dam built forming a small waterhole.

Wearing his hip boots the bishop waded into the water as we stood silently watching. Putting out his hand he helped Glenn step into the pool and kneel. Then dipping his hands into the icy stream he began the same process he'd done inside the building, asking the questions, pouring three handfuls of water over his head, and extending the right hand of fellowship. The deacon helped Glenn out onto the bank into heavy towels and a blanket, as his sister Helen entered the water.

I envied those two young people. I'd begged Mom to let me be baptized with them in the stream. "That's the way Jesus was baptized," I'd argued.

"It's too cold in April," she'd said. "You'll be sick again." Feeling guilty when I continued begging, she'd taken me to our family doctor and asked his opinion. He advised me to wait until June. *I'd be so embarrassed. Nobody is ever baptized in June – only in the spring and fall, at communion time. God wouldn't let me get sick when I was getting baptized.* But Mom's word was final. I was baptized inside the building.

As I watched the shivering teens step onto the bank I knew in my heart Mom had been right. But as we sang a final hymn and their parents hurried them into the backseat of their car and whisked them away home to a warm kitchen and dry clothes I wondered if their baptism hadn't been better.

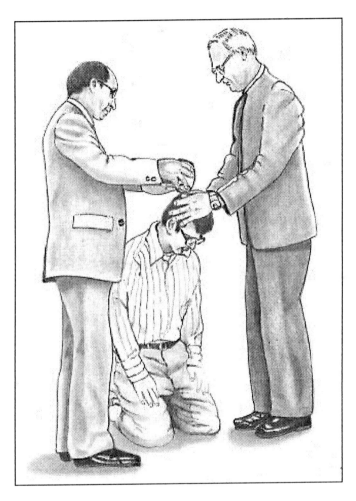

Baptism by pouring in a Lancaster Mennonite
Conference church.

# Baptism in the River
# 1968-1971

Thursday, February 22, 1968

Dear Mom and Daddy,

Witnessing 40 Congolese being baptized in the Tombe River was the highlight of this past weekend. I was surprised because the church here at Ngombe Lutete holds a baptismal service during their bi-annual Baptist Association meetings, just like the Mennonites back home baptize at spring and fall communion.

The candidates attend catechism class as we did growing up; the missionaries usually take turns instructing our students and any other locals who want to be baptized. Instruction for candidates in outlying areas varies from village to village, depending on the pastors. People from a 25-mile radius come to our mission post every February and September to attend these meetings, called Matondo (Thanksgiving). Those who can afford it ride a transport lorry (that's British for truck) but most of them walk to get here.

I know Mennonite bishops and preachers at home discuss the readiness of candidates before they're baptized, but here it's an all-day, two-day affair. Pastors, deacons, and missionaries assemble to interview the candidates and then discuss their lives, whether anyone has seen a difference since they made the decision to join the church. When I asked Lesley, she said someone is rejected occasionally, but not often.

When we arrived for the morning service Charles sat with the schoolboys on their side, and I joined my girls. The 40 baptismal candidates sat together at the front, men on one side, women on the other. All were dressed in unbleached muslin robes that closed in the back with a tie at the neck, like hospital gowns except these were sewn shut from the waist down, probably made by one of the local tailors. And they had a matching belt tied around their waist to give a bit of shape. Some wore a shirt or blouse under their robe and a few of the elderly men also wore trousers, but most just wore the shapeless gown.

One thing surprised me but shouldn't have. The candidates were all barefoot! Congolese walk barefoot everywhere. Lesley told me many of these people walked, carrying their sandals for 25 miles or more, in order to save on wear and tear. They wouldn't want to take their shoes into the river or chance losing them, so they just came barefoot to the service.

After a round of choirs, announcements, and the sermon, the nine-member drum and flute band that had played throughout the weekend welcoming the different village groups picked up their instruments and went out to the narrow dirt path leading to the river. The pastors lined up the baptismal candidates behind them. When they were ready the band began playing traditional African music, flutes and whistles bleating and drums beating. The candidates followed the band marching in two columns down the dirt road to the river. Arms crossed, a hand at each elbow, heads bowed, faces serious, they marched to the beat of those drums, in their mid-calf-length gowns.

Down the road we advanced, band, candidates, pastors,

students in school uniforms, men in trousers and colorful short-sleeved shirts, women in long African-print wrap-around skirts, toddlers and babies on their backs, school children and dogs running in and out of the line. Past mangoes and palms, scrub trees on the grassy hillside, and the cemetery holding graves of missionaries who'd given their lives for the very thing that was happening here today.

"If you cross to the other side you'll have a much better view," Lesley told me. She would know, having attended all the baptisms down here for the last six years. So we picked our way across the uneven little plank bridge just as the flutes and drums came to a sudden halt. And in a moment we felt drawn into that solemn place.

We stood on the opposite shore, facing the candidates lined up in four rows on the riverbank, their dark faces and white gowns reflected in the quiet water. School children hovered near the edge of the water wanting a close-up view when their friends were baptized. The congregation formed an immense crowd behind the candidates. "This must be the way it looked when Jesus preached by the Sea of Galilee," I whispered to Charles. I couldn't stop snapping photos.

We heard nothing but water lapping on the banks and birds chirping in the grasses until Tata Robert began singing and the sweet notes of "Shall We Gather At The River?" floated across the water to us. Tata Ntela read the story of Jesus' baptism, the candidates standing silent under the hot noonday sun, their arms still folded. Five pastors and deacons in muslin gowns waded out into the waist-deep river. Then five-by-five the candidates were called, sent out into the murky water, and baptized as one, a pastor on shore calling out, "In the name of the Father, and of the Son, and of the Holy Spirit." Lady deacons were waiting to welcome the girls and women and to send them dripping on their way up the steep hill.

As soon as the last candidate and pastor left the river, the band began to play and the crowd turned to climb the hill. A dozen little boys waiting for this moment stripped off their shorts and jumped in. "It's holy water," they told us in French as they climbed out grinning and jumped in again. "Because of the baptism." Two ladies stooped in the water on the far bank washing their babies before heading up the path.

By then the colorful congregation was a thin string in the distance, wending its way up the hill. Our students, thinking about dinner, had long since outstripped mothers with sleeping babies tied on their backs and elderly men and women tottering along on canes.

I wonder what Mennonites at home would think. Love, Janet

Sunday afternoon, May 9, 1971

Dear Mom and Daddy,

We just got back from an incredible trip out into the bush. When we had our Matondo, the twice-a-year Baptist Association Meeting here on our mission post in February, two elderly ladies, one of them a 91-year-old, wanted to be baptized. The problem was they live in Kimaza, a village about an hour's drive from our school, and both are too feeble to make the trip. The chief sent word to Tata Ntela, our pastor, and asked if he would come out to their village and baptize them.

"Kimaza has no church," Lesley told me. "Apparently a visiting pastor had stopped in their village and talked with them and that's what prompted their decisions. It's impossible for me to go just now, and I'd be grateful if you and Charles would take Tata Ntela in the VW. He'll show you the way. It's along the road heading toward the Congo River."

"It'll be a bit difficult with Tata Ntela not able to speak French," I said. "But not impossible. I'll talk to Charles."

I couldn't resist the invitation. "Witnessing this baptism would be an experience of a lifetime, Charles," I said. "And just think, we'll get to go out into a real village."

"They'll offer us a meal. Then what'll you do?"

"We'll eat the hot cooked parts and sprinkle on lots of pili-pili peppers," I grinned. "That'll kill any parasites."

"We'll take a bottle of filtered water."

Our destination wasn't all that far and the road was dry, but we bumped up and down and back and forth the whole way out, hitting and skirting potholes, making the twelve miles feel more like 80. "Voilà le village," Tata Ntela finally said, pointing to the top of a distant hill.

The village appeared quite small and poor. The homes were thatched, sun-dried, mud brick houses with dirt floors, ragged children peering around corners to stare. "They're so far out in the bush there's obviously no employment for the men," Charles said. "Not like on our post where we have foreigners needing house help and construction workers."

The chief came out to meet us and ushered us into a room at one end of his whitewashed house where a table and chairs had been set up for us. We shook hands and he offered us bottles of orange Fanta. Charles dislikes room-temperature sodas, and you know I never did care for them warm or cold. But we were polite and drank them. The chief and Tata Ntela chatted in Kikongo as we sipped our drinks, occasionally saying a word or two in French.

I never did find out either of the women's names. One was so ill and weak that four barefoot men had to carry her to the baptismal site at the bottom of a steep path. I don't know how they managed; they certainly were more sure-footed than we were. Maybe we should have taken off our sandals! Charles and I clung to trees on the way down the path, descending almost at a 45-degree angle. Peering through the tall grass we caught sight of a small hand-dug pool fed by the nearby spring.

"It looks like they dug that pool and dammed up water from the spring just for this occasion," Charles said.

They set the old woman down on the ground and Tata Ntela read the account of Phillip's baptism in the book of Acts, in Kikongo of course. He prayed, the men put her in the shallow water, and he baptized her, and then the other one. Afterwards came the job of carrying the poor wet lady back up that steep narrow path. As we followed, dragging ourselves up the winding trail, I wondered about the village women and how they manage to carry home buckets of water on their heads, using this terrible path. The women on our post have it so much better with the river and a spring that can both be reached using the dirt road.

By the time we reached the top the women had disappeared and we were whisked away to the chief's house. They soon reappeared in dry clothes and we sat down together for a short communion service. What an awesome experience sharing their first communion, breaking bread and drinking a bit of grenadine. The setting must have been something like when Jesus broke bread and shared it with believers in the little village of Emmaus.

Afterwards the chief's daughters brought us a delicious chicken stew served with boiled sweet potatoes and chiquangua, a sticky carbohydrate, a bit like chewy bread dough, made from manioc. I don't like its sour smell or taste, but to be polite I smothered a few pieces with the fiery hot chicken broth and was able to clean my plate. I particularly enjoyed the sweet potatoes, a favorite of mine that we don't often get out here. The chief invited us to stay longer, but a storm was threatening and we wanted to get our Volkswagen home in one piece.

I've been reflecting a lot on these baptisms in the river. I worried 20 years ago that maybe my baptism by pouring inside the church wasn't as good as those done in the stream. Here, the candidates must be immersed for membership. Going down into the river and getting wet all over seemed so natural and more like Biblical baptisms. But in the end I believe it's what's in your heart that counts. Love, Janet

Baptismal candidates marching to the river to be immersed.

# Communion and Foot Washing at Stauffers
# April 1952

When I woke up that bright April Sunday morning I heard the teakettle singing and Daddy stoking the wood stove. Mom was calling up the stairs, "Boys, Janet, you better get up. We don't want to be late for church."

Throwing back my quilts I jumped out of bed, hopped across the cold linoleum rug, and pulled back the flowered curtain in front of my closet. My new navy blue cape dress hung pressed and ready with my best white cotton slip. I lifted the hanger from its hook high on the sloped ceiling, pulled the slip over my head, then my dress, and finally the V-necked cape. It closed with snaps on the shoulder and at the side of the attached belt. Church regulations didn't allow us to have buttons on our dresses, only on sweaters and coats, I guess because we bought them.

I hated my long brown cotton stockings rolled just above my knees over garters Mom had made from pieces of elastic. I had to be careful when I got up from the kneeling in church, because they had a tendency to slip down over my skinny knees. I struggled into my stiff black leather oxfords and tied them with double bows.

Looking in the long mirror on my dresser, I combed out my hair, parted it in the middle, fastening each side with a bobby pin, and then pulling it back tight. Twisting it into a bun, I secured it with hairpins the way my sister had taught me. I gently lifted my best white nylon net covering from its resting place on a roll of toilet paper on the dresser. That's where we kept them because they fit perfectly and kept their shape. I placed it over my hair, checking that the corners where the ribbons were attached came right behind each ear, to make sure it wasn't crooked on my head. Picking up two straight pins from the milkglass dish, I pinned my covering to my hair on each side like I was fastening a pattern to material getting ready to cut out a dress.

I did one last inspection, turning this way and that, looking in my hand mirror to see the sides and back of my head. This would be my first communion and I wanted to look right. Satisfied, I headed down the stairs, stuffing the white ribbons down inside the back of my dress. Mom hated when they went flying and I didn't want to tie them; only old ladies did that. I stopped at the washbowl at the end of the kitchen and washed my face and hands before heading to the table.

Mom had spooned globs of hot oatmeal into our cereal bowls from the big pot on the back of the cookstove. A hand of ripe bananas lay in the middle of the colorful oilcloth on the table. "Put your apron on. You don't want anything spilled on your dress this morning," she said when she saw me.

I didn't like oatmeal, but that was our regular Sunday morning fare. I got my flowered feedbag apron and sat down on the bench behind the table, my two brothers each seated at a corner, Mary Anne in her wooden highchair. My older sister Anita was toasting homemade bread in our old-fashioned toaster with a little slanted door on each side, hinged at the bottom, opening down from the top. She'd pull the knob, drop the door, and turn the slice around when the bell dinged. Then she'd close it and wait for the bell again.

Daddy looked around at us, bowed his head, and said, "Our Heavenly Father, we thank Thee for this beautiful morning and for a good night's rest. We thank Thee for our health and sound minds. Bless this food to the nourishment of our bodies. Forgive us our shortcomings. Be with us now as we go to Thy house of worship that what is said and done might be to Thy honor and glory. In Jesus' name we pray. Amen."

We passed the gallon jar, poured Bossy's fresh whole milk onto our cereal, and spooned brown sugar on top. I smothered my toast with butter we'd churned the day before and strawberry jam from last spring's pickings. It helped mask the taste of oatmeal. "Eat a banana with your cereal. It'll be a long time till dinner today," Mom said as she rushed around packing her bag with some crackers and a few toys for Mary Anne. We'd be at church for three hours, maybe more today since we were having communion, so she needed plenty of stuff to keep my little sister quiet.

I noticed the dark dresses as soon as we walked inside the church. Everyone was wearing solid navy blue except the old women, and they were in black. Mom said it was out of respect for the death of Christ. That made sense, because we always wore dark clothes to funerals and we were here to take communion in memory of Jesus' death.

After Sunday school, as usual I tiptoed down the side aisle and found a seat beside one of my favorite old ladies. I didn't even know her name, but she always smiled and made room for me to sit by her at the end of the bench.

Herman Myers left his seat among the young men at the back and strode down the side aisle to lead the singing during preaching. As he laid his open hymnal on the podium I watched him pull his pitchpipe from the side pocket of his coat. "Let's sing two numbers in keeping with the communion service this morning. Please turn to 360 in the hymnal," he said looking at his pitch pipe and turning it round and round in his hand to the right note. Holding it to his mouth, he blew into it, sounding *do* in the key he needed. Then he hummed the note on which the sopranos would begin. Raising his right arm he began to beat time, on the downbeat our hundred and forty voices resounded in four-part harmony.

> *Tis midnight and on Olive's brow,*
> *The star is dimmed that lately shone;*
> *'Tis midnight in the garden now,*
> *The suffering Saviour prays alone.*

During the hymn, Bishop Noah Risser, the two preachers, Sylvan Myers and Walter Oberholtzer, and the deacon, Peter Smith, got up from the front bench on the men's side, mounted the two steps to the platform, and sat down on the long bench behind the wide pulpit. Herman announced a second hymn and led us in Charles Wesley's eighteenth century methodical mournful hymn.

> *Arise, my soul, arise, Shake off thy guilty fears;*
> *A bleeding sacrifice in my behalf appears;*
> *Before thy throne my surety stands,*
> *My name is written on His hands.*

As the last notes died away Brother Sylvan rose. He moved forward to the pulpit, pulled the chain on the little round brass lamp above the slanted top, opened his Bible, and read the account of the Passover and first communion celebrated by Jesus and his disciples. After a few comments we knelt for silent prayer. Some of the oldest ladies with canes had trouble getting down on their knees so they stayed seated. The rest of us faced the bench, hanging over it, our elbows on the seat.

When the preacher said a loud Amen, we got up and sat in our benches. Bishop Risser stood up behind the pulpit to preach the morning sermon. He was elderly and his hands shook. Mom said he had palsy. I looked up the story of the man in the Bible who had palsy that Jesus healed. I wondered about our bishop and if he couldn't be cured.

The bishop recounted the story of Jesus and his disciples observing the first communion in an upper room and how He'd told them to continue to celebrate it in remembrance of his suffering and death for our sins. "It's a memorial to His broken body and His shed blood," the bishop said, looking us in the eye. "We eat the bread and drink the cup so we don't forget. It's a serious thing to partake of communion. We're commanded to examine ourselves to see whether we're in right relationship with God and at peace with the brotherhood and mankind in general. 'He that eateth and drinketh unworthily, eateth and drinketh damnation to himself,'" he quoted from the Bible.

I thought about the students at school and some of the stuff I'd said to my brothers that week. *Am I at peace with everybody? I sure don't want to eat and drink damnation to myself. I asked God to forgive all my sins. But what if I forgot something?*

We knelt again in prayer and the bishop gave us time to confess to God any sin in our lives. Then he prayed for our souls, asking God to forgive us and help us to follow faithfully.

A white cloth covered the entire communion table down in front of the pulpit. Under it I could recognize the outlines of the plate of bread, the bottle of grape juice, and the mugs. Mom said it was one of our deacon's jobs to bring bread and juice for communion. Peter's wife, Nancy, always bought several loaves of homemade white bread and cut them in thick slices after removing the crusts. Mom invariably commented on the cloths. She said Nancy washed them in rainwater to keep them snowy white.

The grape juice was in a funny looking bottle with a straight long neck coming out of the center of a big bulb at the bottom. Daddy said it was an awfully old hand blown decanter, probably going back to Civil War times. I went up to the communion table and looked at it one time. It was light green but Peter Smith always wrapped it in a white cloth that he'd fold a certain way. "It's a ritual," Mom said, but I wondered if it was to keep the juice from running down the bottle when he poured it, or to keep it cool. Two pewter pint mugs stood beside the bottle. Daddy said they were eighteenth century tavern mugs. They were plain, flared out at the bottom, with a handle in the shape of a question mark.

"Before we partake," the bishop said, "I need to remind you that our communion is restricted to members in good standing of our own congregation. Two brothers and a sister from Stricklers, who were sick when they had their communion three weeks ago, are here and may partake with us."

The bishop and Peter Smith came down from the platform and stood in front of the communion table. Peter removed the cloth, picked up the plate of bread, and offered it to the bishop. Brother Risser took a slice and held it in his hand while he recited, "Our Lord, on the night he was delivered over to be crucified, took bread and said, 'Take, eat, this is my body which was broken for you. This do in remembrance of me.'" He broke off a piece and ate it, before giving the next bits to the ministers and deacon. Then breaking off small pieces of the bread he began handing them one by one to the men on the front row and then to the second row. After that he moved to the edge of the communion table and indicated the men should come to him. The third row emptied as they reverently moved toward the center aisle and walked forward to receive their communion. Each man took his piece of bread, held it in his hand, and proceeded toward the outer wall and down the side aisle back to his seat.

The attendance board said one hundred and forty people were present. *This is going to take forever,* I thought. *Oh, good. The bishop asked one of the preachers to continue handing out the bread to the men.* He took another slice from the deacon's plate, walked over to the women's side, and handed pieces to the elderly ladies on the front row. Then the women began coming forward, pausing to take their communion bread from the bishop. Peter Smith hovered around, holding his plate of bread ready for whenever the preacher or bishop needed another slice.

"When the bishop hands you your piece of bread," Mom had told us, "hold out your palm kinda cupped so you don't drop it. Keep it in your hand and take it back to your seat. Don't eat it until the bishop tells you to. We'll all eat it together."

I followed the old ladies to the end of our bench at the center aisle and walked forward to get my bread. The bishop looked startled to see this little girl among the elderly women, but he continued reciting, "'Take, eat, this is my body which was broken for you. This do in remembrance of me,'" as he handed me a piece of bread. I held it loosely in my hand and followed the women around the front of our benches to the wall and then down the side aisle to our seats. I looked at my bread, closed my eyes and prayed, *Forgive me God for anything I've done wrong. I want to do what's right. I don't want to eat damnation to my soul.*

I watched the rest of the middle-aged women go by, followed by the married ladies with children. Most of them had someone hold their baby while they came forward, but once in a while a mother carried her baby with her to receive her communion bread. The young girls walked by, then the older teens, and finally the last rows of young married women. My sister had her head bowed as she passed me.

When everyone was again seated, the bishop took a piece of bread, held it up and again repeated, "'Take eat, this is my body. This do in remembrance of me.'" And all together as a congregation we ate our bread remembering the Lord's suffering for our sins. It was good light fluffy bread, definitely homemade.

The bishop turned and picked up one of the pewter mugs from the communion table and held it while Peter Smith poured grape juice into it from the funny-looking bottle. It took a long time to fill. When it was finally full, Peter wiped the mouth of the bottle and set it back on the table. The bishop held out the cup in front of his face and thanked God for sending his Son and saving our souls. Again he began with the men on the front row. One by one they stood, took the cup, drank, and handed it back to the bishop. It always had to be handed back to the bishop for him to hand to the next person. I remembered the time a young boy who was a convert from a non-Mennonite family took communion and passed the cup to the next person. He was embarrassed when the man refused, telling him to hand it back to the bishop. I wondered about that. Why couldn't it be passed on to the next person?

The bishop continued reciting the words of Christ as the congregation walked forward to receive the cup from him. Then he told Peter Smith to fill the other cup and asked Walter Oberholtzer to offer it to the women. Again I followed the elderly women from our bench and walked among them to the front for my sip of grape juice. "'Drink ye all of it, for this is my blood of the New Testament, which is shed for many for the remission of sins,'" the bishop intoned from the men's side. The preacher bent to hand me the cup. It was heavier than I thought it would be. I think he was afraid I'd drop it, but I held on tightly, my right hand clamped around the question mark handle and my left one steadying the mug.

"Just take a little sip," Mom had told us that morning. "A little swallow. We're not doing this to eat and get filled up. It's a symbol of the blood of Christ. All you need is a little drop."

After I sat back down, I watched the ladies. Mom came by in her new navy blue dress, her head down, without my baby sister. I wondered who was watching Mary Anne. Maybe Anita. Everyone looked so solemn and serious. The bishop started singing a hymn and we all joined in:

> *When I survey the wondrous cross*
> *On which the Prince of Glory died.*
> *My richest gain I count but loss,*
> *And pour contempt on all my pride.*

I thought maybe he was getting tired from reciting all that scripture. He was pretty amazing for an old man to remember all those Bible verses. Mom says it's because he's been doing it for forty years.

As the line continued to inch forward down the aisle, the subdued congregation joined the bishop in singing about the suffering and death of our Lord:

> *Alas, and did my Saviour bleed and did my*
> *    Sovereign die,*
> *Would He devote that sacred head for such a*
> *    worm as I?*

And then:

> *Not all the blood of beasts, On Jewish altars*
> *    slain,*
> *Could give the guilty conscience peace, Or*
> *    wash away the stain.*
> *But Christ, the heavenly Lamb, Takes all our*
> *    sins away,*
> *A sacrifice of nobler name, And richer blood*
> *    than they.*

My Sunday school teacher walked by and smiled at me. When the line finally ended, the preacher went out to the anteroom and gave communion to mothers sitting out there with their babies. Peter Smith put a napkin over the bread, the cork back in the bottle, and the tablecloth over them, before joining the bishop and preachers on the bench behind the pulpit.

Brother Risser stepped forward and addressed us again, "On the same night that Jesus established the communion service, He also instituted the ordinance of feet washing. He rose from the table, girded Himself with a towel, poured some water into a basin, and washed the feet of the twelve apostles. They did not understand the meaning of what He did, and when He began, Peter protested very much against Jesus washing his feet." The bishop stopped and looked out over the congregation.

"Jesus told Peter that if he did not allow Him to wash his feet he could have no part of Him. This is a symbol of our sins being washed with the blood of Jesus. Without that we can have no part with Him. Jesus also showed a fine lesson of humility. He, their Lord and Master, was willing to take the place of servant among them. They should in like manner serve each other.

"The command that we should observe this ordinance is very plain, and all of us should be willing to follow Jesus' example and wash each other's feet just as He washed the feet of His disciples. He promised happiness and blessing to those who do these things that He taught."

The bishop then asked for the tubs and towels to be brought in. He told us we should wash the feet of the person next to us. Several men went out to the anteroom and poured warm water into the tubs from milk cans that a farmer had brought to church that morning in his truck. Others carried in stacks of towels and distributed them around the church. Members all over the sanctuary began taking off their stockings and shoes and setting them under the bench in front of them. Some of the old ladies went out in the anteroom where a couple of tubs had been set for them. I rolled my stockings down over my knees, pulled them off, and laid them on my black oxfords.

This was the first time I'd washed feet with anyone, but I'd often seen it done so I knew what to do. The lady beside me apologized for her feet. I told her it was okay; I wanted to participate. We got in line for a tub, standing around with the other old ladies. Their bare white feet startled me. I was so used to seeing them in black stockings and shoes; I'd never thought about their feet being so pale.

The towels were huge and had strings on one end which the person doing the washing tied around her waist like a half apron. My friend knelt down, put my left foot in the tub, splashed some water on it, rubbed and then dried it with the loose end of the towel. After she'd done both of my feet she stood up, untied the towel, and handed it to me. I tied the strings around my tiny waist, winding them round and round, tying them in a bow at the front. Then I knelt down and washed the old lady's feet, bent with bunions and covered with calluses, and dried them with the end of the towel that was so long it dragged on the floor. We stood up, kissed each other with the kiss of peace and said, "May the Lord bless you." I took off my towel apron, handed it to the next woman in line. We went back to our bench and we pulled on our stockings and shoes. From every corner of the sanctuary we could hear water being gently sloshed over feet and quiet murmurs of "The Lord bless you."

While we were waiting the bishop suggested that the chorister lead us in singing until everyone had finished. I sat there feeling kind of grungy after having had my hands in water that a lot of feet had been washed in, but remembering our Lord had commanded this, I tried not to think about it.

Herman didn't come down front to lead the songs this

time. Instead, someone called out a hymn number, and he
started the song from his seat. We all joined in and continued singing until everyone had finished washing feet. I was
hoping they'd hurry up. My stomach was growling after the
bite of bread and sip of juice.

The bishop told us to remember to practice what we had
just demonstrated: humility and love for our fellow man. We
all stood and with our heads bowed sang

> *Blest Be the Tie that Binds Our Hearts in
> Christian Love.
> The fellowship of kindred minds is like to
> that above.*

And then raising his right arm straight out in front of
him, his hand slightly above his head, the bishop recited the
benediction from the book of Jude, "'Now unto Him that is
able to keep you from falling, and to present you faultless
before the presence of His glory with exceeding joy, to the
only wise God our Savior, be glory and majesty, dominion
and power, both now and ever. Amen.'"

As I turned to pick up my Bible and Sunday school
papers, the old lady next to me shook my hand and congrat-
ulated me on my good behavior for an eleven-year-old.
"Come sit by me any time you want to," she said. I smiled
and nodded, knowing I'd be back every Sunday.

Communion cup and bottle used for many years at
Stauffers Mennonite Church.

# Pomegranate Juice for Communion
# 1968 – 1969

February 22, 1968

Dear Mom and Daddy,

When I left home three years ago I know you were
worried I wouldn't find a church like the ones I'd grown up
in. You were so right. In California, and now out here in
Congo, I've never come across the exact same denomination, but I have found Christians with deep faith in God.

I want to tell you about one of the differences I've
encountered. Communion. The Christians here believe, like
you, that communion is a symbol of our acceptance of the
death and resurrection of Christ. The difference is in the
process: how often, who serves it, how it's served, and
who's invited to partake. I'm more and more inclined to
believe the process isn't that important as long as we have
the right spirit.

Our church here on the mission post observes communion once a month. Many of our students are already
members in their home churches; others go through instruction class here, are baptized in the river, and join this

congregation. They all partake in communion. I can't understand what the pastor says since it's all spoken in Kikongo, but Lesley told me if a person is a believer, even though a member of another denomination, he may participate.

How it's served is the biggest difference I noticed. The first time we were here for communion I was surprised to see a group of about eight or ten ladies wearing white dresses and headscarves, sitting together near the back. Lesley told me the church provides the women deacons with these dresses, but that they are responsible for the scarves. Nobody else wore any special clothes that day, just their regular colorful African print blouses and wrap-around skirts, and short-sleeved shirts for the men.

After the sermon we sang "When I Survey the Wondrous Cross," in Kikongo of course. I know the words in English so I understand what I'm singing as I phonetically read the words from my hymnbook. Here's what it looks like in Kikongo:

> *Vo mbadik'ak'e mpondw'ambi*
> *Twavondelwa o Mvuluzi;*
> *Yawonso yin'ova nza yayi,*
> *Ke yina nkutu mfunu ko.*

Suddenly the group of ladies in white stood as a group, padded barefoot down the center aisle, skirting a sleeping dog on the way, and lined up at the communion table. Two lifted off the large white tablecloth uncovering aluminum plates holding locally made bread that these deacons had cut into small squares before the service, and containers holding individual cups. Given the countless parasites and communicable diseases out here, I was relieved to see those tiny cups instead of a mug to pass around.

At first I found it a bit disconcerting to have women distributing the sacraments. But when I thought about it, women in this culture are in charge of anything to do with food: planting, caring for, and harvesting gardens, carrying water and wood, cooking, serving. Men would never dream of serving a meal unless they were working as a houseboy for a foreigner. So I believe it has to do with culture rather than not being Biblical as some at home might think.

The pastor prayed, in Kikongo of course, asking God's blessing on everyone partaking of the bread and drink, that their hearts and lives would be pure, and that they would remain faithful. The lady deacons then carried the communion bread to the front bench and handed a plate to the person at the end. He or she took a piece, ate, and passed the plate. When it reached the end of the bench another server passed it to the next row.

When all had been served, the ladies took the plates of leftover bread back to the communion table and picked up trays filled with tiny aluminum communion cups, each holding several drops of pink grenadine to represent Jesus' blood. Grapes don't grow here in tropical Africa, which explains the pomegranate-based drink substitute. When I first saw it I remembered a missionary to Africa who visited our church when I was growing up. He told us that in translating the Bible for people living in tropical Africa they had to find a substitute for "whiter than snow" since the readers had never seen snow. They chose "whiter than young cotton."

After a prayer the grenadine was distributed down the rows, each person picking up an individual cup, drinking, and replacing it before passing the tray down the line. The deacons will take the cups home and wash them for next month's communion.

They are my church family, my brothers and sisters in the Lord, for the next several years. In spite of the differences such as drinking grenadine and women serving in this African setting, I found true fellowship with these believers, celebrating Christ's death, burial, and resurrection. Lovingly, Janet

Monday, July 28, 1969

Dear Mom and Daddy,

I decided I must write and tell you about the special service we attended yesterday in the jungles of northeastern Congo. As you know we're up here teaching in a summer school for primary teachers who missed out on a lot of their training due to the recent prolonged civil war. Monsieur Polidor, the superintendent of schools who set up this program, invited the Secretary to the Governor of Oriental Province, the Secretary of Public Works, and the Secretary of Education to come and participate in a special Sunday morning service for our teacher-students here at Yakusu Baptist Church.

This tall brick building with its large bell tower is quite remarkable in itself, being located out here in the bush. But for this stately occasion the church was even more striking, the local membership having decorated it with flags, flowers, and cloths draped from the balcony and the front wall. A Congo flag hung from the pulpit, and a snowy-white cloth covered the communion table.

Most of the dignitaries were dressed in Mobutu-style suits – a sort of shirt-jacket with a small lapel. But Monsieur Polidor wore a black tuxedo, ruffled white shirt, and bow tie. Before the service began, the dignitaries and our faculty, followed by our students, lined up and marched into the church. Monsieur Polidor invited Charles and me to join them, but we told him being foreigners we didn't want to intrude. Besides, Doreen West, an American nurse at the mission hospital was going to sit with us in the balcony and translate. Charles and I, not understanding Lokele, the local language, had no way of knowing what would take place. So we stayed outside greeting dignitaries, students, and locals, snapping photos until everyone had entered.

I've probably already told you our students are poor, coming from jungle villages up and down the river. They too turned out in their Sunday best – a light blue, pink, yellow, or white shirt and dark trousers. Parades play a large part in their culture, so they'd arranged themselves by villages and sectors and marched into the church carrying banners identifying the different areas they represented. We were quite impressed with their flair and organization.

We followed Doreen up the stairs to the nearly empty balcony. The view of the decorations and proceedings was magnificent, we could take photos, and she was also able to translate without disturbing others. The Kisangani Protestant Youth Chorale began the service singing several hymns in Lokele and French. They looked almost professional in their school uniforms – a pleated knee-length blue skirt and a white blouse with matching blue V-shaped choir stole. At the end of their mini-concert, the director turned and asked the congregation to stand as those young people raised their voices to praise the Lord, singing the French translation of Handel's "Hallelujah Chorus." Tears welled in my eyes as I sang along in English. Out here in Congo we rarely hear music from home, so this was a special treat.

Doreen sat between us and, in a loud enough whisper, translated the inspiring sermon on the work of the Holy Spirit in our lives. Local women deacons, dressed in white, most of them wearing shoes for the occasion, served us little squares of homemade bread and pomegranate juice just as they do in our mission church at Ngombe Lutete, 1,000 miles away. I looked over that balcony railing at the rainbow of 225 pastel shirts in the center section representing numerous tribes and political ideals and marveled at how Christ, the core of our religious belief, brought us all together. There we were, worshiping as one, in an equatorial jungle that barely two years before had been wracked with civil strife. Several hundred of the poorest and least-educated Congolese, Africans who'd been educated abroad, government officials, British nurses, and American teachers were all partaking of the same communion. I came away spiritually refreshed and rejuvenated, longing to share this uplifting experience. Love, Janet

Our village church at Ngombe Lutete.

# Honor the Flag
# 1952 – 1963

Unlike the majority of Mennonite children we knew, my siblings and I attended public schools, where our parents insisted we'd get a better education with certified teachers. They thought Christian day schools were too expensive, plus providing transportation would have been difficult for them since we lived some distance from any large Mennonite community.

Starting back in the 1950s my aunt Charlotte McCorkel taught in Christian day schools for more than eighteen years. Hearing that she'd graduated from our local junior college, Mennonite school boards began seeking her out as a prospective teacher since they often had to fill vacancies with young women having as little as a partial high school education.

I recently talked with Aunt Charlotte, wanting to hear her recollections of teaching in Mennonite schools. "I guess my first question is where and what did you teach?" I began.

"My first position was at Erismans teaching 38 students in grades one through eight. That was such a traumatic experience I left at the end of the school term and went to work in a factory. The following spring when a school board member contacted me about a teaching position at Manor Christian School, I refused. But then I had second thoughts and for several months prayed God would have someone else contact me if teaching was to be in my future. One evening at Summer Bible School another board member from the same school asked me to come and teach their first four grades." She paused and smiled. "I spent five years at Manor."

"That's the school I visited as your helper when I was in my early-teens," I said. "After I told you I wanted to be a teacher you invited me to spend a day in your classroom from time to time. You showed me how to make duplicates of pictures for the children to color."

Charlotte laughed. "That was on my Hectograph. I still have it," she said, jumping up and going to another room. In a few minutes she returned with a small metal box, her original 1953 Gelatin Duplicator. The complete set included gel, ink, and sponge for making 9X12 copies in various colors of typewritten or pen and ink originals.

"How did it work?" I asked, gingerly pulling off the lid, revealing a dark hardened substance.

"You sponged the gel with water and wiped it dry. It's all dried up now, but back then it was like extra-thick Jello. The original was placed face down on the gel, smoothed with your palm, and left for 1-3 minutes, depending how many copies you needed. After you pulled off the original you could see the exact reverse impression in the gel. Then you smoothed sheets of clean paper over the gel one after the other until you had as many as you needed. You could get fifty to seventy-five good copies."

"I remember it took a while. But I had fun doing that and you were pleased to have a helper. Where did you get it?"

"In Lancaster. I shopped at the Herr School Supply for items I needed but the school didn't furnish. Look, the price is marked on the back, three dollars and forty cents," she laughed. "I'm going to donate it to the Hershey Historical Society."

"Can you imagine a teacher today buying her own photo copy machine?" I said, gently closing this 50-year-old treasure. "Where else did you teach?"

"Next I went to Paradise Christian School near Hagerstown, Maryland, for four years, until I married. Most of the parents at Paradise were related. They all belonged to the same Mennonite conference and went to church together. So everyone knew each other. The teachers were constantly invited out to eat in the homes of their students. That school really was one big family."

"So after you married you quit teaching?"

"Yes. The children came along and John supported us. After his death, I needed to work again, but I couldn't bring myself to teach." I remembered John's sudden accidental death, leaving Aunt Charlotte and the whole family in a state of shock. "Priscilla and John were toddlers," she continued, "so for a time I cleaned houses, taking them with me. When they were in elementary school I put them in Dohners, a Christian day school with grades one through nine, and I took a job there teaching the youngest children."

"I remember Dohners," I said. "The one-room white frame school with a bell on top stood across the road from the church. I used to wonder what it would be like to attend school in a building like Laura Ingalls Wilder described in *Little House on the Prairie*: a stove in the center, ancient alphabet letters parading across the top of the blackboard, an aged globe in the corner, rows of double desks with curly iron work on the sides all connected together on long runners on bare wide pine floor boards. But I guess I'm too nostalgic."

"Don't forget going out to wash at the pump in winter weather and carrying in buckets of water to fill the cooler at the back of the room," Charlotte giggled. "Dohners has been upgraded a lot since then. They built onto the school and had three rooms with inside plumbing when I taught there. But with Priscilla going into tenth grade I had to find a school that included senior high school. I taught three years at Emmanuel Christian School until she graduated."

"So your specialty became the first three grades?" I asked.

"Twice I had one through eight, but usually I had first grade or a combined classroom of first through third with about thirty pupils, although one year I had 43, the most I ever taught."

"Besides the fact that many were one- or two-room buildings, how were they different from the public schools you attended as a child?" I asked.

"The main difference would be the Bible reading and prayer. When we were growing up in public schools, the teacher read a scripture and we repeated the Lord's Prayer. But in Christian schools we discussed the passage, making it more personal and practical. We also had prayer before our meals."

"Did you salute the flag? I remember that was controversial. My parents thought it was all right for us to say the pledge, although they didn't believe in participating in the military. 'It would be sinful to be a traitor,' Daddy argued. So I crossed my heart and saluted the flag, glancing sidelong at the Jehovah's Witness girl beside me who just stood there, her arms at her sides. I think she was surprised I didn't join her."

"We didn't always have a flag in the classroom but when we did we never pledged allegiance to it," Charlotte said. "Our students were taught to respect the flag as a symbol of our country. We don't vote, believing that as Christians we're set apart from the world and can't participate in government or politics. But in school we prayed on a regular basis for the President and those in authority as we're taught to do in the Scriptures. And from time to time we did a project on the flag, its origin, and meaning."

"So you respected the flag but couldn't pledge your allegiance to it?"

"Yes, that's right. We pledge our allegiance to God."

"Were you teaching when President Kennedy was shot?"

"No. I'd gotten married that spring and didn't take a job that fall. The day school finished on May 22, 1963, I got in my car and drove home. John and I were married at our minister's house that evening," Charlotte laughed.

"The same day school ended?" I asked, my eyes wide.

"That's right," Charlotte giggled. "You remember Mother wasn't well and couldn't attend, so I decided to have a private wedding."

"And you didn't go back to teach in the fall?"

"No, I didn't. We were living back there at the orchard where John worked. Someone stopped by our house that November day and told me about the President's death."

"I was teaching in Pennsylvania. They turned the radio onto the speaker system and we listened to Walter Cronkite the rest of the afternoon. I was devastated. My landlady and I were glued to the television for the next four days. School was closed until after the funeral on Monday," I said, shaking my head, reliving one of the saddest moments in our country's history. " What do you think happened that day in Mennonite Christian day schools?"

"Unless a parent heard and called in they probably weren't informed that day. Our news comes from newspapers, so they would have read about it the next day. The administration would have left it to the teachers to answer students' questions. Social studies teachers would have talked about it more than others. Since the faculty was all of a common faith they weren't too strict about what the teachers would say; they trusted us. They would have prayed for the widow and the President's family."

"What about music in school?" I asked, suddenly chang-ing the subject.

"We sang hymns and some other songs that showed God in nature, for example. But at recess it was okay for them to sing 'London Bridge' or 'Farmer in the Dell' with their games. They also used the jump rope poems we chanted as children."

"I remember," I said. "Teddy Bear, Teddy Bear turn out the light, Teddy Bear, Teddy Bear say good night."

"That's it," Charlotte said. "Innocent songs for play were all right. We also placed greater emphasis on good manners and respect. And unlike in public schools where you were one Mennonite out of hundreds, these children felt accepted – they were among their own and were like a big family. I was always impressed by the loyalty of brothers and sisters to each other, such as wasn't seen in our grow-ing-up years in public schools."

"I can identify with that," I said. "After I joined the Mennonite church in fifth grade I was the only plain child in our whole elementary school. Students sometimes asked me about my clothes, but a number of them were Brethren and wore prayer veilings on Sunday, so they understood. The Italian Catholics regarded me as a little nun. You know, back in those days nuns wore long black habits and veils."

"I had somewhat the same experience. But I was in junior college when I joined. A lady at church made me a dress with a cape and then I copied her pattern and made another one. For a while I tried to get along wearing those two cape-dresses to school two or three days a week and my regular dresses the rest of the time. One day some hockey players saw me coming out of the building and laughed when they saw me in a stylish dress with a covering on my head. I guess it did look odd," Charlotte giggled, "so after that I got busy and made several more and switched over to all plain dresses for school."

"What do you recall as the best and worst of Christian day schools?"

"One thing I will never forget is the wonderful warm Christian hospitality. Often I was invited to a student's home for supper and even to stay overnight. They always served a hearty meal with lots of desserts at the end. I found it enjoyable getting to know the student's family. As a result the children were freer to share interesting events or even difficulties with their teacher."

"And the worst?"

"Some parents created problems," she said. "One morning I was busy getting ready for the day when a mother came in and told me that while the supervising teacher was out of the room during lunch the day before, someone had put salt on her second grade son's food. I still remember her words, 'That didn't seem like a Christian attitude.' I guess compared to problems in schools today that was mild. And I must say those kinds of incidents were rare."

"On the whole were parents interested in their children's education?"

"Oh, yes. And I felt a real challenge to see that each child was learning to the best of his or her ability since many of them quit school at the end of the eighth, ninth, or tenth grade. That's when they left school to work on the farm. Their parents expected them to study hard and learn as much as they could in those few short years. Those who were allowed to go on were expected to place high in state tests. Some continued at home and even finished their high school classes, using the Christian Light Publications' correspondence materials under an older person's supervision."

"I guess a lot of them married by the time they were 18."

"No, they didn't. Most were not allowed to start dating until they were 18. Having a family and buying a farm was a lot of responsibility, so most didn't marry until they were about 20."

"Do Mennonites still have strong elementary and secondary Christian day school programs?" I asked, looking up from my notes.

"Oh, yes. I'd say better. The Teachers' Institutes are so improved and Mennonite publishing houses provide excellent teaching manuals and methodology books for day schools and home schooling. Marla Martin, for example, is a quiet yet excellent teacher in Lancaster County. She's written wonderful children's reading books and a phonetics series."

"Do Mennonite schools still hire teachers without a degree?"

"Lancaster Conference Mennonite schools require their teachers to have degrees. But in our Mid-Atlantic Conference we have a number of teachers who finished their high school education through correspondence and home schooling. Sometimes even while they're working on it, they begin teaching. I've heard some say they're one step ahead of the students. But they can be effective if they follow the manuals, attend workshops, and work hard. Mennonite school boards have to search to find teachers, especially those with any college education."

"I know you've recently been doing some substitute teaching in your conference's schools. Are there differences, especially in behavior, from in the 1960s or 70s?"

"I haven't seen differences. In 2000 and 2001 I worked at New Haven School where the students come from five or six of our conservative Mennonite churches. Parents are 100 per cent involved in backing teachers and in financial support, and they teach discipline at home and in church. The children are good, very well-behaved," Aunt Charlotte emphasized, nodding her head.

"I'm sure parental backing is the answer to many of our school problems! By the late-1990s teaching had become a chore for me. Lack of interest in learning and discipline problems in our high school were the two main factors why

I retired and I've had no desire to return. So I'm anxious to hear about your experiences substituting in the Hershey Public Schools."

"This is my fourth term working there. I most often shadow a child with severe allergies. There are many of these bright children in the early grades who could die if they ate even a piece of a nut. I walk around with an epi-pen ready to act in case of emergency. I've spent several entire days watching one child in a regular second grade classroom."

"And how do those classes compare to your Christian day schools?"

"I see extremely good behavior. The teachers try to out-do each other being calm and gentle with their students, reminding them to put up their hand and be recognized, not to speak out of turn. They don't raise their voices at the children. They're good, quality teachers."

"The teacher's attitude and competence has a lot to do with good classroom management."

"I think a lot of it depends on the teacher but also how well the administration and school board backs them. Twenty is the normal class size. During recess on the playground, special aides supervise the students, using a whistle if anyone gets too rough. They have gym, music, and art teachers for scheduled classes. The classroom teachers are free during those times to plan for the subjects they teach," Aunt Charlotte smiled. "Oh, and I must tell you, I've been in their beautiful new gym twice to watch a student. I was so impressed with the exercise program."

"I'm impressed with what you're telling me," I said, shaking my head. "Hershey schools must be well-funded to have staff for what many here in our county in Virginia consider elective classes. Our local elementary teachers would give their eyeteeth for that kind of situation."

"Yes, they are fortunate in that way. And I believe it does help them work to be better teachers."

"I have one more question. Did you encounter any problems getting a job substituting in a public school wearing your big covering and cape dress?" I asked my aunt.

"None whatsoever. The issue was never raised."

"Times have sure changed," I said, shaking my head again. "In 1962 when I tried to get a teaching position in Pennsylvania I was turned down by several public school districts because I wore a small white net covering on the back of my head. I'd given up my plain Mennonite dresses while I was in college. Even though my clothes and shoes looked like any other professional's, I was told I couldn't teach wearing my little covering because it came under the category of religious symbols, which were illegal for teachers to display. One week before school began I was hired to teach French at Northeastern High School in a rural community outside of York. When I asked the superintendent about my covering, he told me if it didn't bother me it wouldn't bother him! I taught there for three years without incident. I guess that would come under the category of religious discrimination today."

"I've had no problems. No one has ever mentioned it. The children are respectful and I feel I have a good relationship with the teachers," she said.

I'd been sure she'd say behavior had deteriorated over the past 50 years. Nowadays we hear so much about poor discipline, especially in our public schools. On the other hand, with total backing from parents and administration, hers were excellent illustrations of teachers able to do a first-rate job. And I could imagine the children responding respectfully to this gentle 70-year-old grandmother, her voice almost a whisper, a genuine example of a soft answer turning away anger.

Dohners Mennonite School, as it appeared in the 1960s and where Aunt Charlotte taught in the 1970s.

# Teaching In The Bush
# 1968 - 1971

"**D**id you know that when Congo got its independence from Belgium in 1960, out of 15 million Congolese, only twelve men were university graduates?" Ian Secrett, the British director of our secondary school, asked as he drove west from Kinshasa toward the mission where we'd be spending the next six years teaching African youth.

"Congolese representatives at the United Nations gave us that same statistic during our orientation in the States," Charles said, his eyes never leaving the passing countryside of small villages, mango trees, and palms nestled in valleys between rolling hills covered with tall grass.

"The Belgian government has a long history of educating African children through six years of primary school, enough for them to read, write, and do simple arithmetic, but not sufficient for them to move into positions of leadership in the lucrative diamond or copper industries. Before independence only a few of the brightest attended, never mind finished, secondary school," Ian said, veering to the edge of the two-lane paved road as an enormous army transport truck bore down on us.

"Of course, Catholicism being their major religion, for

years the Belgians subsidized only Catholic schools in Congo. As a result, Protestant schools are terribly neglected except for those few fortunate enough to be funded by churches or organizations abroad. These days about 40 per cent of the children attend school. One out of four graduate."

Reality began to sink in. Ian drove through tiny villages and we saw poverty first hand. Thatched mud huts the size of an American kitchen were home to large extended families. Poor adobe structures with dirt floors served as schools for elementary children.

"That brick one is the Catholic school," Ian said. "Look across the road. Here's the Protestant one." I couldn't believe my eyes as he stopped the Jeep truck near the door of a shack made of sticks – tree branches an inch or two thick laced horizontally between fatter vertical ones hammered into the ground. Mud plaster had been applied but much of it was cracked and crumbling, exposing the skeleton under a decaying thatched roof. Open holes served as windows. Scantily dressed children wiggled on hand-made crude wood benches without desks, watching the teacher at the front as he tried to teach the squirming mass from one of the few books in the room.

"It's like in Bible times," I whispered to Charles. "He reads and they repeat until they have it memorized." Ian spoke briefly with the teacher who introduced us to his shy wide-eyed pupils. They stood at attention and he explained to them in his broken French that we were Americans who'd come to teach in the secondary school at Ngombe Lutete. We nodded and smiled and said "Bonjour." They sang a song for us.

Heading down the road Ian turned and said, "That's an Angolan refugee village. The parents are doing the best they can with no government assistance. Even the brightest of those poor children will never pass the Cycle d'Orientation entrance tests." We knew what he meant – the equivalent of seventh and eighth grade in America. Congolese children had to pass a test to get into middle school and another for high school.

"I don't know how they could," Charles said. "That was pitiful."

"The competition is tremendous," Ian said. "Just this year we had 500 applications for the 90 openings in our secondary school."

I nodded. "That's why we're here."

Our school director went on, "When Congo got its independence, all primary schools were turned over to African directorship. Many of the teachers are former middle school dropouts. Although some of the elementary principals are good, many don't know how to lead and run a school, which only exacerbates the problem of inadequate teachers. Just keep in mind, foreigners were strictly forbidden to interfere in primary education."

As Ian pulled onto the campus at Ngombe Lutete and drove across the grounds, we were relieved to see our middle and secondary schools were built of solid cinderblocks with glass panes in the windows and corrugated tin roofs. "This post was established in the 1880s and has been supported by the British Baptist Missionary Society since its inception," he said.

Our arrival near the end of first semester would lighten the loads of our over-worked colleagues but gave us no time to become acclimated to Congolese culture and a different education system. We quickly unpacked and tried to adjust to our little four-room house, no electricity, no running water, an outside toilet, and a houseboy.

Ian assured us Mpanzu was well trained and could clean, wash dishes, do our laundry, iron, and carry water. "He can even cook a little. You won't have time to do housework with your full teaching load," he said. "He needs the job, you're paying him, so let him do what he knows.

Later if you want to change something you can."

We hurriedly prepared lesson plans for a full schedule of classes – subjects we'd never taught before. Two days later we walked cold turkey into our classrooms trying to use the Belgian method of writing our lectures in French on the chalkboard for students to copy into notebooks, memorize, and regurgitate at exam time.

"The hardest part is having to teach in French," I said to Charles over dinner. "Those four months studying in Paris probably helped, but I still make too many mistakes when I speak. And I can't understand half of what these kids say."

"I know," he said. "It's the African accent. And the Kikongo names. I don't think I'll ever learn them."

Michel Liard, the stern Belgian Latin teacher, came by our house. "Sometimes I pretend to understand," I confided, "but when someone asks a question I *have* to answer. Other students sometimes jump in and say, 'In other words, Madame, he means …' and they try to explain. And then there's the problem of grammatical errors in the notes I write on the board." He nodded, pursed his lips, and stared out the window. "Can you help me, Michel?" I asked.

"J'en veux bien," he said. "I'd love to. Why don't you write out your geography lectures and I'll correct your grammar? Would that help?"

"It would be an answer to prayer," I said, my heart pounding. I was embarrassed to let him see how poor my French was, but I wanted to improve. Being a lonely bachelor about our age, Michel enjoyed the interaction with Charles and me in our home every afternoon speaking French, our only means of communication. In spite of his harsh nature, he understood my sensitivity and was gentle with me, and I made progress.

Our school was a literary section with an emphasis on languages. The seniors carried an incredibly difficult schedule: French IV, Latin IV, English V, geography, history, trigonometry, calculus, physics, bio-chemistry, sociology, religion, and philosophy. And for each class they were given pages and pages of notes to copy from the blackboard into their notebooks to memorize during free time and evening study hours.

"The juniors and seniors have such extensive exams I don't know how they cope with it all," I wrote home. "They carry a notebook everywhere they go, constantly reading and memorizing. And no wonder; exams count half of their grade. The amount of time they spend taking exams is mind-boggling: ten hours of Latin, eight of French, five and a half of English, two and a half of history, two each of philosophy and geography, one and a half of religion, not to mention math and science. We have ten days allotted to taking exams after a full week of review."

"How'd your morning exams go?" Charles asked as we sat down to a lunch of rice and canned beef about three weeks after our arrival.

"I was so embarrassed. I handed out a sheet of paper to each of the 30 students in my ninth grade class like Ian had told us to do. Then I wrote the six questions on the board for them to answer. I sat at the teacher's table down front and watched them furiously writing long essays to answer the questions. All I could think about was how long it would take me to grade those papers. After a while a boy raised his hand and said something. It sounded like 'Faye.' Just one word. I had no idea what he meant."

"What did you do?"

"I wrinkled my forehead and scratched my head. He kept repeating 'Faye.' The other boys looked up. Finally he came down to my table and pointed to the stack of clean paper. He needed a second sheet of paper! Apparently the teacher is supposed to take paper to them when they need more. Do you know that word in French?"

"Oh," Charles laughed. "He should have said *une feuille de papier* with a fur sound instead of fay," Charles laughed.

"I feel so ignorant. But I guarantee I won't miss that one again."

"Our students have to write two research papers using our meager closet-sized library, which fortunately does contain *Grand Larousse*, a complete French encyclopedia set," I wrote home to our mothers. "And at the end of the school year they'll have to pass written and oral state exams to get their high school diplomas and for entrance into the state-run university system."

"What are you typing?" Charles asked, as I clacked away on the manual typewriter one of the British missionary teachers had given me to use.

"An aerogramme. Actually I'm writing two at a time using a sheet of carbon paper. One for your mom and one for mine. Do you want to add anything?"

"Not now. I need to finish grading papers for tomorrow."

"They do their own laundry, washing their clothes and themselves in the Tombe at the foot of the hill," I continued typing. "As far as I can ascertain, everyone goes to the river for a bath before mandatory 'prayers' in the chapel at 6:45 every morning. They spread their shirts and pants on the grass to dry and later iron them with a charcoal iron." Our mothers wanted lots of details, so I tried to oblige them.

"Two hours a week every student must do a manual labor class. We teachers take turns one afternoon a week overseeing their work. Charles is in charge of the tenth grade boys and I supervise the eighth grade girls. During that time they carry firewood and water from the river to their school kitchen or to faculty members' homes. They also clean around campus, cutting grass with machetes and sweeping paths with brushes they make from palm tree branches. The boys carry rocks from the river and put them on piles to be hauled to the new building site. Students vie for the job of walking four miles round trip to Ngombe Matadi to get bread for our faculty from the Catholic Mission. That's a real break for them to get off campus and go into the village."

"Why do you need bicycles?" my mother wrote. "Is it too far to walk?"

"Our middle school, a four-classroom building for seventh and eighth graders, is located at the west end of the mission post," I wrote back. "Boys and girls at that level are taught separately. The four high school classes, located in the secondary school about a quarter of a mile away, are mixed but rarely include more than one or two girls. (Girls are expected to marry and have children, so most parents don't see the point in educating them beyond primary or middle school.) Our little brick house is located in between; we ride our bikes back and forth on the mango tree-lined dusty path between the two schools. Charles has a box on the back of his to carry books or groceries when we ride to market at Ngombe Matadi. I have a big wicker basket strapped to my handle bars."

"Wouldn't you know the generator's down when it's our turn to supervise study hall?" Charles said one Friday evening. The generator was often down. That meant we had to go early and light a Coleman pressure lantern to set on a five-foot-tall stool in the center of each of the four classrooms. Sometimes one wouldn't function and a class or even two had to do without, using instead their own personal kerosene lanterns.

That evening, as usual, I sat at the teacher's table at the front of the girls' refectory, my back to the wall, facing the girls. I hunched over my work, preparing for Saturday morning classes. Small hurricane lamps on our desks lit reading material, but cast deep shadows into the corners.

I was engrossed in my paperwork when I felt something crawling over the top of my instep. I jerked, shaking my foot hard, and then looked down to see the little animal I'd flung off to the side, his tail waving high above his body. Maleka and Kina jumped from their seats and grabbed a stick to kill my attacker.

"Wait," I said. "What is it?"

"A scorpion, Madame," they said, astounded I wasn't afraid. "Didn't he sting you?"

"I didn't feel anything."

"You were lucky," Maleka said.

"Don't smash him. I want to preserve him for zoology class," I said as I ran to get a jar and alcohol from the office cupboard. When they were sure he was dead the girls were able to settle down to their studies again. After I looked up scorpions in my zoology book I understood their fear. *A member of the spider family, the sting is usually more painful than dangerous*, I read, *but some tropical species are highly poisonous.*

That same week my black cat jumped down from our attic eaves with a bat in her mouth. Kitty, totally trusting, allowed me to pick up her prey. I thanked her and dropped it into a jar of alcohol, telling her I needed it as an example in my eighth grade zoology class. My poor cat spent the rest of the day searching for her victim, but I had a fine bat specimen for science.

I stayed busy trying to keep up with planning lessons for ten different subjects, writing Belgian-style notes for my students to copy, rewriting them with Michel's corrections, making maps for geography classes, getting sewing projects ready, preparing tests, grading papers, and supervising extra-curricular activities.

When my parents' Mennonite church in Pennsylvania sent us a bit of money to use in our school, we bought ditto masters and paper so we could duplicate our notes for the students to copy into their notebooks later, freeing us up to have more time for classroom discussion. We also invested in soccer balls and basketballs, and Charles had a basketball court constructed in a flat clay area. Tata Maluka, our school construction foreman, set tall hardwood six by six boards into concrete and hung baskets for physical education classes and free time.

Every morning at seven o'clock when we got back from prayers Charles turned on our short wave radio and we listened to Voice of America, our major news source. The Congolese got theirs in Lingala from the national station, beamed out into the bush from Radio Kinshasa. Being extremely interested in American politics, the students came seeking our point of view. They were overjoyed to learn Lyndon Johnson wasn't running for a second term and cheered for Monsieur Kennedy's little brother Bobby when he became a candidate.

Camelot and the mystique of that era had spread even into the far corners of Africa. Africans idolized John F. Kennedy, the man who'd sent Peace Corps workers and funds to rebuild Congo after years of civil war in the northeast. They'd been stunned by his assassination five years earlier and were suspicious of the man who replaced him.

Then on Tuesday, April 4, 1968, the news that Dr. Martin Luther King had been gunned down blasted around the world. Our seniors sat stunned in their classroom as though here, on the other side of the planet, they too were attending his wake.

"There're a lot of assassins in America," Bilongo murmured, after I'd come in and set down my book bag. Coming back from a holiday they'd talk about having seen John Wayne and his cowboys gunning down Indians. Try as I might to convince them that was fantasy in the movies, they never believed we Americans didn't live like that.

"America is a dangerous place to live," Mabwaka said, nodding in agreement. They poured over my weekly "Newsweek" airmailed out from Europe, looking at the photos and able to read much of the text.

But only two months later, on June 5, the day Bobby Kennedy's murder was announced, their faith in our American system of government was shaken to the core. When I went to the seniors' classroom that day, they had Bobby's name written on their blackboard. They wanted to talk. "Why, Madame?" they asked. I didn't know the answer and could only shake my head. They said they didn't understand these killings in America, the world's leader of democracy. How could it happen? Embarrassed for my country, I told them I didn't comprehend it either. I wondered if anybody did.

"Americans have too many guns," Kalu suggested.

"We don't have guns here. They're illegal," Ntalu said.

They mourned for Bobby and his family, but especially for his mother. "How can she stand to lose two sons?" they asked, ever mindful of their own suffering mothers and grandmothers. Bobby's name remained on their chalkboard for several weeks.

The following summer, in July 1969, Americans put the first man on the moon. We'd read and discussed the space race in geography classes. They heard about it on Radio Kinshasa. Charles and I listened to Voice of America and read reports and looked at photos in "Newsweek."

"Madame, it's impossible," Ntalu, a senior in my geography class told me one day as we were discussing this extraordinary feat. "I don't believe it actually happened."

Several students agreed with him. "Look at the moon," they said. "How could anybody send a spaceship that far and precisely to that spot in the universe?"

"How do you know it really happened?" Nsemi asked.

"People were there when the space ship blasted off at Cape Canaveral. They heard the astronauts speaking from outer space, saw movies of them walking on the moon's surface, and were there to see them reenter and land in Florida."

But some remained skeptical. "They had actors make a movie to pretend they did this," Ntalu insisted.

"Don't argue with them," Charles said when I told him. "Some Americans don't even believe it! So how can you expect people in a third-world country, without electricity or running water, to accept such a phenomenon?"

One morning just a week before Christmas vacation as we were getting ready to leave for morning prayers, Lesley rode up to our house. She jumped off her bicycle, and pounded on the back door. "What's the matter, Lesley?" I asked, opening for her.

"Oh, it's a terrible thing," she whispered, her hands shaking. "The new chappy from Belgium. The one that arrived six weeks ago. He died last night."

"Come, come," I said, pulling her inside the kitchen. "What on earth happened?" I asked as Charles came from the bedroom, buttoning his shirt.

"We're not sure. Morning classes are to be cancelled. The students are going to prayers so they'll be told there. John and Margot have gone off to Ngombe Matadi to fetch the police du secteur. Would you go over to the house? Bob could use you over there. I'll see to your duties at the church," she said, turning to leave.

We shook our heads, finished dressing, and breathed a prayer before jumping on our bikes and heading across campus to the sprawling brick house where our newest Belgian teacher had been living. His housemates, Guy, our upper-level French teacher, and Bob, a 20-year-old American conscientious objector sent out by Mennonite

Central Committee to help with our building program, had been trying with little success to make Jean-Pierre feel at home out here in the bush.

Bob came out to meet us, shaking his head. "I woke up late. Guy was already up and getting dressed for prayers. I didn't see Jean-Pierre so I hollered and knocked on his door. He didn't answer so a few minutes later I went back and knocked again. Finally, I opened his door. It was awful," he said, putting his head in his hands.

Guy came down the steps as we parked our bicycles. "We knew he had a lot of problems. But I didn't realize he was this depressed. If we'd had any idea ...," he trailed off. "Thank goodness he left a note so there's no question about what happened. He was overwhelmed and couldn't cope."

Charles became an errand boy, running back and forth between the school, the director, and the house. I made tea and sat and listened as the guys paced and talked. The police arrived and looked at the room. Nothing could be disturbed until the magistrates and coroner came from Mbanza Ngungu. A casket was being sent from Kinshasa. We'd have to wait. The room remained dark and closed.

Students came and stood on the lawns, not knowing what to make of their science teacher taking his own life. Village people also came to wait in front of the house.

Bob asked me several times to go in with him. "I want you to see it," he said.

"No, Bob. I can't. I don't need to cope with that scene in my head the rest of my life." I made him another cup of tea. He talked about what he'd seen in the room. What Jean-Pierre had done.

Nobody could eat. We waited, and waited, and waited. Lunchtime came and went. And then a large transport truck pulled up, a casket on the back. Our ordeal was coming to a close. Roommates were interviewed, notes written, documents signed, and the body was taken away. Guy went out and talked to the students, thanked them for caring about their teacher, told them to go back to their dormitories, eat some lunch, and take the rest of the day to study.

"We want all of you to come over to our house," I told the teachers and Bob. "I have lots of eggs and fresh bread I baked yesterday. I'll make lunch for everyone."

I knew food was cathartic and eating together in our house, in a different location, would be healing. I scrambled eggs, opened a can of cheddar cheese, sliced my bread and several tomatoes I'd found in the market the day before. Lesley helped me cut up mangos, bananas, avocados, and a pineapple for a tropical fruit salad. And we brewed more tea. We talked and ate and eventually we felt strong enough to pick up the pieces.

Month after month Congolese celebrated not only the regular holidays, but on the spur of the moment added a jour férié – a day off – announced in Lingala on the radio that morning: the President's mother's birthday, a special anniversary, a visiting senator. At times we didn't know what we were celebrating. We'd find out at prayers that all schools were closed for the day and classes were forbidden to meet. If the students weren't required to march in a parade for a visiting dignitary under our supervision, I'd spend part of the day sewing in the girls' refectory. Many would join me and we'd talk while cutting out blocks and making pillows or baby quilts. I showed them how to put backs on blankets and tie them with yarn. We'd mend their school uniforms or they'd cut out and sew new dresses.

Charles spent many of his afternoons and holidays hauling water or rock or sand or bricks in the temperamental Jeep truck for Tata Maluka who was building badly needed outhouses behind the dormitories, a new kitchen for the boys, and a new duplex for teachers. Several of Maluka's helpers would ride down to the river on the back of the Jeep.

While they dug sand out of the river and loaded it on the truck bed, Charles sat under a tree and graded papers or prepared lessons. The workers were paid the equivalent of six cents each for every load they brought in. One day he told me they made five runs, so the men earned 30 cents apiece for the day, better money than they could make anywhere else.

Students carried rocks from the river and piled them on the bank during their weekly manual labor class. The workers would later heave them into the truck bed. Charles brought load after load of rock to the construction sites where Maluka's men cracked them with hammers into gravel-sized stones to be mixed in the cement. The sand was combined with cement to manufacture cinderblocks by hand using a little mold.

The Congolese used the murky Tombe River at the bottom of the hill for everything: baptizing, soaking manioc, bathing, washing clothes, doing dishes. But the women, swaying gracefully even as they climbed the steep hill, carried home on their heads buckets of water from the spring for drinking and cooking. Although the spring water was clean, we foreigners still needed to boil and filter it.

During the various dry seasons when cisterns were empty, students carried buckets of water to their school kitchens. Charles and John Russell, a single British missionary teacher, spent hours hauling barrels of spring water to faculty members' homes, especially during school vacations.

"You're home early," I said when he came in after only a couple of hours one afternoon. "Did the truck break down?"

"Nope. We're done."

"Done? You've filled all the teachers' cisterns?"

"Yep," he answered, looking a bit smug.

"So how'd you do it that fast?"

"John found a hose so we rigged up a pipe line. He connected one end to the spring. We strung it across the river and stuck the other end in a barrel on the truck. Then we sat around and waited for it to do its job! Sure beats finding people to help with a bucket brigade."

One afternoon when I'd finished teaching my last class I jumped on my bike and headed home. "Did you hear about the snake?" someone asked as I rode up the path.

"Snake? What kind of snake?"

"A python! Domingo has it up at the garage."

I pedaled home and grabbed my camera. "Did you hear about the snake?" I asked Mpanzu as he placed firewood under two buckets of water on a little metal frame in our back yard. Charles would light it about five o'clock so we could have hot baths before dark.

"Yes, I saw it, Madame. It's as big as the one that killed our dog in my wife's peanut garden." I hurried off to the garage, shivering at the thought it could have been his toddler.

I photographed Domingo holding the snake draped over the pipe that had killed it. Charles arrived and snapped a picture of me holding that python's tail high over my head, its body stretching out nine feet in front of me. "Hurry," I said. "This thing is heavy!"

"And dangerous. Look how big and thick its body is."

"Where was he and how did you kill him, Domingo?"

"I heard a noise, like cracking bones. I thought maybe it was a cat eating one of my chickens. They've been disappearing recently, you know. So I tiptoed toward the noise in the woods behind your house and there at the edge of your back yard I found him wrapped around a chicken. I grabbed up a piece of pipe and went back and smashed his head. He was coiled around the chicken and had started to swallow it so he couldn't get away. I hit him until he was dead."

"At the edge of our back yard?" I asked, my mouth hanging open.

"Yes, I'm so glad we got him. He could have killed one

of the children or even an adult."

Domingo kept the valuable skin but gave the meat to several students who came from central Congo where snake is a delicacy. They made a stew by boiling the white flesh with onions, tomatoes, and hot peppers and served it up with their chiquanga. I knew I'd often be asked how python tasted, so I tried a bite of the meat. "Like a cross between chicken and fish," I'd say. "And I didn't mind one bit helping eat that reptile."

"A letter came from the state," Ian said one morning, pulling us aside at prayers. "We need to send four teachers from our school to help correct entrance exams at Kimpese. I want you two to go."

"It'll be a lot of work," I said to Charles at breakfast. "But I don't mind going to Kimpese. Ian said we'll stay at the hospital guesthouse. Just think, a real shower!"

"Well, that's a selling point."

"And on the way home we can stop at the central market in Mbanza Ngungu and buy veggies and fruit."

"And fresh meat at the butcher shop."

And so, early on the morning of May sixth we rode the 100 miles, along with John and Lesley, in our school's VW Bug to the correction site. On the way, Lesley talked about the impact of the exams. "Very few girls continue their education beyond middle school even if they make high enough scores," she said. "Education is expensive and most parents prefer to send only their sons on to high school since their boys will be the ones taking care of them in their old age."

"So what happens to the girls?" I asked.

"They drop out, teach primary school for a year or two, and then marry. If they hold a middle school diploma they have a better chance of marrying an educated man."

"That would definitely put them in a higher standard-of-living bracket than if they remained in their village," I said.

"The other problem is finding enough places even for the boys. We have 60 students in our middle school taking the test, but places in the upper school for only 30. We'll want to choose the very best students."

We corrected French exams from Monday noon until Tuesday night. "One of our boys placed seventh out of 859 who sat for the exam," Lesley confided when the scoring was completed.

"We definitely want him back, don't we?" Charles said.

"Absolutely. Tomorrow we'll choose. We must consider the student's character if we know him, his scores, and the schools he prefers to attend. We know our own boys' dispositions, so we'll take as many of them as possible. Although we want the highest all around scores possible, we'll be looking closely at their French and English grades since ours is a literary section."

On Wednesday we chose our candidates and then headed up the two-lane paved road to Mbanza Ngungu where we stopped at the market for fresh vegetables. I was delighted to find colored embroidery thread in a tiny tailor's shop. Lesley told me it hadn't been available since independence, eight years earlier. We bought some meat and canned food in the shops and went by the post office to pick up our mail before tackling the 35-mile pot-holed dirt road to our mission post.

Throughout the next several weeks I told Charles over and over, "I hope I don't have to go to Mbanza Ngungu to give oral state exams to the seniors."

"They won't give oral *geography* exams. You'd think they'd do something like French or science. So don't worry about it," he kept telling me.

But Ian had different news. My name was on the list of participating teachers sent by the state department. We'd been chosen to administer oral geography exams to seniors from our area at a high school in Mbanza Ngungu the last week of June. Patterned after the French and Belgian systems, these exams would decide who received a state secondary school diploma. Without it they could not attend a Congolese university.

Not having ever taken an oral exam myself and not being a geography specialist, I felt ignorant and was probably more traumatized than my students, worrying I'd not taught them all they needed to know. Three of us teachers – an African, a Belgian, and I – watched while a student entered the room, walked to our table where we'd spread out, upside down, state-supplied questions typed on strips of paper. The student had to choose, like we pick letters for playing scrabble. "Take two slips," the Belgian would say. "Look at the questions, keep the one you prefer to answer. Lay the other one back on the table."

Some stared, their hands trembling before choosing, others just grabbed. But each one picked up two slips of paper, turned them over, and read. Some shook their heads, others broke into a wide grin before returning one slip. "You have several minutes to prepare," the Belgian would say. "Sit down and organize your thoughts." In three minutes he'd call the student to come and stand before us to explain his answer.

We took notes and then jotted down the grade we thought he deserved. After he left the room we shared our decisions, and averaged the three grades. A student's state geography exam grade was thus signed, sealed, and delivered in a matter of minutes, a system Europeans have used for centuries.

Every year we became more proficient in our spoken and written French, improved the quality of our lesson notes, learned more about the system, and became more comfortable with African culture and our surroundings. In the end I came to realize they'd taught me far more than I was ever able to give in return.

Domingo, a gifted Angolan refugee who oversaw
our school's maintenance program.

Fetching water from the Tombe River.

# Mennonite Childbirth:
# A Baby Sister
# 1948-1956

"**D**id you know Mennonites have bigger families than other people?" I asked my mother one spring afternoon not long after she and Daddy had joined Stauffer Mennonite Church. I was seven years old.

"Really?" Mom said, looking up from kneading bread on the enamel board of her Hoosier kitchen cabinet.

"At school when I say there're four of us children, my friends think we have a big family. But to Mennonites, it's small."

"What about the Stricklers? They have only three children," Mom said, turning the little handle on the flour bin to sift more flour into the crock below. She reached in and took a handful, shook it over the board, and continued kneading the ball of dough.

"Yeah, but what about the Brubakers? They have eight," I crowed. And to prove my point I started counting them off on my fingers: "Wilbur, Allen, Helen, Glenn, Mildred, Roy, Charles, Mark, and their new baby Nancy."

"Well, I have nine brothers and sisters," Mom said, "and

my parents aren't Mennonites.

"But that doesn't count," I said. "Because your *grandma* was! Mom, Mennonites have lots of babies. Why can't we have one too?"

My mother just looked at me, a little smile playing at the edge of her lips. "Have one what?" she asked, placing the dough in a pan and covering it with a cloth.

"You know, Mom, a baby sister! Why can't we have a baby sister?"

We didn't have a nursery at our Mennonite church. Mothers sat in the center section and held their little ones on their laps during preaching. There were so many that Mom was usually sitting in a row with a mother and baby. She didn't mind as long as other women were sitting between the child and us, because she was afraid I'd try to play with it and make it bawl. I leaned front to watch the mother pull things out of her diaper bag: Cheerios in a little jar for baby to pick up one by one, a cloth picture book, a plastic teething ring to chew. Watching babies was one of my favorite things.

Halfway through the service the mother would lay the baby on his back on her lap and give him a toy or pop a pacifier in his mouth. She'd pull down his rubber pants and unpin the little garters clipped to the tops of his long white stockings. Then she'd undo the big pins and slip off the wet diaper under cover of the clean dry one. Those mothers were experts. Nothing ever showed. And in two minutes the new diaper was pinned, stockings reattached, rubber pants pulled back in place, and the cute little suit buttoned up. She'd roll up the wet diaper and slip it into a plastic compartment of her diaper bag, and voilà, baby was fresh as lilacs in spring.

When baby fussed, his mama would reach in from the side, under her cape, and open her dress. Then she'd snuggle baby's head in the crook of her arm and, his face hidden beneath her wide cape, he'd breastfeed and go to sleep. Then I'd sit back and open the metal clasp on my little navy blue quilted pocketbook and look at my stuff: two Sunday school tickets – one red, one blue; two shiny pennies; a clean hanky; a rainbow tablet; and a pencil. I'd sort and rearrange my stuff, and maybe print some words or draw in my notebook, waiting for the end of the sermon or for a baby to wake up.

Mennonites were different from the children we knew in public school. Mennonites knew the real meaning of family and belonging; they taught their children integrity and responsibility. Everyone helped everyone else. Older children looked after little ones, especially the toddlers and babies. And I wanted to be like them, to fit in. To me, as an eight-year-old, that meant we needed a baby.

Like most Mennonite women in the 1930s and 40s, my mother had given birth to her first four children at home, old Doc Horn and Daddy attending. Her labors were long and hard, but she never had complications. After I was born no more babies came.

In the autumn of 1948, when my siblings and I were in elementary school, my ten-year-old brother Dennis was diagnosed with that most dreaded disease, polio. His back and neck were stiff; he could hardly walk. The doctor had Mom put him in the bathtub and soak him in hot water. Nobody knew how polio was contracted or how to stop it. Mom blamed the creek water we'd played in during the hot summer months.

Someone came out from Hershey in a big car and tacked a sign on the side of our barn. We were quarantined. "You're not allowed to leave the premises," the man said. "Anyone who comes in will have to stay. You may not send out letters or give anything, not even money, to anyone."

"Can we go get the mail?" my older brother Carl asked.

"Out at the end of the lane?" My brother nodded. "Absolutely not. You may not leave your property. Don't go in the woods either. You might come in contact with someone." Daddy came home from work and didn't go back. We had no telephone; we felt truly isolated.

Neighbors, relatives, and friends were terrified. They brought food and our mail and set it on the wall by the barn, fearful to come any closer. We'd stand on the other side of the barnyard and holler back and forth, just to have somebody different to talk to. Grandma wrote Mom a letter and sent it up the hill with Aunt Shirley. Grandma had reason to worry about her oldest daughter; she knew something we siblings didn't know. Mom was going to have a baby and that baby was at high risk for polio.

Mrs. Hanford, our neighbor on the hill, drove down in her wood-sided station wagon. She brought groceries and paid our bills. She told Daddy not to worry; he could pay her later.

Then Far-Grandma came on the bus from Virginia. We called her Far-Grandma because she lived so far away. Mom said that way we'd know which Grandma was meant. Uncle Lloyd brought her in his car from the station. She thanked him, picked up her black cardboard suitcase, and started down the walk.

"Far-Grandma," I said. "You can't go in. If you do you can't leave."

"I came to stay. I'm going to help your mother." And in she went. She carried her bag upstairs and took Carl's empty twin bed across the room from Dennis. From then on she looked after my brother at night and helped Mom and Daddy tend him during the day. She gathered up the ends of the garden before frost hit, cooked for us, washed our clothes in the old wringer washer, and hung them out to dry. We gobbled up her pumpkin pies and homemade light yeast bread.

Dennis got better, the quarantine was lifted after a couple of weeks, and we went back to school. Eventually my brother was strong enough to walk, and oddly outgrew his slight limp in a few months. Years later a specialist told him he probably didn't have polio, that it had most likely been misdiagnosed for spinal meningitis, another deadly disease in those days before antibiotics.

"Where's Mom?" I asked Far-Grandma when I got up that Saturday morning in mid-October.

"Your mom went to the hospital to get a baby," she grinned, knowing I'd been begging my mother for a baby sister.

I stood there in disbelief. "You're teasing," I said. But Far-Grandma explained that this was the real reason why she'd come, to take care of us while Mom was in the hospital. I was elated and danced around the house, singing and whooping. "I knew it! I knew it! I just knew Mom would get a baby." Suddenly I stopped. "Is it a boy or a girl?"

"We don't know yet," Far-Grandma said. "We're still waiting for it to arrive. Just eat your breakfast and then find something to do. It'll be here before you know."

Years later, after my own son had been born, my mother told me how terrified she'd been of losing her ten-year-old son. In spite of being in the last trimester of pregnancy, she nursed Dennis through his illness, carrying him back and forth to the tub, massaging his back and neck, changing his bed, urging him to take liquids. Dr. Lodge had come every day and given orders.

She said that the doctor, fearing for her and the baby she was carrying, gave her no choice but to go to the hospital for this delivery. A private room had been set up for her at the Harrisburg General Hospital. They were prepared for the worst scenario – a mother and newborn with polio.

Mom hated being in the hospital. She'd never been away from home, didn't like the food, and wasn't used to being served; she'd always played the role of a servant. And she had a bad experience with Twilight Sleep, as she called it – an anesthesia administered during the last hours of labor, before her daughter was finally born early Sunday morning. "I felt like I was floating," she said. "I hated it. I always wanted to be fully awake and aware, to hear my baby's first cry."

That Sunday morning I proudly marched into Sunday school with Daddy, my siblings, and Far-Grandma, announcing that we had a new little sister named Mary Anne after our grandma.

Far-Grandma said, "I reckon" and baked green tomato pies. We made faces but Daddy said we had to try it, that it was better than apple pie. And he was right. Far-Grandma had put in sugar and cinnamon and it tasted just like an applesauce pie.

"I reckon if you want breakfast you'd better bring in some kindling and stack it in the woodbox so I can make fire in the morning," she told my brothers.

We whispered to each other, wondering what "I reckon" meant. "Ask her," my brothers said. "She'll tell you."

So I sidled up to her and asked, "Far-Grandma, what does 'I reckon' mean?"

"I'll I reckon you if you don't get out there and bring in that kindling right this minute," she shouted and we scurried to the woodshed. We never did find out what it meant until weeks later after she'd gone back to Virginia and we asked Mom.

I hung around the house watching my mother tend our black-eyed baby – bathing, feeding, and changing her. After Mom had the boys bring the old baby coach down from the attic I spent hours pushing my little sister back and forth to put her to sleep.

When I was 15 years old Mom didn't tell us she was going to have another baby. Back then "pregnant" was a medical term. "She's expecting," Mom would say. Or Daddy might ask, "Is she in the family way?" With four teenagers, Mom was embarrassed and kept silent in 1955 when she learned she was pregnant. Being somewhat over-weight, she was able to hide her pregnancy behind her loose skirts. Everyone thought she'd just gotten heavier.

Not having had a baby in seven years, Mom didn't have hand-me-downs. While we were at school she secretly made preparations, sewing flannel kimonos, cotton diapers, and bellybands, buying undershirts, rubber pants, a folding cot for herself, and a big wicker clothesbasket for the newborn. She made arrangements with our family physician to come to the house, and generally lined up things, as she would say. Daddy had birthed many farm animals and had attended his first four children's arrivals, so he knew what to do. Mom, even at 41, wasn't afraid to have another baby at home.

One Friday evening in late January when I came in from school I could tell my mother wasn't feeling well. I heard her talking on the phone to our doctor's nurse. "Margie, my water broke, but it'll be a long labor. Mine always are. I just want you to be ready; I'll probably need you tomorrow," she said.

"Would you get the sweeper out and clean downstairs?" Mom asked me. "The doctor's coming." That's the closest she ever came to telling me she was having a baby. My sister Anita arrived from college and in her quiet way was a comfort to Mom.

The next morning Mom was still in labor and asked me to take seven-year-old Mary Anne outside. "Don't tell her. She'll want to come inside to see. I need some rest."

I dressed Mary Anne in her winter coat and leggings, sliding the side zippers down to her ankles, pulling up her boots and fastening the clasps to make them snug. I put on a pair of daddy's overalls under my coat before tying wool bandanas on our heads.

We walked though the woods and I thought of Robert Frost's poem we'd read in English class.

> *He will not see me stopping here*
> *To watch the woods fill up with snow ...*
>
> *The only other sound's the sweep*
> *Of easy wind and downy flake.*
>
> *The woods are lovely, dark and deep.*
> *But I have promises to keep,*
> *And miles to go before I sleep,*
> *And miles to go before I sleep.*

We played for hours in the meadow, scuffing and kicking our way through the deepest snowdrifts, lying down and making snow angels. We rolled enormous balls and built snowmen until we were chilled. I took my little sister to the barn and for a while we played with the goats. Finally, hoping the baby had come, I gave in to my sister's begging and brought her to the house for lunch.

"You'll have to take her down to Grandma's," Mom said, still pacing the floor as we ate sandwiches and soup Anita had warmed on the cookstove, next to two teakettles simmering at the back.

We put on dry clothes and hiked out the slippery lane and through the snowy fields to our grandparents' dairy farm. Grandma warmed us by the cookstove and fed us hard pretzels. Aunt Shirley took us upstairs to her bedroom and read to us and we entertained Mary Anne with her dolls. Hours later the phone rang and Grandma came and told us Mom had given birth to a baby girl; we could go home. Mary Anne felt betrayed. "Why didn't you tell me? Why didn't anyone tell me?" she asked. I told her I had only found out the night before. None of us had known.

Mom was lying on her folding cot in the living room when we came in, and a tiny pink baby snuggled in snowy white blankets in the basket on the piano bench. We hung over the edge, watching our two-hour-old sister's tiny chest rise and fall as she slept. "Don't bother her," Mom said. "She needs to sleep. When she wakes up you can hold her."

Later we watched as Mom sat in a soft chair and breast-fed this tiny creature with a loud voice, her dark brown eyes following us as we circled around her. "Do you know how the doctor measured her?" Anita asked. We shook our heads and she showed us two Sears Roebuck catalogs still lying on the table. "He put the baby between them, stretched her out, and then measured the distance, 18 ½ inches!"

"Tell them how Margie got here," Mom said as we came back into the living room. I was as incredulous as my seven-year-old sister, gazing at our tiny sister and stroking her puff of dark hair.

"Dennis had to go get Margie," Anita giggled, looking at our brother. "She was afraid to drive in the snow, especially to come down our lane." Dennis shrugged, pleased to have played a role in this little drama.

I touched our baby's perfectly formed miniscule fingers and marveled at the wee nails and miniature ears. Mom let me change her diaper when she'd finished nursing. "Just don't stick her with the pin," she said. "Put your finger underneath."

"What are we going to call her?" I asked, gently pulling on her newborn-sized rubber pants. Mary Anne stroked her soft crocheted booties. We straightened her flannel kimono and then wrapped her securely in her brand new receiving blanket for support and warmth.

"Your father says he wants to name her after Ruth in the Bible, because she was such a Godly woman. But we can choose the middle name." In the end we all liked the sound of Ruth Ellen. So we chose Ellen. Several weeks later we

received a note from Far-Grandma in Virginia, telling us
how pleased she was we'd given her middle name to our
new baby sister.

The house and well on the old home place.

The barn and chicken house.

# A Gift: Our Son
# September 1972

"They want to introduce you," Lesley leaned over and whispered to Charles and me. "Stand up." We stood and the pastor talked to the large congregation in Kikongo, gesturing toward us. All eyes were on us, the first Americans many had seen.

When the women responded with a humming sound, we sat down and I turned to Lesley and hissed, "What's he saying?"

"They're Americans. They've come here to Ngombe Lutete to teach in the secondary school. They're very young and have just married, so they have no children yet," she translated.

Charles and I looked at each other and giggled. We'd been married three years and were 27 and 30 years old, well beyond what these Congolese would tolerate in a childless marriage. They wouldn't have believed it if we told them we'd decided before we married to wait until we were ready to settle down before having a child.

One day ran into another as we dealt with the daily struggles of preparation and teaching in a second language and an unfamiliar culture. We made two summer trips back to the States. Three years had passed. Many changes had taken place in Congo, which was now called Zaïre.

The women in the village, their eyes cast down, pitied me for my childlessness. Living in a country where many children died before the age of two, they had no comprehension of birth control or why a woman would choose to wait. In their society a woman without a child was scorned and often divorced.

After I turned 30 I started thinking more like my African sisters and began to worry that perhaps I'd never conceive a child. Another year and a half passed. Then word swept through the post that Nengua Patton was going to have a baby. In the market women smiled at me or laughed and said, "Ahh, kiamboti, Nengua," followed by a string of Kikongo. I knew they were congratulating me. Sometimes one would pat my tummy as she laughed and pointed to the child on her back.

The lady deacons told the director of our school that it was unseemly for me to wear short skirts when I was going to be a mother. Not wanting to offend them I made several well-below-the-knee maternity dresses for teaching and an ankle-length African print skirt for walking around the post.

As my baby grew inside of me, I put away my bicycle and walked, paying attention to where I stepped, keeping an eye out for snakes and scorpions. Avoiding contracting intestinal parasites became critical; I scrutinized what I ate and drank, overseeing the boiling of our drinking water and cleaning the filter.

I began making and searching for baby clothes, to the point of begging Ede Thompson, the director of CARE in our area, to let me have two-dozen Birdseye cotton diapers. She agreed when I promised to pass them on to Congolese women on our post. In the market week after week I sifted through piles of American baby clothes and bought an undershirt here, a kimono or sleeper there, and once even found a little pair of blue corduroy overalls for the dry season when mornings would be cold.

My husband went to Tata Maluka, the local carpenter, and gave him measurements and drawings for a crib, a dressing table, and a rocking chair. I talked to Mama Lukau, an Angolan mid-wife who'd lost her job in the dispensary. She was also expecting a baby in September and would need a job afterwards. I begged her to work for me taking care of our babies while I taught school. We were an answer to each other's prayers.

Worried about my health, once a week I walked over to see Tata Pedro, an Angolan nurse who worked in the dispensary on our station, and asked him to check my blood pressure. He was a kind capable man, frustrated with the lack of medicines and equipment for his clinic. Occasionally when the mud road was dry, I drove the four miles to Ngombe Matadi to consult with the wrinkled Belgian nun dressed in a black habit and a long white apron. This elderly woman of God was all that remained of a once important clinic in our corner of Congo. I found her kind and supportive and went home comforted.

Every couple of months Charles drove us in our little blue Renault to the large hospital-nursing school, Institute Médical Evangélique, known as IME, in Kimpese. Although we usually experienced several harrowing episodes on the 35 miles of pot-holed dirt roads and the 75 more of two-lane curvy paved highway where we dodged passing busses and transport trucks, I always looked forward to our overnight stay with American friends. There I consulted with Betty Shelly, my American Mennonite obstetrician. She reassured me each time but advised me to come to the hospital compound to live the last month before my September 1 due date. And then in July she and her family went back to the States.

For my last prenatal visits I saw a round of international

doctors. One from Holland ordered X-rays in August to see
how the baby was doing. After that I saw Dr. Kvernes, a
general practitioner who'd just arrived from Sweden.

At Kimpese we house-sat for a British pharmacist who
had gone home on a two-month furlough. I especially
enjoyed interacting with our American, Canadian, and
British neighbors and attending English services with them.

One afternoon during our daily walk around the
compound, Charles suddenly barked, "Stop." I stopped dead
in my tracks and turned to stare into the eyes of a viper,
coiled and ready to strike, no more than eight feet in front of
me. Having seen the deadly affects of this snake before, I
knew my baby certainly would have died had I been bitten. I
thanked God and my husband for protecting us.

September 1 came and went. Charles took the Renault
and returned to Ngombe Lutete for the beginning of the new
school year. Tina Warkentin, a Canadian secretary, came to
stay with me that night, but my labor started. She sent word
to a Congolese houseboy with whom we had an agreement
to go and fetch Charles. I gave him transport money and a
practical note I'd scribbled to my husband, "My water broke
this evening at six o'clock so I guess you can turn around
and come back. I'm going to stay in the hospital guesthouse
tonight. Don't panic - just come through safely and bring
enough shirts and pants to stay several days."

The houseboy couldn't find transport that evening.
Eighteen hours later Charles walked into my room at the
hospital guesthouse where I'd spent the night pacing the
floor. Six more hours passed. I was exhausted with painful
back labor. Charles stayed beside me, wiping the sweat
from my face, rubbing my back.

A retired American orthopedic surgeon appeared at my
side. This dear man with an artificial leg himself had come
to Congo to help the less fortunate after his retirement.
"Twenty-six hours is too long to be in labor," he said. "Your

baby can't be born naturally. You need a Cesarean-section."
He shook his head and looked into my eyes. "I'd be glad to
do it for you, but I've been in the operating room all day and
I'm just too tired. We're going to give you a sedative and let
you rest for an hour until we can assemble a team and get
the operating room ready. And we need to find some blood
donors." He told Charles to go take a shower and get something to eat and come back at eight o'clock.

"Who'll do the surgery?" Charles asked.

"We can put together a fine team with Dr. Jim Evans, a
Canadian general practitioner on our staff, doing the surgery
and Dr. Kvernes assisting him."

Dr. Evans came forward and bent over me. "I'll be
happy to do the surgery for you, if you want. But I feel obligated to tell you I'm not a surgeon; I have never performed a
Cesarean-section on a white woman."

"Have you done any?"

"Oh, yes, several hundred here in Congo."

"Okay," I said, "I'm ready when you are." I'd heard of Dr.
Evans before; he and his wife Patty had worked on the Good
Ship Hope before coming to Congo and had excellent reputa-
tions as compassionate health care workers. I wasn't afraid.

Before I went into surgery a hospital mid-wife stopped
by my bed and asked if I'd heard Mama Lukau was also
there and ready to deliver. She wanted me to know. I sent
her my best wishes.

Minutes after they placed me on the operating table I
heard my baby's first tired whimper. "It's a boy," Dr. Evans
said, handing the bruised child to a nurse who swaddled him
in a green cloth, stopping only to give me a fleeting glance
of my battered son before she carried him away. Tears
welled in my eyes.

My six-pound baby boy had been through a war before
his birth. Sedatives and long labor had taken their toll on
him to the point that he couldn't coordinate his mouth to

suck. I'd grown up with babies at church and two much younger sisters at home. I knew what to do and patiently guided my son through his difficult first few weeks.

Two days after his birth I developed a high fever. "Oh, no," Dot, the American nurse from Oregon who ran the guesthouse, said. "You either have milk fever or malaria. Have you been taking your prophylaxis?"

I thought back over the last several days and realized that Nivaquine had never entered my mind. My first experience with malaria quickly passed when I restarted my medication. Dot kept an eye on my son and me after Charles had to go back to school at Ngombe Lutete. But Averil Cooper, a British nurse/mid-wife, sustained me through the blues, inviting me to her house for chicken suppers and lending me a Sears catalog, urging me to look at the latest fashions.

When Charles returned on the weekend he said, "Michel wants to know if there's anything he can do for you."

"Tell him to have dinner ready when I get there. That's the best present I can think of." I was grateful to our Belgian colleague who cared.

Ann Marie Nordby, a public health nurse from Norway, gave me a little yellow book, an International Certificate of Vaccination, and told me when to bring my baby back for his shots.

Three weeks after Chucky's birth our little family drove back to our station in the bush, one hundred miles from medical help. Michel welcomed us with roast pork, oven browned potatoes, canned peas, and a tender flan. He came every evening to our house and we spoke French. He held our baby and we called him Oncle Michel.

One afternoon I came home from class to find Mama Lukau bouncing Chucky, tied African style on her back. "He was crying so I put him on my back," she explained in her broken French.

"And Valentine likes to sit in the crib," I laughed. "It's

okay. Just keep them happy." Watching my son grow and develop consumed my waking hours. My diary describes him blowing bubbles, sleeping through the night, rolling over.

"He's so funny," I wrote to his grandmas. "I wish you could see him. He gets up on his hands and knees and rocks; he can go backwards but hasn't figured out yet how to go forward. His eyes light up and he smiles and coos when I come in from class and my heart does summersaults."

The first Sunday we carried Chucky to church for the morning worship service, remembering Congolese women wrap their babies even in ninety-degree weather, I draped him with the dainty crocheted yellow blanket his grandma had sent from California.

Nervous that he might cry, we sat together near the back of the men's section, taking turns holding him upright so he could see. The women across the aisle turned and looked from time to time, curious to watch this blond fair-skinned child who looked so different from their own curly-haired brown babies. He was quiet for the first hour, his big blue eyes investigating everything around him, especially the students who tried to get his attention and the dog that wandered down the aisle.

As soon as he started fussing I took him out and found Mama Lukau and several other mothers sitting in a row on the side veranda under the open windows. I smiled at them thinking, *so this is where the moms hang out with their babies!* They wanted to get me a chair but I slid down beside them on the brick floor, our backs against the outside wall of the church. They watched, waiting for me to pull a bottle from my diaper bag, amazed when I flipped the yellow blanket over my shoulder and began breast-feeding, just like they were.

When some little kids came strolling by and saw the mundele feeding her white baby they stopped, snickered, and pointed. Mama Lukau looked up and in a loud whisper hissed, "Katuka!" and they scattered like chickens she chased from the garden. Giggling with these women, I felt a closeness that couldn't have happened without the birth of my son.

Mama Lukau caring for Chucky.

# Home For Dinner
# 1948 – 1956

B eing invited home for dinner was the highlight of any Sunday for me as a child. Most Mennonites lived on big farms and had large families so I could depend on playing with lots of children and babies. Many of us back in the 1940s and early 50s didn't have telephones so the invitation was usually extended after preaching service, although occasionally we were asked a week in advance.

We liked knowing ahead of time so we could take old clothes and shoes along for jumping rope, playing hopscotch, or taking walks in the meadow, while the boys jumped in the haymow, rode bicycles, or played ball. Otherwise after dinner we'd put puzzles together in the parlor or play board games. But my favorite thing was rocking an infant. I loved babies and planned to have ten when I grew up.

We never went out to eat when I was growing up. I was in college before I even had a fast food hamburger. Mom loved to cook, using our homegrown vegetables and fruits. She thought eating in a restaurant would be a waste of money. Besides she didn't think the food would be as good as hers.

Not always knowing when we'd be invited or when she'd need to bring visitors home, my mother always tried to be ready. Sunday dinner was a big deal to Mom anyway, company or no company. Preparations began on Saturday and ended when we sat down to eat.

Saturday mornings my older sister Anita and I mopped, dusted, vacuumed, and scrubbed, while Mom made pies. Later she took down her big cut glass dish from the top of the china cupboard. After dissolving three boxes of either orange-pineapple or strawberry-banana Jello in boiling water, we gently poured the mixture into the cherished dish, a gift from Grandma. Finally we added crushed pineapples or strawberries, our favorites.

Mom believed in keeping Sunday a holy day and not doing any unnecessary work. We could wash dishes, sweep up spills, and cook certain parts of our dinner on Sunday. But according to Mom there were certain things that had to be prepared on Saturday: pies, cakes, Jello, bread, cookies, and puddings. I often made a Boston cream pie for our dinner. Mom didn't mind if I added the cream filling and icing on Sunday, but the cake had to be baked on Saturday.

We knew the rules and wouldn't have dreamed of whipping up a batch of cookies on Sunday afternoon. Sunday was for church, resting, reading, writing, walking, or quiet games. We never sewed, cleaned, or worked in the garden. Some Mennonites included schoolwork on their list, but not Mom; to her schoolwork was in the category of reading. If a question came up about wanting to do something she called work, she'd break out into a little chorus:

> *You must not work on Sunday*
> *Sunday, Sunday,*
> *You must not work on Sunday*
> *Because it is a sin.*

On Sunday mornings Mom put a pork shoulder, a chicken, or a piece of beef in the oven to slow roast while we were at church. When we got home Anita and I threw on pretty feedbag aprons and helped get dinner on the table. Mashed potatoes were a must for Mom's Sunday dinners, so while she peeled, Anita brought a jar of corn, peas, or green beans from the back cellar. Later after we bought our big chest freezer, Mom would say, "Get a pack of limas," or "bring a container of corn from the freezer." She never did like frozen beans and continued canning them to the end.

Mom turned off the oven, set the dark blue speckled granite roaster on the enamel sink, and lifted out the meat. The broth was divided between two pans, one for cooking a big dish of egg noodles with onion and the other for gravy. Anita had more patience than Mom or me, so she always stirred until the gravy thickened.

I rubbed some homemade soap on a dishrag and washed the flowered oilcloth that covered our kitchen table. I set it with Mom's mismatched Virginia Rose and other old-fashioned plates and real silver utensils. Mom and Daddy drank water, but I filled the rest of the short fat barrel glasses with Bossy's creamy milk that'd been strained and set to cool in gallon jars in our Kelvinator refrigerator. Sunday dinner wasn't complete without a jar of Mom's home canned pickles, a dish of sour beets and red beet eggs that had been hardboiled and soaked in the juice overnight, a plate of sliced homemade bread, a pat of butter we'd churned the night before, and a jar of homemade strawberry jam.

When the potatoes were cooked soft, Mom mashed them with her old-fashioned metal masher with a wooden handle, pounding it up and down on top of the potato chunks until the big lumps disappeared. She added a little cream, butter, and salt and whipped them with a wooden spoon to make the potatoes smooth. When Mom eventually bought an electric mixer for making cakes I took over mashing the potatoes. I'd beat them until they were a fluffy puff. Mom never did like them that way, always preferring them mashed by hand, the way she'd grown up.

One Sunday Mom invited our elderly Bishop Noah Risser and his wife Elsie home for dinner. Other guests had come as well so our dinner table was stretched as far as it would go. I whipped the mashed potatoes in the new mixer until they stood in peaks like meringue. As usual Mom served so many different foods it looked like Christmas dinner. Everyone finally sat back and chatted, having eaten until they could hold no more. My mother, looking around at our guests asked, " What else can I get for you? Would you like another piece of pie?"

The gentle bishop grinned, and shyly said, "If you don't mind, I'd like some more of those mashed potatoes. They're the best I've ever eaten."

I was jubilant. My mother laughed and told our bishop he had me to thank. And he did, beaming as he ate another helping of my whipped potatoes at the end of that enormous meal.

Our house was small compared to the ten-room farmhouses most Mennonite farming families lived in. Sometimes they'd invite two families, and have as many as 25 or 30 people, including babies, at the table. Daddy didn't like big crowds and he disapproved of having so many guests they couldn't all sit down together. So we'd invite one large or two small families.

I particularly remember two young families coming home for dinner with us. Afterwards, we went outside and sat under the apple tree. It was a beautiful warm lazy afternoon. I was elated playing with babies and toddlers, and my parents were enjoying interacting with those farm couples. As the sun began sliding toward the mountains, and they started talking about going home to do the evening milking, Daddy jumped up and asked, "How about some popcorn before you go?"

Daddy was a popcorn aficionado. Not only did he grow his own popcorn, he planted several varieties and knew their names. That afternoon he brought out a sampling of his corn and asked which kind they wanted: plain yellow, white, red, or what I called the spiky kind. He recommended that prickly corn, the kind that hurt our hands when we broke the kernels off the cob. As we shelled, he went inside and popped and filled huge white oval enamel dishpans with the most delicious and fluffiest cream-colored popcorn our guests had ever eaten.

Since our parents converted when they were both past 30, ours was not always a typical Mennonite household. But one place where Mom did fit in was with cooking. She loved to cook and had inherited some recipes from her Mennonite grandmother. But for the most part, Mom's recipes came from her high school Home Economics class. She'd copied them into a notebook without directions, in the style of that era, many of them written in shorthand.

In the early years of her marriage she bought a *Household Searchlight Recipe Book* printed in 1938, a big black book she kept in the top of the china cupboard and used throughout her life. One of her favorite recipes from it was Vanilla Wafers. She'd serve them with creamy tapioca or chocolate pudding, or we'd have several with just plain milk.

### *Vanilla Wafers*

| | |
|---|---|
| *2 eggs* | *½ cup shortening* |
| *1 tsp cream of tarter* | *1 ½ - 2 cups flour* |
| *½ teaspoon baking soda* | *½ teaspoon salt* |
| *1 cup sugar* | *½ tsp vanilla.* |

*Cream sugar and shortening, add well beaten egg yolks, sift flour, add ½ cup of flour and sift with cream of tarter, salt, and baking soda. Combine with egg mixture; mix throughly. Add stiffly beaten egg whites and flavoring. Add sufficient flour to make a soft dough. Turn onto lightly floured board. Roll in a sheet 1/8 inch thick. Cut with floured cookie cutters. Place on slightly oiled baking sheet. Bake in hot oven 400 degrees for 10 min. Makes 50 servings.*

For many years Daddy worked evenings in the Hershey Chocolate Factory and we'd see him only on weekends. So on school nights after the milking and barn chores were finished, Mom often made a quick and easy supper for us children: eggs scrambled with fried potatoes, served with tomato sauce; a dried beef cream gravy over toast; or one of her favorite soups: beef bean, chicken corn, vegetable, or potato soup.

To make these quick evening meals a bit more special, Mom would sometimes prepare ice cream in the tiny freezer compartment in the upper left corner of our Kelvinator refrigerator. She'd pull the floppy metal separators out of a couple of ice cube trays and fill them with her ice cream mixture, using a recipe in *Household Searchlight Recipe Book*. She'd add a fruit that was in season or canned pineapples. Anita and I would crowd around as she lifted the trays out onto the sink to stir the partially frozen mixture from time to time, knowing we'd each get a tiny taste. On hot summer evenings we couldn't have asked for a better treat than half a cup of Mom's strawberry ice cream with vanilla wafers.

### Ice Cream

*2 cups crushed strawberries       1 cup milk*
*1 ½ c thin cream                  1 ¼ c sugar*

*Combine strawberries and sugar, let stand 30 minutes. Stir ingredients together. Freeze. Stir occasionally during freezing process.*

One afternoon in early November 2002 I e-mailed three of my siblings. "I'm writing an essay about being invited home for dinner when we were children back on the farm in Pennsylvania. What do you remember?"

"I've eaten many meals with Mennonite families," my older sister Anita wrote from Guatemala. "When we were children we were often invited to supper if we went to another church for their All Day Meeting. Do you remember going home for supper with the Schnupps?"

"I remember one time we were invited to someone's house for supper and they served us fried eggs," Dennis wrote from South Carolina. "Mom talked about that for a long time which is probably why I recall it."

"By the time I came along," wrote my youngest sister Ruth, "Lancaster Conference Mennonites had changed and weren't inviting people home for dinner anymore. Now we have full kitchens in our church basements and do fellowship meals instead. Sometimes people are assigned to bring something, other times two or three families get together and plan and serve a meal."

"We still get lots of invitations to go home for dinner with Mennonites when we're in the States," Anita wrote. "But they're members of more conservative conferences that support our mission. I do notice that nowadays many families have cut back and don't serve so many different foods at one meal."

Growing up, one of my favorite things was going to an All Day Meeting or Weekend Bible Conference, beginning Saturday afternoon and ending Sunday evening. The acappella singing was awesome especially when the church was packed with young people, and the speakers had been chosen from among the best preachers in our conference.

John W. Hess and Aaron Shank, for example, drew enormous crowds.

If the church had a basement, for the Sunday noon meal the ministers' and deacons' wives would organize a cold picnic-type lunch and serve it on long tables used for Sunday school and sewing circle. These meals were functional foods, easily prepared ahead, and meant just to hold you over. They seldom varied: ham or bologna sandwiches, cheese chunks, crackers, celery and carrot sticks, pickles, homemade applesauce, pretzels, tapioca pudding, cake, cookies. Water and coffee were normally the only beverages served in cups matching the heavy plain church china. The meal was quickly served and eaten, and by one o'clock we were back in the sanctuary for a half-hour song service before the sermon.

Between the afternoon and evening sessions, since families needed to do their milking and other barn chores, they invited visitors home for supper. Children especially enjoyed this three-hour break for playing and eating.

One afternoon when I was seven years old, we attended an All Day Meeting in a neighboring church district and were invited by a family we didn't know well. As Daddy drove behind them to their house Mom warned the four of us she expected impeccable behavior. "I don't want to hear any comments about the food. And you'll eat everything they offer you," she said, looking over her shoulder at us in the back seat of our 1935 Chevy. "And clean your plate."

My brothers disappeared as soon as we arrived, probably to the barn to watch the boys doing chores. The girls in this family, older than Anita and me, scurried around the kitchen and dining room, preparing supper and setting the table. So we had to sit in the living room beside Mom with the adults.

Finally we were called to the table. I was seated between Mom and my brothers. Each place was set with a plate, silverware, and a glass of water. Salt, pepper, butter, and two big bowls of cracker stew stood in the center of the huge table. My heart sank when I saw them. I remembered hearing Mom tell us, "You should be thankful for the good meals I make. Some families have only cracker stew for supper." Mom didn't care for it any more than I did. "Crackers soaked in sugar and milk just isn't nutritious," she'd say. I liked my crackers crunchy. I wouldn't even crumble them in soup like Mom and Daddy did, let alone soak them in milk.

Two tall thin girls came to the table and began taking orders down the line for fried egg. I didn't like dippy eggs; Mom always scrambled mine. I heard my mother say, "Two eggs, please," and then it was my turn. Everybody was looking at me. "How many eggs would you like?" the dark-haired girl asked.

I shook my head. I didn't dare ask if the yolks would be runny or hard. It was so quiet at that table I couldn't even whisper to Mom. I knew I wasn't allowed to ask for something different, so I decided to take my chances on the rest of the meal that was sure to appear. "No, thank you," I whispered.

A prayer was said and fried eggs and sliced homemade bread were brought in. The cracker stew was passed and people spooned some onto their plates. Up and down the table everyone was dipping pieces of bread in the runny fried egg yolks. I ate a piece of bread. And then the plates were being taken away.

Suddenly I went into a panic. *That's it? Fried eggs and cracker stew was supper? I'll starve on just a piece of bread. Maybe I better eat a dippy egg after all.* I pulled on Mom's sleeve and started to whisper to her. Mom knitted her brows and shook her head. I knew what she meant. Our hostess, mother of the ten quiet obedient children seated around the table, insisted on knowing what I wanted. I said

I'd changed my mind and would eat an egg after all. My brothers later told me they wanted to crawl under the table.

The tall girls went back to the kitchen, cooked my egg, and served me. Everyone sat at the table watching and waiting until I finished. I knew Mom was furious, embarrassed beyond belief as she told me in the car on the way back to church for the evening service. But I was more worried about my growling stomach. When I finished choking down my egg, the dark-haired girl came and took my plate. And then the kitchen door swung open and they brought in roast beef, noodles, and cooked vegetables.

The first weekend of June in 1950 we attended the Annual Mission Meeting for the Lebanon County district at Shirksville Mennonite Church. Our whole family wanted to hear George R. Brunk, the well-known evangelist from Denbeigh, Virginia. That evening for supper we were invited home for dinner with the Schnupp family. It was a beautiful sunny day and their daughter Mary Catherine took Anita and me for a walk in the lane through the meadow. When we came back her mother and Mom were sitting at the kitchen table chatting like they'd known each other for years. Mrs. Schnupp was taking meat off the bones of chicken she'd cooked earlier and stored in the refrigerator.

"You don't mind that I'm pulling the meat off with my fingers, do you?" I heard her ask my mother.

"I don't know any other way to do it," Mom giggled, offering to help. But our bubbly hostess said there really wasn't that much to do to make the soup – dump in the chicken and some corn, cut up an onion, and make rivels. Mrs. Schnupp just wanted Mom to sit there with her and talk. Along with her delicious soup she served ham and cheese sandwiches, pickles, and celery sticks.

"You're welcome to more soup," Mrs. Schnupp said, "but I want to warn you I still have a chocolate cake and peaches to bring out." We felt at home with this family and enjoyed their simple meal. I hoped they'd invite us the next time we came to their church for All Day Meeting.

### Chicken Corn Soup

*3 chicken legs and thighs (or equivalent)*      *3 quarts water*
*salt and parsley to taste*      *2 cups corn*
*1 stalk celery and leaves, diced*      *1 large onion, diced*

*1 carrot, diced or grated*      *rivels*

*Cook chicken and salt in water until meat falls off bones. Remove bones, skin and fat. (The meat may be cooked a day ahead and cooled.) Add carrot, corn, celery, and onions. Boil 20-30 minutes. Add rivels to boiling soup. Continue boiling about 15-20 minutes.*

### Rivels
*Place about 1 cup of flour in a bowl. Make a "well" (a hole) in the center and break an egg into it. Using a fork beat the egg gradually adding more and more flour until the mixture turns into small balls. Drop them slowly a few at a time into boiling broth.*

One recent evening I called my friend Vera Zook in Pennsylvania. She was surprised to hear from me. After I left for college we drifted apart even though we'd been bosom pals at North Lebanon Mennonite Church during our early teen years. "Do you have time to talk?" I asked. "I want to reminisce about going home for dinner."

"Home for dinner?" she asked.

"You know, someone at church would invite you home for dinner after church."

Vera laughed. "We did that a lot. My mother always

prepared for extras on Sunday. If no visitors came to church that day she'd invite a family from our church. If we had more than expected, she'd make a larger pot of noodles, fix extra cooked vegetables, and put out another loaf of home-made bread."

"Sounds like at our house," I said. "What kind of meat did she prepare?"

"Almost always beef roast or meatloaf. There were ten of us children so she'd have to make two roasts for Sunday. She'd put them in the oven in a roaster with a tight lid at 250 degrees and they'd slow roast until we got home from church. The whole house would be filled with the aroma of that meat. Our stomachs would be growling. We'd yank out the table, stretch it out as far as it would go, cover it with several white tablecloths, and set out our best plates, silver-ware, and tumblers. The children drank milk. Everyone else had water. We never served sodas or tea."

"Did you make mashed potatoes?"

"Mom used noodles on Sundays instead of potatoes because they took too much time to peel and prepare. Nowadays I put a pan of scalloped potatoes in the oven on Sunday morning with the timer. But Mom didn't have a timer."

"Mom had one tradition that I never really understood," Vera said. "She'd put a plate of Ritz crackers and slices of Velveeta cheese on the table for Sunday dinner."

"Maybe to stretch the meal when there were extra people?"

"I don't think so. She always did it. And she often made potato salad. We'd make that on Saturday so we could just pull the prepared dish out of the refrigerator on Sunday."

"We learned about potato salad at your house. Mom had never heard of it but thought your mother's was delicious. She went home and tried it and afterwards often made it. Back in 1995 my youngest sister Ruth talked to Mom and wrote down her best recipes. A lot of Mom's recipes were a scoop of this, a dribble of that. Ruth measured what Mom told her and put together a nice little booklet called 'Mostly Mom's Cooking.' Potato Salad is in there! Probably the recipe your mother told her!"

### Potato Salad

| | |
|---|---|
| *8 medium-sized potatoes* | *4 hard cooked eggs, sliced* |
| *1 cup diced celery* | *Salt, parsley, garlic, and pepper to taste* |
| *1 medium-sized onion, diced* | *½ cup cooked salad dressing* |
| *¼ cup grated carrots* | |

*Cook potatoes in skin until soft. Cool, peel, and dice. Mix together potatoes, eggs, onion, carrots, and celery. Add seasonings and cooked salad dressing.*

### Cooked Salad Dressing

| | |
|---|---|
| *½ cup sugar* | *½ cup apple cider vinegar* |
| *½ cup water* | *1 teaspoon salt* |
| *1 tablespoon prepared mustard* | *1 tablespoon flour* |
| *2 eggs* | |

*Combine sugar, salt, mustard, and flour. Add eggs and vinegar. Mix well. Add water and stir until smooth. Cook until thickened. Cool. Pour over potato salad and mix lightly.*

"What kind of raw vegetables did she serve?"

"Cole slaw was quite popular because we could keep heads of cabbage in the vegetable cellar well into winter. Celery, sliced tomatoes, and lettuce were served in summer – during the growing season."

"Did your mother make a dressing for the lettuce?"

"Oh, yes. We didn't use any bought salad dressings. Mom made a homemade sauce with cream, vinegar, a bit of sugar and poured it over fresh leaf lettuce. In the fall she made a hot bacon and hardboiled egg dressing and put it on endive."

"Sounds like my mom. That's part of our Swiss German heritage. In summer we always had cucumbers and onions too, seasoned with a bit of cream, vinegar, and sugar. Another question I have, did your mother make tapioca with fruit?"

"Of course she did. Mom used tapioca for pies, to thicken her rhubarb sauce, and she made fruit tapioca. She'd open a can of pineapple juice and bring it to a boil. Then she'd add some pearl tapioca (soaked in water to soften them a bit), boil it until it was clear and thick, cool it, and then add a can of crushed pineapple."

"Mmmm. Sounds delicious. I remember pink or purple tapioca at your house. Did she ever make it with grape?"

"Oh, yes. She'd use her home-canned grape juice. But she didn't add any fruit to that."

"That's what I'm sure I had. I told my mother about it, but she liked creamy tapioca. She always made hers with milk."

"We did that too, but my mother's standard dessert for Sunday was a chocolate cake and peaches."

"My mom too! Home-canned peaches of course! When I got married Mom gave me her recipe for Silver Sea Foam Cake that her mother had given her. She said Grandma always baked it in a tube pan. Sometimes they sliced the cake in half, filled it with peaches, and took it along on a picnic. Did your mother have other cakes she made as a change?"

"Once in a while she made an Angel Food Cake, but almost without fail, it was her chocolate cake. Always the same recipe. She had it memorized and never measured. She used lard for shortening, dipped some out in her hand, looked at it and decided when she had enough. The same for all the other ingredients. Oh, and with peanut butter icing!"

"I think that was a standard in Mennonite homes," I laughed.

### *Chocolate Peanut Butter Frosting*

| | |
|---|---|
| *½ butter* | *3 cups confectioner's sugar* |
| *⅓ cup milk* | *⅔ cup baking cocoa powder* |
| *1 teaspoon vanilla* | *¼ cup peanut butter* |

*Beat butter until soft. Add sugar, milk, cocoa, vanilla, and peanut butter.*
*Beat with electric beater until smooth and creamy. Spread on cake.*

The Hoosier kitchen cabinet bought in 1934
when Mom married.

## Shirksville Mennonite Church
### Near Fredericksburg
## Annual Mission Meeting of Lebanon County
### June 3-4, 1950

### Saturday Evening

7:15 Song Service and Devotions
7:30 "The Bible for Youth Today"      George R. Brunk,
Denbeigh, Va.

### Sunday Morning

9:00 Sunday school Lesson      Paul R. Weaver,
Narvon, Pa.

10:00 "The Field is the World"      J. Paul Sauder,
Mt. Joy, Pa.

10:40 Romans 1:1      George R. Brunk

### Afternoon Service

1:15 Song Service and Devotions
1:30 Children's Period      Clarence Neff
2:00 "One Soweth Another Reapeth"      J. Paul Sauder
2:40 "Every Congregation a
       Missionary Center"      George R. Brunk

### Evening Service

7:00 Song Service and Devotions
7:15 "Occupy 'Till I Come"      George R. Brunk
8:00 Evangelistic Sermon      Richard Danner,
Hanover, Pa.

Paul R. Weaver, Moderator
Clarence Neff, Robert Vogelsong, Choristers
**Evangelistic meetings to continue**      **Everybody Welcome**

# Finding Food In Congo
# Fall 1968

When Charles and I arrived in Congo, we each had two suitcases and a book bag. Our barrel was following by ship. We had no idea when it would arrive. "You'll need to buy enough food to last several months," Ian Secrett, our British school director, said when he met us that first evening at our mission headquarters in the capital. "It's the rainy season and the roads are often impassable."

We were surprised by the large well-stocked grocery store in Kinshasa where he took us to buy basic foodstuffs, although almost everything looked foreign, being imported from Portugal, Belgium, or South Africa. "Won't we be able to buy fresh vegetables and fruits in an outdoor village market?" I asked.

"The women come to our village market in Kivianga twice a week," Ian said. "You'll find onions, a few local rather bitter tomatoes, hot peppers, bananas, occasionally several small eggs. A baker in the village makes bread every day, but it's not the best."

"Are there any grocery stores?"

"Not in Kivianga. But the village of Ngombe Matadi, about two miles from our school, has a few shops. You'll find canned sardines, candles, soap, matches, perhaps some coarse Congolese sugar, items they can sell to the locals."

Since Mennonite Central Committee would be paying for our food, John Gaedert, our director in Kinshasa, had prepared several boxes of staples and supplies for us: cans of vegetables and fruits, evaporated milk, powdered whole milk, dried packs of spaghetti sauce, sacks of rice, bags of dried beans, pasta, toilet paper, a propane tank for our apartment-sized kitchen range. "Since you'll be out in the bush I'm including some MCC canned meat," he said, handing us a container.

"Oh, I can't believe it. Charles, look at this," I said, staring at the fat two-pound cans wrapped in yellow paper with black printing. From time to time, growing up in Pennsylvania, my older sister had helped MCC can meat donated by area farmers. She would join a volunteer crew to process it for the world's poor. "Beef, pork, chicken, lard, tomato juice, and even vegetable soup. I never dreamed I'd be a recipient."

"It's okay," John said. "Since you're located so far out in the bush, you qualify. You'll need meat to keep up your strength, and with a full teaching load you won't have time to be worrying about how to get food. We ordered a kerosene-run refrigerator for you, and bicycles," he added. "But we have no idea when they'll be here."

When we arrived at our school, Ian sold us tins of dried veggies a missionary family had left behind when they went back to England before the end of their term. Tins they'd brought with them when they came out to Congo on a ship several years earlier. The dried green beans smelled like new-mown hay. "Soak them in cool water and then cook them just like you would fresh beans," Lesley Fuller, one of our British colleagues, told me.

"At least we can have dessert for a while," Charles grinned

from inside our little pantry as he stocked shelves with British goodies: one can of brown sugar, a partial can of confectioner's sugar, a small box of baking chocolate, a package of cornstarch, several tins of white flour, and spices.

"And look at this, canned cheddar cheese and whipping cream!" I said, handing him several three-ounce cans. "I guess it's canned like evaporated milk."

"Now we can have whipped cream on our desserts," he laughed.

"I wish the MCC cans of meat were smaller," I said, handing him several of the fat yellow tins. "I don't want to waste any, but without a refrigerator ...," I trailed off.

"Ian said to boil cooked meat for twenty minutes once a day and that'll preserve it unrefrigerated for two or three days."

"We could always give some to our houseboy. I'm sure his kids wouldn't have any trouble finishing it off. But my biggest question is what to *do* with canned meat," I said. "I remember when I was a kid, before anybody had freezers, and Daddy butchered a pig in the fall, Mom always canned some of the meat in jars."

"Write and ask," Charles said.

Our mothers quickly responded. "Thicken the broth with a flour paste, stir in some meat, and have gravy over rice," Mom wrote back. "Use it like hamburger and make chili beans or spaghetti sauce."

"Make beef stew," my mother-in-law said in her letter. I combined dried diced potatoes with dried carrots, added onion flakes and dried peas from my small stock and made stew. If I found a fresh onion or a few tomatoes in our tiny market I made soup. Charles mixed vinegar, sugar, tomato paste, and palm oil with the beef and made Sloppy Joes.

Our English-speaking staff gathered together every Sunday evening for an English worship service, and to celebrate birthdays. It was a nice break from speaking French all day and the singles especially needed some social interaction with their colleagues. The host at these gatherings usually provided simple refreshments.

"I'm sure glad I brought my Mennonite Community Cookbook along out here," I said to Charles one afternoon as I was looking for ideas. "You know the Pennsylvania Dutch always dried apples. Apple schnitz, they called it and used it in pies. Why wouldn't dried peaches work the same way?"

"I don't know why not," he agreed. "Just add extra sugar and lots of cinnamon."

I made two crusts, soaked the bitter peaches in warm sugar water, boiled them with a bit of cornstarch, added several teaspoons of cinnamon, and turned out a scrumptious pie for an afternoon tea. Charles found a recipe for yeast potato doughnuts, which became my stand-by for these gatherings.

When I mentioned the boredom of eating the same canned beef or pork every day, Lesley's eyes lit up. "Come by my house on your way home from school this afternoon. I'll be happy to exchange something from my pantry." So from time to time we opened a flat pie-shaped can of her steak and kidney pie or chicken pie, or shepherd's pie, removed the lid with a can opener, and heated it in our little oven for supper – like a TV dinner.

During the first few days after our arrival we received gifts from several Congolese. The village chief sent us three pineapples. So I made him a pineapple upside-down cake and sent it to his house. I only realized much later the sacrifice people had made to welcome us by sending four small eggs or a squash. Irene told me her houseboy tried for the longest time one day to catch a rat. She knew he wanted to eat it.

Occasionally a Congolese lady with a baby tied on her back and a large white enamel dishpan on her head stopped by the house asking for two or three makutas for some mushrooms, half a dozen tiny chicken eggs, or fresh spinach wrapped in a bit of paper. Mpanzu taught me to put the eggs in cool water. "If they float they're no good," he said.

Several times we rode our bikes on paths out of the village to the fields where the women grew their gardens. Newly planted plots of manioc reminded me of the little mounds my daddy made to plant sweet potatoes back in Pennsylvania – "sweet potato hills," he called them. And their manioc grew into an underground tubular vegetable, much like a large white sweet potato.

The part above became a small tree, about five feet tall, bearing dark green leaves which the women picked, sliced into fine strips, and cooked with onion, palm oil, dried salt fish, and hot pili-pili peppers to prepare a vitamin-rich dish the locals called saka-saka. From the beginning I enjoyed saka-saka with rice, but could never bring myself to eat the pasty sour chiquanga made from the root.

The women worked hard hoeing and tending their gardens. But it didn't end there. After the manioc was mature, they dug it, soaked it in stagnant water for three days to release its poisonous cyanide gas, dried it in the sun, and hauled it home. There they placed the manioc in a large wooden trough, much like the kind early American women used to make bread dough, mixed it with water and made a sticky glob. They divided the dough into balls, about the size of an American football. Each was securely wrapped in special leaves they'd brought from the forest and tied securely with strings they'd stripped from palm branches.

After carrying water from the spring and gathering fire-wood, the women stacked these oblong packages in a sawed-off barrel, covered them with water, and boiled them for three hours over an outdoor wood fire. The result was a pile of chiquanga, a sticky sour carbohydrate with little food value, but which filled hungry stomachs. Unwrapped, chiquanga would keep for about five days. The women would sit in the market place and earn a few makutas selling what they didn't need for their families.

Charles and I were teachers, not administrators, so we didn't know much about our students' dormitories or food service. They often complained to us about the monotony of the meals served in the refectory – their dining hall. But that was to be expected; American students habitually complained about school food.

"Madame, if we have chiquanga and brown beans for lunch then we have chiquanga and dried fish for dinner. Every day. Whichever one we have at noon, we eat the other in the evening."

"If I had to eat chiquanga every day, I'd croak," I told Charles.

"But they're used to it. It's like the Chinese eating rice everyday. That's what they do," he argued.

I found the sour smell of the sticky chiquanga lumps quite distasteful. "I could eat rice every day, twice a day, but chiquanga – I'd probably starve," I said.

"I don't think chiquanga is the problem with the students," Charles said. "It's not having variety to go with it."

We asked Ian about the students' food service. "They're right, the food is monotonous," he agreed. "But it's wholesome and filling. The beans and fish provide protein and the manioc gives them energy. Most of them eat better here than they do at home. Many Congolese families can't afford to feed their children more than one meal a day. They're fortunate to have a cup of black tea for breakfast."

Every morning two students walked to the village bakery for the school's standing order of "pistolets," bread rolls shaped like hot dog buns with the consistency of two-day-old bread. And it never smelled fresh, not even when newly baked. At times we suspected someone added manioc flour to stretch the more expensive wheat flour. Or maybe the flour was just old and buggy.

Under a picnic shelter-like structure, Tata Jean, the school cook, made fires, using wood the students fetched for punishments or as their job during manual labor class. Every morning Tata Jean placed a huge pot of water over a fire, brought it to a boil, dumped in a measure of tea, and added several cans of sweetened condensed milk. When it was ready the students walked by holding out their tin cups as the cook ladled out his sweet brew.

"That's awful how much sugar they consume in their tea," I complained to Charles.

"It's the only sugar they get!" he said. "Let them enjoy it."

We bought the same bread for our breakfasts and spread it with peanut butter and a bit of marmalade from our British collection. Being good Americans we loved peanut butter, especially the old-fashioned chunky kind made by crushing peanuts and adding a bit of salt. We hired Mama Louise, our houseboy's wife, to keep us supplied.

"Do you know how she grinds the peanuts?" I asked Charles. "She rolls a coke bottle back and forth over dried peanuts, like a rolling pin when you make pie shells."

The British spread their morning bread with Marmite, a slimy dark brown paste with a strong salty flavor. "It's an extract of yeast, a by-product of the brewing industry," Lesley explained." She gave me one of her three-inch high bulb-shaped jars with a bright yellow lid. "Try it. Marmite is highly recommended for its protein."

"No, I don't want any sludge," Charles would say when I teased, asking if he'd like some Marmite as a change. I also found it distasteful and stuck with peanut butter and jam.

"Not to worry," Lesley said, when we admitted to disliking Marmite. "It's a love-it-or-hate-it food in the U.K. But out here in Africa we try to eat it regularly as a source of Vitamin B – to prevent anemia."

Every morning I placed several spoonfuls of loose Congolese tea in my china teapot and then added filtered water I'd boiled on our propane stove. Following British instructions I covered my teapot with a padded tea cozy they'd provided to keep the water hot as possible while the tea steeped. Charles sweetened his with the coarsely refined Congolese sugar we could buy locally. But, like my British colleagues, I preferred to add a bit of powdered milk to mine.

Student unrest about their monotonous food built until they selected a committee from among the seniors – boys who were leaders in the dorms – and sent them as spokesmen to Ian, asking that beef be added to their diet. So the school tried to provide meat from time to time, but it was expensive and the students paid so little tuition. We suspected Ian often subsidized it from his own pocket.

The first time Ian furnished all 131 students with fresh beef I went down to the school kitchen to see how it had been prepared. "Good idea. Tata Jean made stew," I said, looking at the small pieces, like beef tips, that he'd boiled with onions, tomatoes, and hot peppers, and served as a sauce with their chunks of chiquanga.

"Oh, Madame, it's *delicious*," the students said, inviting me to join them as the cook ladled out six pieces of meat in a bit of sauce per person.

Someone gave me a spoon and I tasted their spicy stew as they watched. "It *is* delicious," I said, licking the spoon, "but we have our portion at home. I don't want to eat your meat." I wished them "Bon appétit" as they savored their gourmet meal.

That evening after Charles and I had supervised study hall at our middle school, the girls walked to their dorms singing in Kikongo at the top of their lungs. I remarked to several students sweeping out their classrooms, "The girls seem happy tonight."

"Ah, oui, Madame, they had beef for supper!" they chorused.

Ian arranged with some women to bring greens, which Tata Jean cooked with peanuts for lunch every Thursday. Congolese women scoured the fields to gather greens like redroot to sell in the market. Plants Daddy had always considered weeds and fed to the pigs and chickens, I now learned made a rather tasty and healthful dish. So we asked Mama Louise to prepare it for us from time to time.

Sunday was the cook's day off. So after a long morning in church, for their Sunday noon meal along with the usual portion of chiquanga the students were given a can of pilchards – a fish from South Africa – or more rarely corned beef. Each can was divided among four students. Some of the more creative ones gathered wood and cooked a stew.

When I saw their monotonous simple diet I was ashamed that I'd complained and was embarrassed to let the Congolese know how much we had. Ian told us to keep our storeroom locked, not that our houseboy was not trustworthy, but because it was wrong to put such temptation before him. Although we were volunteers with MCC and each received only $25 a month spending money, our mission paid all our bills. And from time to time our director sent us treats: popcorn, jello, or even a cake mix.

I often grappled with why I'd been born American and lived in luxury compared to the rest of the world. Ian understood, but he told us not to overwhelm our houseboy. "If you subsidize him too much, how will he cope when you go home?" So I tried to find a happy medium, making sure his family had the necessities and a few treats from time to time, providing medical help when they needed it, and assisting with school tuition.

One afternoon I was supervising a group of eighth grade girls cleaning the path in front of my house. They'd cut palm branches to sweep away leaves and branches left by recent storms. Suddenly I realized someone was missing. "Where's Mvunzi?" I asked. The girls bent over their brooms and worked with a will.

"I'm here, Madame," she answered, sliding down a tree trunk.

"What are you hiding?"

"Oh, please, Madame, don't take it away." She reluctantly held out a scrap of paper wrapped around several wriggling furry four-inch caterpillars she'd found in a mango tree.

"What are you going to do with them?"

Her eyebrows shot up and her eyes widened. "Eat them, of course!"

I ran home and grabbed my camera, took a picture, and then asked her to finish her job. She worried about her worms escaping so I gave her a little box with a lid.

"How will you prepare them?" I asked.

"We'll boil them with tomatoes and onions and make a delicious soup," Mvunzi said.

"Why don't you come and eat with us?" Maleka added.

During the supper hour I walked down to the school refectory to see their worm soup, which added a little variety to their daily monotonous fare.

"It's so delicious, Madame. Don't you want some?" they giggled, watching my face. I declined but told them I'd read in "Newsweek" that caterpillars were extremely high in protein and therefore very good for them, that they should enjoy their soup.

During a long holiday when all the students and missionaries were gone, Charles and I were left in charge of the mission keys. So we went exploring, poking into areas we'd never seen. In the school storeroom we found a stash of corn meal. I'd grown up eating cornmeal mush and milk. "This would fill'em up," I said, eyeing the US Aid sacks. I stopped as I heard a plaintive whine. "What is it?" I asked, looking at Charles, just as a small pathetically thin coal black cat jumped across the bags.

"A cat. Oh, no. We're not taking a cat home," he said firmly as I spoke to the poor animal.

"But look at her. She's starving," I said. It didn't matter what we said. Kitty followed us home, always keeping her distance and constantly alert to her surroundings. When I offered her leftovers from the kitchen she swallowed whole chunks of food and lapped up the milk.

Two weeks later our Kitty was firmly entrenched. She jumped up onto our water barrel lid, and then with an enormous bound leaped into the open end of our attic. She made herself at home up there, caught mice and brought them down to show off, landing with a thud on the barrel. Charles was convinced we should keep her when she brought a rat she'd caught in her attic home.

One day when we were studying cats in our zoology class, I told my girls I wanted them to come to my house and watch my cat eat. Their eyes got wide and round and I sensed their fear. "Your cat's a witch," one girl said.

"A witch?" I asked, looking at them over the top of my glasses.

"She's black and we heard she understands English!"

Laughing, I told them it wasn't true and she wouldn't hurt them. I finally convinced them to walk to my house to observe her actions. I whispered to them to sit quietly on the grass in my front yard. "Don't talk or move no matter what she does," I said. "She's afraid of you and will run away if you scare her." After explaining what I planned to do and warning them again to be silent, I shouted in English, "Hey, Kitty. You want your dinner?"

In two seconds we heard her bounding across the attic floorboards and three seconds later her face appeared from under the eaves. When she peered at the girls I again warned them to be quiet. "Come on down, Kitty," I said. "It's okay. They just want to watch you eat." She hesitated and then jumped down to the barrel and onto the ground. I stationed her sideways so they could watch her lap milk with her tongue, and crunch toast with her long sharp teeth. I didn't give her any meat because they'd never have understood how I could feed meat to an animal when they themselves seldom had any. When she finished I petted her and told her to go back up to her loft and she did.

"It's proof," Mayamba said. "Not a white hair on her body and she understands when you talk to her."

"She's definitely a witch," said Malemba.

"How'd she know you were talking to her if she didn't understand?" asked Wombisa.

"She heard my voice," I explained. "She knows when I shout that I have food for her. It's our routine. But she doesn't understand the words."

"Yeah, right," they said. "Madame, she's a witch." I doubt they learned anything about the cat's body or habits that day.

When we asked Ian if we could have some of the cornmeal he told us to help ourselves. "After all," he said, "your country sent it here. We don't know what to do with it and neither do the Africans."

"I'll see if I can change that," I said.

When Charles brought a bag home and opened it, I was aghast at the wiggling yellow worms wallowing in our wonderful corn meal. "We'll just have to strain them out," Charles said. Pouring small amounts at a time into a metal strainer and shaking it gently, we were able to remove the larvae and most of the nits, which we threw out to the

Congolese neighborhood chickens scratching in our back yard.

Ian laughed when we told him. "I have a story for you," he said. "We can always tell a new missionary from an old one. When a new missionary comes to Congo and sees a bug in his soup, he's repulsed and throws out the soup. After he's been there for a while and finds a bug in his soup, he picks it out and eats the soup. After a few years when he finds a bug in his soup, realizing it's good protein, he eats it along with the soup. A veteran missionary can easily be spotted. He can't eat the soup because there're no bugs in it." We laughed, realizing we were making progress.

Once cleaned, our corn meal looked good enough. I experimented and made quite edible cornbread, crunchy fried corn meal pancakes which we spread with jam, and creamy mush seasoned with cinnamon to give it a fresher taste. I found a recipe for tamales and made a quite tasty tamale pie, using MCC canned beef and hot peppers to mask the odor of bugs.

"Let's invite my class over and teach them how to make mush," Charles said. "We'll build a fire outside and cook it in a pot just as they would in their camp. Then they can teach the others."

And so one Saturday evening 15 tenth grade boys showed up at our door with their bowls and spoons in hand. We took them round to the side of our house where the fire that had heated our evening bath water was still smoldering. The boys built it up and soon had a large pot of water boiling.

"You need to mix the corn meal with a little cold water. Never dump the meal directly into boiling water or it'll form a hard lump that's inedible," I explained as I slowly poured the soupy raw corn meal into the boiling pot, Bilongo and Kalu stirring with long-handled wooden spoons. "And don't forget about half a teaspoon of salt for each cup of meal," I said, sprinkling a measure of salt into the boiling porridge.

The fragrant aroma of steaming corn wafted around us and the boys inched closer smiling and grinning, licking their lips like we used to do waiting for Daddy to tell us the freezer of ice cream was finished. I tasted the mush every now and then and finally was satisfied it had boiled enough. As they passed by the simmering pot, Charles ladled out a portion onto each plate. I gave them sweetened condensed milk to pour over their creamy warm mush.

I think they savored that bowl of mush as much as we ever enjoyed Daddy's homemade peach ice cream on a hot July afternoon. "It's delicious, Madame," Nsemi said scraping the bottom of his dish. "We're going to cook it in camp now that we know how."

"We didn't know what to do with it before," Mabwaka said.

"If you have any left over you can save it to fry for breakfast," I said, showing them how to form the cooled mush into patties and brown them on each side in an iron skillet. "They're delicious with pineapple jam," I said.

"But Madame, jam is too expensive," Nsemi said.

"Uhh," I stammered, "maybe you could put some sugar on it.

One afternoon when I had a scrawny tough Congolese rooster to cook I asked Mpanzu how the Congolese prepared poultry. He told me they didn't eat chicken very often because meat was expensive and they liked to keep their hens for eggs. "So chicken is for special occasions?" I asked.

"Oui, Madame," he said.

"But I want to know how you prepare it." And so my culinary lesson began.

"We make chicken soup," Mpanzu said. "We call it Muamba (soup) Nsusu (chicken). I watched him make the dish, jotting down his delicious recipe for future reference.

"Do you often eat this at your house?" I naively asked.

"Oh, no, Madame. It's too expensive. We eat it only for special holidays." He carefully gathered the entrails, the feet, and the head and wrapped them in a bit of paper to carry home with him. I quickly learned the pleasure of sending his family several of "my" pieces as well.

### Muamba Nsusu

*Clean and cut the chicken in pieces. Boil with salt until tender.*
*Remove chicken from broth. Skim fat.*
*Sauté a chopped onion in palm oil. Add to chicken broth.*
*Add a cup of peanut butter and a can of tomato paste.*
*Stir until smooth. Bring to a boil.*
*Return chicken to the soup and simmer for about an hour.*
*Season with hot dried pili-pili pepper to taste.*

Kitty at our house in Ngombe Lutete.

Mvunzi displaying her caterpillars before stewing them with tomatoes and onions.

# Big Red
# February 1973

"Ko, Ko, Ko. Phyl. It's me," I called out in the singsong Kikongo greeting to our British missionary neighbor who lived behind our home, just across the garden. I climbed the back steps of her sprawling frame 19th century missionary house, my five-month-old baby in one arm, a basket of eggs on the other.

"Hello, Janet," I heard from within the attached kitchen where I found Phyl pulling a tin of muffins from her wood cookstove. "I'm just taking some scones from the oven. Hello, Chucky," she added, tickling my bouncing boy under the chin.

"Oh, they smell so good," I said, wiping perspiration from my face and shifting my baby to the other hip. "But aren't you hot? This humidity's about worn me out."

"It is quite warm this afternoon, isn't it?" she said, tucking back a strand of graying hair. "Won't you come in and join me for tea? I've got it ready in the dining room. Margot should be back from Mbanza Ngungu any minute."

I tagged behind her across the veranda into the dim interior of the main house where she lived with her roommate. "I should have made tea when I got back from class, but I thought I'd check first to see if Margot had come with mail. And I brought you a present," I said, setting my little basket of big brown eggs on her long dining room table.

Phyl's eyes lit up. "How good of you, Janet. An omelet would be perfect for high tea. So your chickens are laying well?"

"They are. We're having barbequed chicken for supper tonight."

"One of your roosters?"

"Yep, Big Red. He attacked Chucky and me on our way up here. Mpanzu's taking care of him right now," I said, satisfaction dripping from my voice.

I laid Chucky on a blanket on the cement floor and dropped into one of Phyl's straw-stuffed living room chairs. The large wrap-around porch kept her house cooler than ours, and the upsweep of air to the vent across the peak was as refreshing as an electric fan.

Holding a strainer over a pretty china cup, she poured a bit of black tea from the first teapot, and then added boiling water from the second. "A spot of milk?" she asked, peering over her sagging glasses.

"Yes, please," I said. It'd taken me three years to be able to answer in this direct English style.

"Sugar?" she asked, handing me the dish of cubes and a small tongs.

"No, thank you," I said, holding up my hand.

Early on Charles and I had felt their annoyance when, trying to be polite, we would hedge saying, "I wouldn't mind," or "That would be nice." Ian in his frank way had told us to say, "No, thank you," or "Yes, please." So we tried to learn their ways.

Phyl placed my cup and saucer on a little table beside my chair and then hurried back with a plate of scones and apricot jam – jam she'd brought out with her on the ship from England.

"It's very nice," she said. "I opened it just yesterday. I could have eaten half a dozen of her warm muffins smothered in butter and preserves but I didn't say so. Our British missionary staff, mostly single women, generously shared their hard-to-come-by stores. Rich by Congolese standards, they were poor compared to the average American.

After several years of eating mostly canned food, Charles decided to raise chickens. "Just think," he said, "we could have fresh barbequed chicken, stuffed roasted chicken, fried chicken, and all the eggs we want."

Having grown up in Los Angeles he knew nothing about farming. So he went to see Mr. Pitkethley, a British missionary at CEDECO, an American based program for small-animal-raising projects. He was given a booklet on raising poultry and urged to get Congolese involved and help train them.

So Charles worked with the local church to start a moneymaking project, raising Rhode Island Reds. The school carpenter helped him renovate an abandoned building, they added fence for an outdoor chicken run, and he bought laying mash from CEDECO. But after the Reds arrived he couldn't find anyone to faithfully feed, water, and shut them in their house at night.

Used to letting their Cornish hen-sized chickens run loose to feed on insects and seeds, and to sleep in trees, the Congolese didn't seem to grasp the fact that these large hybrid American hens needed to be pampered. Tending chickens and selling eggs for the church became another job on Charles' already overloaded schedule. But at least we had a steady supply of eggs to buy.

Eventually the church abandoned the project and sold off their chickens. With our sudden loss of eggs, Charles decided to raise a few of his *own* Reds. He hired a man to build a little house with roosts and a small fenced-in pen at the back of our yard. When he arrived with a dozen tiny chicks and feed from CEDECO, I put the babies in a box in the kitchen and tended them until they were old enough to live in their outdoor pen. Before long we were again enjoying egg custard, omelets, and barbequed rooster.

Mpanzu's dark eyes got wide and he grinned, showing all his teeth, at the size of our huge roosters. After he'd killed, plucked, and cleaned the bird, I'd oversee the butchering, preferring the American method of cutting pieces at the joints instead of chopping the bones in half as Congolese normally did.

"This is yours," I'd say, indicating the neck and head. He'd put them with the innards and feet in his bowl.

"Sebastien likes chicken soup," he'd say, always using his older son as an excuse.

"We can't eat this much," I'd say, eyeing the huge drumsticks. "Here, take the back for Mama Louise and part of the breast for Marie."

"More tea?" Phyl asked, breaking in on my reverie, teapot in hand. Glancing down I saw my baby, lulled by the coolness, had fallen asleep at my feet.

"Oh yes, please," I said, holding out my cup. "And the scones are delicious. I feel refreshed already."

"A cup of hot tea always brings down one's temperature," Phyl stated. It'd taken me a while to accept what I'd first believed to be fantasy. But after a few months in this steamy tropical climate I'd found the British were right.

Earlier that day I'd come back from teaching my afternoon classes, thanked Mama Lukau for watching my baby, and told her I'd see her the next morning. She gathered her things and walked down the garden path, past the hedge, to the road behind our house. Mpanzu would stay until he finished ironing.

"Margot should be back with the mail by now," I said, picking up Chucky. "So I'm going over to check if we got any letters. And I'm taking six eggs along for her and Phyl."

"Okay, I'll see you," Charles called from his office. "Why don't you come out and make sure that old rooster doesn't bother us?"

"The chickens are penned up. You'll be all right," he said.

"Famous last words," I mumbled, carrying my baby and the little basket of eggs out onto the veranda. Even though Charles had plugged all the holes in the fence, that power-hungry chicken could still manage to squirm through. I stood there a moment and scanned the back yard for Big Red. He held the Number One position in our chickens' pecking order. But he was nowhere in sight. Not having a free hand to carry my big stick I decided to leave it propped against the side of the house and stepped out into the sunshine, Chucky bouncing on my arm.

Big Red behaved just like my mother's old roosters had back on the farm in Pennsylvania when I was a little girl and Mom sent me to the hen house to gather eggs. Sensing my fear, they never failed to attack unless I threw grain out for them to hunt in the straw. I think Big Red was always listening for my voice and my footsteps, and then watched to see if I picked up my stick. I felt secure with that cane in my hand and he never approached me when he saw it.

I headed down the path, keeping an eye on the pen at the far side of the garden. The chickens were contentedly pecking at their feed or dusting themselves in dirt holes. We stopped at the open window in the out-building where Mpanzu was ironing a shirt with the big charcoal iron.

"Ah, Kiambote, Nengua. Kiambote, Chucky," he said with his usual wide grin.

"Kiambote, Tata," I answered. "Chucky and I are going to Phyl's house for the mail. I hope that rooster doesn't bother us."

"Ah, non, Madame. They're eating," he laughed. "They won't bother you." So I continued down the garden path beside the hedge.

Halfway there I spotted a red whirlwind coming from the right. Big Red was running so fast he fairly bounced up and down as though a pack of hounds were pursuing him, heading straight for my baby and me.

"Mpanzu! Charles!" I yelled. That rooster had seen me coming without my stick and had waited until I was too far from the house to retreat. Coming to a screeching halt at my side he began jumping up and down, flapping his wings, scratching my legs with his sharp spurs, and clawing my arms with his long toenails. With each flapping bounce he pecked and flopped his huge wings at my baby. I screamed and screamed, turning round and round to keep my back to him, holding Chucky and the basket of eggs as high as I could, leaving my sides unprotected as that bundle of red feathers danced around us.

"Katuka!" Mpanzu shouted, as he raced across the lawn, his iron in hand.

As Big Red retreated, I screamed, "Tue-le! Tue-le. Il est mort."

"Oh, Madame, you don't really mean to kill him," Mpanzu said. "He's so beautiful."

"You bet I mean for you to kill him. He's dead meat. It's one thing for him to assault me, but to attack my baby is walking death. I can't wait to eat his barbequed legs. Forget the ironing. We're having chicken for supper."

"Won't you have another scone?" Phyl asked, as I picked up my baby.

"I'd better not. I need to go home and get the barbeque sauce ready," I said, my eyes twinkling. "At least I don't have to worry about Big Red attacking us on the way home."

"That's the best chicken I ever ate," I said, wiping my mouth and putting my cloth napkin back in its ring.

"I sure wasn't expecting a barbeque tonight," Charles laughed.

"It's not funny," I said. "Big Red could have pecked out Chucky's eyes. What did he think he was doing anyhow?"

"He thought you were a big chicken he could control. He wanted to put you in the right pecking order," Charles grinned.

"Well, he had another think coming, didn't he?"

# Service

Even so faith,
if it hath not works,
is dead.
James 2:17

# Sewing Circle
# 1948 - 1965

"How'd you learn to sew?" my eleven-year-old friend, Shannon Morse asked one Saturday as she helped me tie out a baby blanket to send to Guatemala. I'd been bringing Shannon to our home every now and then since she'd moved to Virginia in 1995 when she was three. Not having any grandchildren of my own, I made her my special project, trying to instill in her a love for sewing and helping the needy.

"When I was about your age my mother taught me to sew by hand so I could hem the dresses she made me. She sewed all our clothes on her old treadle machine," I said. "We had to move the wide pedal with our feet to make it go. And, for your information, backstitch and zigzag didn't exist. All we had was a straight stitch."

"Did you sew on it?" she asked, her eyes widening.

"Absolutely. Until I went away to college we used that machine to sew all our clothes."

"So your mom taught you to sew?"

"Partially. When I was in 7<sup>th</sup> grade all the girls in our public school in Hershey had a two-hour block each week for Home Ec. You know, sewing, cooking, serving meals, good grooming. But there we sewed on electric machines. I taught you the same way I learned, first following lines on a piece of paper with no thread until we could make straight seams. Then we threaded the machine and sewed on scraps of fabric."

"Did you make anything in your class?" Shannon asked.

"Yes, and I still have it!" I took her to a closet and there among my collection of dresser scarves and doilies was a little blue half-apron sprinkled with tiny pink flowers. "Miss Hershburger, our teacher, told us to bring half a yard of material to class. Mom said I could buy it myself. So one day during lunch hour I walked downtown, about two blocks, to the Hershey Department Store. At the front of the store, just off of Chocolate Avenue, I rummaged around in piece goods looking for the perfect material. They had so many bolts of cotton prints I couldn't make up my mind. Finally, it was getting late so I chose this one."

"I like it. Did you use your apron?"

"We had to wear them during the cooking part of our class. I worked hard to make the seams straight. I didn't do too badly, did I?"

"It's pretty," Shannon said, fingering the material. "Did you make anything else?"

"In 8$^{th}$ grade we were supposed to make a dress with a collar and buttons. The teacher wanted us to learn to make buttonholes too – by hand. Problem was, my family and I were Mennonites and back in those days we didn't wear collars or buttons on our dresses."

"Why not?" Shannon asked, wrinkling her nose.

"That's what the church believed. The women all wore the same plain dress style with a round or V-shaped neckline. My mother told me to ask the teacher if I could make a long nightgown. Miss Hershburger agreed, so I bought a pattern with a yoke, a collar, buttons, and cuffs on the sleeves. I still have it in my pattern box."

"And you sewed it on a machine at school?"

"That's right. An electric one with a handle we pressed our knee against to make it run. But that's not where I learned to piece quilts and knot comforters. I learned that in sewing circle."

"What's sewing circle?"

From the time my parents joined the Mennonite Church in 1948, my mother attended sewing circle. A group of ladies met the first Tuesday of every month in different churches in our district to sew for the needy. Mom took me along to Stauffers' circle in summer or whenever I didn't have school. We'd drive around the side of the church and park by the horse sheds.

"Why do they have them?" I asked.

"They're left over from horse and buggy days," Mom told me. "My grandmother brought me here to church when I was a little girl and that's where we tied our horse, out of the hot sun or the rain." I wondered what it would be like to ride to church in a buggy and hitch your horse under that shelter where bits of hay still trailed in the troughs.

We walked to the back of the church, past the water pump, and entered the long low basement. Two windows on the end didn't give much light, so it was more like a musty shadowy cellar. But I was used to that since my Sunday school class met down there every week.

My favorite thing at sewing circle was watching wrinkled elderly women bent over a beautiful quilt stretched out on a big frame, spools of white quilting thread and tiny pointed scissors bouncing as they sewed. Sometimes as many as six surrounded it, but little Fannie Lehman, peering through her round spectacles, was always there. They quilted with minuscule needles, taking tiny even stitches, in and out, in and out, pushing with a thimble on their third fingers, and then pulling the thread through before starting again. The process looked so easy – in and out, in and out, pull the thread through. "May I help quilt?" I finally ventured.

The startled ladies' needles stopped in mid-air. They stared at this small blond eight-year-old, then laughed and went back to work, shaking their heads. Fannie Lehman gently explained that although quilting looked easy, in fact to do an excellent job, it took years of practice. "Why don't you help the women over there knot comforters?" she suggested, pointing me toward the other quilt frame. "That's where beginners usually start."

So I joined the knotters. "This pattern's too pretty to just knot," Ada Lehman said, shaking her head. I watched as she helped her daughter Rhoda, and Mary Rutt, and Arlene Kreider stretch a pieced Bow Tie top and pin it to a frame, using a flannel sheet for padding and printed cotton for the back.

"But MCC needs blankets *now* for their fall shipment," Elsie Risser called out, looking up from the dress she was sewing at a machine on the other side of the room. "We don't have time to quilt it." She was our bishop's wife and was in charge of our sewing circle.

"We know," Arlene said. "But we still think it's too pretty to just knot!"

Mennonite ladies saved all their scraps when they cut out clothes. Mom kept hers too. "Those little old ladies don't waste anything," Mom would say as she rolled up even the tiniest "snibbles" as she called them, and tied the little bundle with a thin string of fabric. "They use them to make nine-block squares for comforters. And Fannie Lehman and several others take even the tiniest leftovers and cut miniature patches and piece the most beautiful quilts." I listened and learned the names of their favorite quilts: Double Wedding Ring, Irish Chain, Lone Star.

Anna Mary Lehman and her sister helped pin the comforter in place and then we all sat down to knot. Using a large needle and crochet thread the ladies skillfully pulled the heavy thread through the taut layers. Ada showed me how to securely tie, knot, and clip the threads to a uniform length.

While the ladies' fingers flew across the comforter, they chatted quietly about daily life on the farm, their children and grandchildren, cute things the babies had done. Their potatoes had bloomed, the corn was almost ready, and they'd canned jars and jars of bread and butter pickles. The gardens were dry; we needed to pray for rain. Old Mrs. Risser was poorly.

Lined up along the far wall, the half dozen sewing machines hummed like bumblebees in a field of clover. All morning Elsie Risser, Jennie Strickler, Etta Brubaker, and Mom sewed children's dresses from pre-cut fabric, brought from the cutting room, they said. I wanted to go along to see it, but Mom said that was way down country and we'd just leave it to the leaders to take the finished clothes and pick up more that were cut and ready to sew.

About noon the ladies started talking about food. "I think it must be time for dinner," Arlene Kreider said, leaning back from tying the last knot in our third comforter. "That was a good morning's work."

The sewing machines stopped purring and the wizened ladies around the quilt put down their thimbles. We sat on backless benches along a checkered oilcloth-covered table, our brown paper bags in front of us. Someone had made coffee in a percolator and Jennie poured water into glasses from an aluminum pitcher she'd filled at the pump outside. Etta Brubaker said a prayer of thanksgiving and then we opened our sacks and pulled out sandwiches, fruit, and cookies. Mom had spread peanut butter on celery sticks for me. And I'd helped her scrape and slice a big fat carrot from the garden.

Afterwards the bishop's wife read a scripture and said another prayer before we all went back to work: thimbles again clicking on needles and sewing machines singing by the wall.

"Where can I get information and statistics about Mennonite sewing circles?" I asked my younger sister Ruth one afternoon when I was visiting her in Pennsylvania.

"Oh, that's easy. Let's go visit my friend Ruth Fry. She's the sewing historian at Gingrich's Church. She can tell you whatever you want to know."

When we arrived at her house, Mrs. Fry pulled out several albums filled with snapshots of quilts and comforters, and ladies who'd made them over the years. "Our sewing circle was started in 1918 and continued actively until 1980. Sewing circle was always a very important feature of the church, but it's dwindling," she said, shaking her head and pursing her lips. "Not many of the older ones are left and the younger women work and can't come."

"Today people find it so much easier to just buy what they need," my sister said, looking over my shoulder at the photos.

"That's right," Mrs. Fry agreed. "And since most of us no longer wear plain dresses, a lot of Mennonite girls aren't learning to sew. There're only three of us left in our circle. We piece tops for comforters in our spare time at home and then get together the first Tuesday of the month and knot them. Five or six a month is about all we get done. This is a problem across Lancaster Conference, not just in our congregation."

"Did young people come to the circles back in the 1940s and 50s?" I asked. "I seem to remember mainly old ladies."

"Sewing circles were an all-day affair, from nine in the morning to about three o'clock in the afternoon. They were made up of women whose children were in school or grown. Young mothers didn't bring babies or toddlers. Girls still in school couldn't attend except in summer. Several districts tried holding junior sewing circles for teenagers in the evening. Here, it's all in my record books." Mrs. Fry said, pulling out spiral notebooks with years and years of sewing circle minutes.

"Wow," I said. "Look at this. In January 1951 seven young people attended and made four dresses. And on another date they went to the Good Samaritan Hospital and mended 375 pieces. In February at their regular meeting they made six bloomers, two dresses, six slips and twelve baby supporters."

"What are baby supporters?" Ruth asked.

Mrs. Fry and I looked at each other and laughed. "A strip of material was wound snuggly around a newborn's tummy and pinned so it wouldn't slip. It was to keep his naval intact. Mom called them belly bands," I said, grinning at my sister's wide eyes. "Here's more. Every month the teens went to the hospital and mended or made new gowns – anywhere from 100 to 200 or more pieces. That's impressive."

"Three women at Minersvillage Church began a circle for young ladies who didn't know how to sew," Mrs. Fry said. "You probably knew them: Lizzie Bomberger, Susan Brumbach, and Irene Witmer. They started by teaching the girls hand sewing. Later they had them make quilt patches and hem diapers on the machines."

"I knew those women very well. At some time in my growing-up years each of them was my Sunday school teacher at Minersvillage. They were always concerned about the youth and were great examples for us."

"Can you tell me about sewing circles from the mid-1940s and into the early 1960s?" I asked. "That's when I attended with my mother at Stauffers."

"Much of our conference's sewing was sent to Mennonite Central Committee's Clothing Center at Ephrata and shipped overseas during that time. But women regularly went to the Good Samaritan Hospital in Lebanon or Saint Joseph's in Lancaster to mend. They also made new gowns or whatever was needed. Their time and work was donated by the church.

Can you imagine that happening today?" she asked.

"No, not with the way our health care system has become such big business," I said, looking over the minutes. "Mending started at the Good Samaritan Hospital in 1949. And it looks like it continued into the 1960s. Listen to this. In 1964 four or more ladies met twelve times at the hospital and sewed a total of 1,862 pieces of mended and new items."

"Sewing circles didn't have much money. Our budget for a year was usually less than 100 dollars. We used that to buy safety pins, thread, needles, elastic, pre-cut garments, and some fabric. Occasionally we bought some new clothes that we wouldn't normally make."

"Look at this. In 1951 they bought six pairs of knickers for a dollar each, six union suits at 50 cents a piece, two pairs of wool underwear for four dollars, and woolens for five dollars. What were woolens?" I asked.

"And why would they want wool underwear?" my sister giggled.

"That most likely would have been winter clothing for refugee families," Mrs. Fry explained. "For someone who worked outside."

"Oh, of course. Refugees from World War II. That makes sense," I said. "And the woolens?

"They would buy wool material and make coats, trousers, jackets. Even blankets. Houses didn't have central heat back then and people used wool blankets on their beds."

"So it could have been for any of those. I remember sleeping in an unheated upstairs bedroom snuggled under a lambs' wool blanket. I noticed you made coverings, bonnets, and plain cape dresses. Who were they for?"

"For people who joined the outreach mission in Philadelphia."

"I hadn't thought of that," I said. "They wouldn't have had access to Mennonite clothes, and if they didn't sew ...."

"That's right. Area churches sent what was needed to the missionaries in Philadelphia and they kept a cupboard stocked for their members."

"I remember making MCC Christmas bundles and school kits as a youngster," I said. "We bought or made the items on the list and put them together at home with Mom. I think Sewing Circle collected them. After I married and moved to Virginia I had my sons help me make school kits for several years. I sewed the little drawstring bags and they filled them with pens, pencils, crayons, a ruler, whatever was on the list."

"Mennonite Central Committee still sends different kinds of kits. You're right; they have listings of exactly what goes in each bundle: layettes for newborns, refugee kits, sewing kits, school kits, and Christmas bundles," Ruth said.

"Samaritan's Purse has a similar Christmas project with their shoebox ministry. That's what our churches down in southwestern Virginia support."

"MCC's bundles are the same idea except you wrap everything in a big towel and pin it. They're labeled for a boy or girl and for whatever age the clothing will fit. Women in sewing circles made dresses or shirts and pants for bundles."

"I was just a little girl but I remember helping make up kits for refugees after World War II. And Mom used to bring home pre-cut baby diapers, kimonos, and saques to sew for newborns. I can see her now, sitting there at her treadle Singer in front of the window in the back room, overlooking the meadow, hemming piles and piles of snowy white diapers and sewing those little gowns."

"Lots of women who couldn't attend circle meetings did that. MCC just finished collecting 16,000 refugee kits to send to Afghanistan. We put in bar soap, 4 towels, toothpaste and brush, shampoo, laundry soap, comb and brush, nail clipper, Band-Aids. Enough to get a refugee family started. Area churches have a drive on now to collect school kits for Iraqi children. Some people contribute money, but most get together and make kits."

"I was talking to Jenny Strickler at the Mennonite Home the other day. She was my Sunday school teacher at Stauffers Church and attended their sewing circle. She remembered one time she made 30 children's dresses in twelve days, including the buttonholes! That's a lot of sewing. She said half of their sewing went to MCC for relief and half went to The Missionary Closet."

"That's right. Our circle was the same. Mrs. Paul Gehman had a room in her house in Manheim. When missionaries came home from overseas they could go there and get new clothing free. She kept all different sizes stocked."

"I've heard several people mention The Cutting Room. Do you know what it is?"

"Two ladies, Emma and Miriam Hershey, lived together at Paradise, near Lancaster. They had a room at their home called the MCC Cutting Room. Emma operated a machine that could cut through about 10 layers of material at a time."

"What did they cut?"

"Anything that was needed: baby saques and kimonos, diapers, different sized dresses, shirts, pants. Representatives of sewing circles could go there and buy the pre-cut patterns and take them back to their churches to be sewn. Emma and Miriam got bolts of material at wholesale prices so it was cheaper and faster for sewing circles to buy from them. They did this as their ministry at no profit to themselves. By 1990 they were elderly and it was discontinued."

"So The Cutting Room no longer exists?"

"Oh, yes. But now they call it the MCC Material Aid Center. It's in a large warehouse where bundles, blankets, and clothes are packaged and sent out. The cutting machine is there and is still used to cut outfits, especially for newborns. Representatives of sewing circles still go there.

We pay to cover the cost of the material, take home pre-cut items to sew, and then return the finished products. They also sell material by the bolt to use for the backs of comforters. It's much cheaper that way. Then everything is sent back to MCC to be shipped overseas."

"Do all different groups of Mennonites support MCC nowadays?"

"A couple of conservative break-away groups have their own relief programs. But most everyone else, including the Amish, supports them."

"The Amish?"

"Oh, yes. Amish women come to the Material Aid Center and work on quilts to be sold for MCC. And you know the Amish are tops as quilters. Those quilts are auctioned in the Harrisburg Relief Sale the first weekend of April. Some of them bring in several thousand dollars."

"I knew about the sale but didn't realize Amish women did a lot of the quilting."

"And the Amish men help with packing and the girls check kits to make sure all are correct. You know, back in the 40s and 50s quilts were sent overseas along with the comforters as blankets for the needy. Nowadays one quilt brings in enough money to buy stacks of blankets for refugees."

"When Charles and I were teaching in Congo under MCC's Teacher Abroad Program, our country director lent us pots and pans, dishes, silverware, and bedding. His wife told me to look in a barrel and pick out what I wanted for a bedspread. I found a gorgeous double wedding ring quilt. She insisted I take it. I was grateful to the ladies who'd made it. That quilt brought me fond memories of home out there in the bush."

"That was the idea of MCC's programs, to help the needy, in the name of Christ."

"I wish I could have gone with you to sewing circle," Shannon said as we finished tying our baby blanket. "You must have had a lot of fun."

"I did. The old ladies were kind and let me help. But I didn't get to go as often as I wanted because of school."

"Did your mom teach you to quilt?"

"No, she never made quilts or pieced comforters. I learned to do that after I got married. My mother-in-law was an expert quilter and showed me how to make tiny even stitches, but I'll never be able to do it as well as she did. Here, look at these," I said, showing my little friend the quilts hanging on a rack at the foot of my bed.

"They're beautiful," she said, running her finger over the stitches Grandma Patton had made years before Shannon was even born.

"She showed me different patterns she'd collected and taught me how to piece them, using scraps of material. I think her favorites were Bowtie, Around the World, and Double-Wedding Ring. At least those are the ones she made the most. She borrowed patterns, drew them on cardboard, traced them on her material, and cut all the pieces individually with her scissors. Back then cutting boards and rotary cutters hadn't even been invented."

"And then you taught your students in Africa how to make quilts, didn't you?"

"That's right. And now I'm teaching you. That's what life's about. Passing along what you know to the next generation."

Mennonite women quilting at sewing circle.

# Sewing, Kikongo, and the Dog
# 1968 - 1969

"**D**id you do much sewing when you were in Africa?" my friend Sue Livick asked one Monday morning as our quilting group pieced samplers.

"Oh, yes. As a matter of fact I was the number one seamstress, Home Ec teacher, and sewing machine mechanic for six years," I laughed.

"You taught sewing in your school?" Irene Merrell, our pastor's mother, asked.

"None of the other faculty or staff sewed much so when I volunteered I was in. I even had to write my own curriculum. Three months after our arrival the director of our school asked me to teach the church women's sewing as well."

"I guess teaching out there was a lot different from here in the States," Sue commented.

"I'll bring some excerpts from my diary for you to read," I laughed.

### March, 1968

*I'm writing this by candlelight since it's already past ten o'clock. The generator runs from seven to nine-thirty each evening during the students' study hours. We have two kerosene lamps in our house but I don't like to use them; they tend to smoke.*

*Last week Ian, our headmaster, asked if I'd be willing to teach more sewing. "It's part of the local church's program for women," he said. "We try to offer a sewing class for them every year, but there's been nobody to teach it for quite a while." He told me to meet with Lesley Fuller, that she would explain it to me.*

*After talking it over with Charles, I agreed to try. So Lesley and I drove to Mbanza Ngungu after our Friday morning classes to do some shopping. We bought 30 yards of cotton cloth, which the church paid for. I'll cut out and sew some outfits to show the women several patterns I have available for them to make. They'll have to pay a minimal charge for each item they choose, for example a little dress is generally about 30 cents.*

When Charles and I applied to teach in Congo, we were asked what we could or would be willing to teach in addition to French, Spanish, and English – our areas of certification. I wrote geography, religion, and sewing on my application. My qualifications for teaching them were almost non-existent: I liked geography even though I hadn't had a class in it since eighth grade; I had almost a minor in religion from Eastern Mennonite College; and growing-up I'd attended Mennonite sewing circles, taken Home Ec in junior high school, and made my own clothes.

"Every teacher in our school has been anticipating your arrival since classes began last month," Ian, our director told me. "We've had no geographer for several years so each faculty member takes one geography class. Now you'll be doing them all – eight hours a week."

"I'm no specialist, you know," I said, "I just *like* geography."

"And neither are we, and we *dislike* it!" he laughed.

"Okay. What else will I be teaching?"

"Sewing, for one thing, some religion. We have plenty of English teachers. Charles will be doing French and some math."

Lesley, one of the long-term British missionary teachers, showed me around the Cycle d'Orientation, where the first and second year classes met – the equivalent of American seventh and eighth grades.

"Our 38 girls are taught separately from the boys. Their classrooms are at the far end of the building," she said, stepping onto the veranda that ran the length of the cinderblock structure housing four classrooms and an office.

"The second year girls' classes meet here at the front of the refectory," she continued, swinging open a grimy wood door. I was shocked by the appearance of the long high-ceilinged dingy room. Homemade desks and backless stools faced a scratched chalkboard at one end. A tall wooden cupboard and half a dozen treadle sewing machines lined the sides beneath large metal-framed windows. Four uneven greasy tables stood at the back. The stale odor of fish and something I couldn't identify hung in the air. The only nice piece of furniture was the teacher's desk, a long smooth wood table.

"Here's where they eat their meals," Lesley said, gesturing to the tables as she walked toward the back door, opened it, and descended several steps to the brick kitchen attached by a narrow breezeway. At one end a large pot of brown beans was simmering over a small fire on the floor. "Mama Makuzayi Neli is the girls' cook. We call her Mama Neli. She's around here somewhere."

"Tell me about the sewing classes," I said, turning back to the dining hall.

"We haven't had any since Lena Pringle went back to Scotland last year," Lesley said, shaking her head. "The machines are no longer in working order, so you'll have to do hand sewing with the girls. They know how to sew by hand; you'll just need to organize projects." I was disappointed. Anticipating teaching machine sewing, I'd brought different sizes of patterns for little dresses, shirts and shorts.

I'd never sewn a garment by hand, but when I was growing up we'd had a German neighbor who made her daughter a beautiful little navy dress all by hand. When I'd asked her about it she showed me the stitches she used to make strong seams. I guessed now this was how the women in Congo sewed. Later, going through the cupboard in the refectory I found several samples of hand sewn projects using the same stitches my German friend had done years before. Besides a few sewing supplies and patterns for baby clothes left behind by Miss Pringle, the cupboard was stocked with patterns, knitting needles, embroidery and crochet thread, and on the bottom shelf piles of jumbled yarn. Wool, Lesley called it.

"I was hoping to find some material," I told Charles. "I guess they taught the girls to knit and crochet so they could make things to sell."

I went home and practiced making neat even stitches by hand. The slow going annoyed me and I was grateful when Lesley offered to lend me Lena Pringle's treadle sewing machine. "Lena sold it before she left," Lesley said. "But the chappy has never come to pick it up. You're welcome to use it until he shows."

"This is the best news I've had since we got here," I told Charles at lunch. "Can you round up some students to bring it over this afternoon? I can't wait." We set it in front of our south bedroom window and elated, I used Lena's wonderful Singer to finish my examples for class.

## April 1968

*I finally got my foyer (that's the French word for a group of people who get together, and it's what they call the church-sponsored women's sewing class) started for the women. They meet every Monday afternoon at my house. Today eleven were present after they'd all dribbled in. I'd had no idea how many would come or even what would happen. Our house is so tiny we have to meet outside, but the women don't seem to mind; they're used to sitting outside on the ground to grind manioc, shell peanuts, or cook over campfires behind their houses.*

*Charles helped me carry our little dining room table out into the front yard. I set it under our only tree and displayed my samples. Mama Wumba, the wife of an elementary school teacher, called the ladies to order and began with a short scripture reading and prayer in Kikongo.*

*Since I don't speak Kikongo and they don't speak much French, a former primary school monitrice is supposed to help translate. She came, but didn't seem to know much of the vocabulary we needed. I had written the prices on pieces of paper and pinned them to the garments. One by one they came to my table and made their choices, usually with a child in arms to show me the size they needed. I was surprised how much French some of the others understood. Between them they figured out most of what I was telling them. I wrote their names in my notebook and noted the outfit and size they preferred. I'll have them all cut out and ready for them to begin sewing next week.*

At our first class session, as the school girls sat around their dining hall tables, I told them my ideas of having them begin by making small projects, showing them the little outfits I'd made. They agreed baby clothes would be a good place to start since they were small, easy to make, and everyone had babies in their families.

"We'll start by making a sewing bag with a drawstring to hold the project you're working on," I said.

Kiabembo raised her hand. "Madame, are you going to teach us to sew on the machines first?"

"I'm so sorry," I told them. "None of the machines work. The bobbins and bobbin cases are missing and we're going to have to sew by hand." The girls groaned and shook their heads, disappointment written on their faces. I bashed on.

"We'll use embroidery thread from the cupboard to cross-stitch your name on the front. When you finish that project you can cut out and sew these," I said, holding up a little bonnet fastened at the back with two buttons and handmade buttonholes, and a pair of booties tied with ribbons I'd made.

They laughed and said those would be useful. "All Congolese babies wear hats," they said.

## May 1968

*I've seen some of the women in my foyer at my next-door neighbor Thérèse's house, sitting in her front yard, babies in their laps, doing each other's hair. After combing out their long tresses, they part them into many small sections. Then taking one bunch at a time, starting at the skull, they wind black thread round and around the hair until it stretches out from their heads like a little stick. When all are completed they tie the ends of the "sticks" together to make a solid framework, which they cover with a puffy scarf called a kitambula. It resembles a beehive hairdo and is quite attractive.*

*These women work hard every day trying to provide food for their families, carrying water from the spring at the bottom of the hill, bringing in firewood, hoeing their gardens, harvesting manioc and preparing it to eat, selling in the market to earn a few makutas for soap and candles. When I see them walk past my front door, their backs and necks ramrod straight, bearing the weight of a bundle of firewood or a bucket of water on their head, they look so graceful and relaxed. But I've seen the steep hill they climb from the spring and the distance they walk to find fuel on the depleted hills, so I understand why they welcome an afternoon of rest, sitting in the shade of my tree, visiting with each other, and sewing.*

Sewing and manual labor classes both met on Tuesday and Thursday afternoons. While another teacher supervised one girls' class sweeping, cleaning latrines, fetching water from the spring, bringing bundles of wood to the kitchen from out in the bush, I taught the other group sewing – about nineteen students each time. Several girls quickly finished the blue and white checked bags, cut out hats and booties, sewed them up, made ties, worked the two button-holes, and wanted more to do.

"I need a project to keep the advanced students busy while the others catch up," I told Lesley. "I've been thinking about having them cut out quilt blocks to make a baby blanket."

"That sounds like a wonderful idea. Let's see if we can help you find scraps."

I gathered up odds and ends from anyone who'd ever done any sewing: Irene had leftovers from making maternity dresses, Edna gave me a couple of good skirts she didn't wear, Ian even came up with a bag of pieces left behind in his wife's sewing basket when she'd gone back to England with the children. I showed the girls how to trace a three-and-a-half-inch template, placing it carefully on the material to reduce waste, and then to meticulously cut on the line so the blocks would fit together uniformly.

"We'll make my mother-in-law's favorite quilt pattern," I told the girls. "It's called 'Around the World' because the colors go round and round the center."

"Is it hard to make?" Wombisa asked, a bit apprehensive.

"Oh no. It's easy. This is a good pattern for using up scraps, and it'll be beautiful."

"Can we give the blanket to Madame Woosnam when she has her baby?" Mayamba suggested, pressing material with a flat iron heated in the kitchen fire.

"Great idea," Mfunu said, looking up from the pieces she was sorting. "She's nice. We'd like to give her something from our class." I agreed, knowing Irene, a British pharmacist, would be touched by such a personal gift.

### June 1968

*The women's sewing group has grown from the initial 11 to 32 in less than four months. I can hardly keep up with getting projects ready. When a new lady comes she wants me to cut an outfit for her right then and there. I can't because I need to be available to help with problems. Thérèse is good about explaining they will have to wait for me to cut it until the next meeting. But I can understand they don't want to just sit there without a project. I wish I could tell them how I feel in their own language.*

*Today a woman came with a large light brown dog. Looking for a bit of shade, he promptly stretched out on his side under my table. I'm sure the lady and dog had walked a great distance and both were tired and hot. Not wanting to be disturbed, he growled whenever my foot touched him as I moved around. My nervousness showed, and one of the women shouted, "Katuka," at him. A small fuss broke out but ended in laughter and the dog stayed.*

*By pointing, smiling, using "oui" and "non," they manage to tell me what they want. They giggle at each other's poor attempts to use French, but I encourage them to try to communicate with me. When they have a problem with their stitches they bring it to me and I have them watch while I straighten it out. I wish I had Kikongo words to accompany my hand movements.*

*Many are serious about their sewing and bring along a child to watch their toddlers, others make little progress with squirmy infants on their laps, their loose blouses pulled down, breasts exposed, the babies feeding at will.*

*Occasionally a frustrated mother will stand and tie her baby on her back, rock back and forth until he falls asleep and she can sew in peace.*

At the end of our first year, I sent a shopping list for thread, scissors, pins, needles, and patterns with Edna who was flying home to England for the summer. As soon as the last student had gone I told Charles, "I need to teach the girls machine sewing in the fall, especially since I'll have eight ninth graders taking Sewing III. Now that I have time I'm going down to the refectory and see what I can do with those messed-up machines. Edna said she had a letter from Lena Pringle saying the parts are all there in the sewing cupboard; I just have to search for them."

We parked our bikes in front of the school, unlocked the refectory, and threw open the windows, hoping fresh breezes would puff away the sour smell lingering from countless meals of chiquangua and dried salt fish. "First of all the cupboard needs to be organized," I said, eying the heaps of jumbled thread and yarn intertwined with bits of cloth and knitting needles. I sorted the contents into piles on the girls' desks. Hours later when I got to the bottom shelf under a heap of yarn I found a box of bobbins and bobbin cases.

"Oh, wow, Charles! Look! She was right. Here they are. Now to figure out which one goes where," I said, arranging them by size and style. "I recognize the Singer ones. They're the easiest."

"Then that's where we should start."

"Look at this poor thing," I shouted, looking up from the first machine. "Somebody jammed in the wrong bobbin case." Charles spent the rest of the morning gently but firmly pulling and prying cases out of machines while I ran back and forth checking and fitting, matching them with several owners manuals we'd found in the cupboard. Once we'd figured out what went where we spent hours oiling, cleaning, and adjusting.

Within five days we had all nine machines running smoothly, three hand-cranked and six treadles. The tension was bad on one; I'd have to go back and play with that later. Singer needles broke in the Pfaff, and the German machine, although it sounded wonderful, refused to form stitches.

I wrote home to our mothers. "Charles and I've been overhauling our school's sewing machines so I can teach the girls machine sewing this fall. I need some Pfaff needles for one. Can either of you find me some?" They both sent me a pack in each of their next two letters.

"I have no idea what to tell you about that German machine," my mother-in-law wrote. "Just keep playing with it; you'll figure it out."

### September 1968

*Every Monday afternoon, unless it's raining, the women come and sit on my front lawn from two-thirty until four o'clock. Their foyer has become the high point of my week. I have women working on six different kinds of outfits: hats and booties, shirts, shorts, and several styles of dresses for their small children and babies.*

*Some of the better seamstresses don't like the cheap cotton cloth Lesley and I bought in Mbanza Ngungu. They want a better quality material for their little outfits. So I pulled out some odds and ends from my personal stock, left-over pieces large enough to make a child's dress or shirt. I hope this doesn't cause a problem. If only I could speak to them. I'd like to talk to them – tell them things I know and learn from them.*

*That light brown dog comes almost every week, flops down in the same spot under my table week after week, and sleeps the whole time we're sewing. I'd prefer for him not to be there, but I don't mind his presence as much as I did. He doesn't growl anymore so maybe he's getting used to me.*

*Last week Thérèse pointed out a woman who walks almost six miles to be in my class. I found that humbling and determined to always be there for them and to have their little outfits cut out and ready on time in spite of my many other obligations. I've learned which ones are beginners and can't sew straight seams, so I draw pencil lines for them to follow.*

*At the beginning of last week's session I had noticed several women were motioning to Thérèse and asking her something. Finally she said, "They want you to read the scripture to them in Kikongo."*

*I laughed, but knowing I could quickly learn to read a passage in their phonetically written language, I said, "Tell them I need to prepare, but I will read next week."*

*They all nodded and laughed and said, "Ahh and Mmm."*

*So I practiced reading John 3:16-17 in Kikongo. My houseboy Mpanzu helped with my pronunciation. "That's good, Madame," he laughed. "You sound like a real Congolese."*

*Today they remembered. Thérèse told me but I could see anticipation written on their faces. I picked up my Kikongo New Testament and when I easily read the verses, these illiterate women were astounded. Talking broke out among them. "How can she read with perfect pronunciation and yet not be able to speak our language?" they asked Thérèse.*

*"Tell them because the writing is phonetic," I said. But they didn't understand. Mama Dioko prayed and they got quiet. But the whispered questions continued throughout our session. I won't read the scripture anymore at the foyer. I'm leaving it to the deacons' wives where it belongs.*

When the girls arrived back at school in September they were elated to find the machines working. "The students in Sewing II and III started on the machines," I wrote our mothers. "They prefer the hand ones but are getting used to the treadles. First I had them sew straight lines and circles on paper, then on material with colored thread, just like I'd learned in Miss Hershburger's Home Ec classes when I was in junior high. I prepared lessons from a French sewing manual I bought in Belgium and gave them notes to study and then a written test on the names of all the parts and how to use the machine. They learned it but are more interested in making a new sewing bag. Sometimes they get so excited about using the machines they sing and waltz around the room. Some find it impossible to coordinate their feet to use the treadles but can use the hand ones. Others are adept at both."

All but the tailor's machine had a wooden box-like cover that fit over the head and could be locked. On holidays and during free time, I gave the keys to certain skilled students who would oversee their classmates wanting to sew. One day in early October I complained in class, aggravated that only six of the nine machines were in working order: once again an aged leather belt was broken on a treadle, the tailor's machine was again jammed, and the German one still wasn't forming stitches.

"Madame, why don't you turn the wheel toward the back?" Kiabembo Christine asked as I tried once again to make it sew.

"Kiabembo, anyone who works with sewing machines knows the fly wheel must turn toward the front. Otherwise the threads will jam."

"But, Madame, I think this one's different."

Annoyed at her idiotic suggestion, I said, "Okay. Watch. The threads'll jam." I put a piece of material under the needle, turned the flywheel backwards, and lo and behold there before the entire class I had to eat my words. That machine worked like a charm, producing a series of the finest stitches anyone could ask for. I jumped up and down and danced around the room with Kiabembo. "You're a genius," I shouted. We laughed for weeks over the backwards German machine. Several girls enjoyed using it and had no trouble making it work.

The day I dreaded finally came. Lesley stopped me as I headed to my morning classes and told me to get Lena Pringle's sewing machine ready. "The chappy who bought it turned up this morning. He wants to leave at noon."

"I can't live without a sewing machine," I whined to Charles at lunch.

"Why don't you get the one in the girls' refectory that you can't lock up? You complain every week that it's jammed and can't be used."

He was right, so that same afternoon I had several students help him carry the heavy treadle machine and cabinet to our house and set it in my office. That wonderful commercial machine with backstitch was a dream, a Mercedes of sewing machines. After whipping it back in shape, I spent holidays and weekends making curtains for the girls' dormitories, mending school uniforms, or sewing blocks together to make quilts and cushions for birthdays.

I felt sorry for Mpanzu's raggedy little girls, Marie and Angelique, when he occasionally brought them to work with him. So I made them each a dress out of material scraps. They would sit out back watching my every move, so afraid of me they'd hide behind their daddy when I approached. I started offering them snacks, a piece of jelly bread or a cookie. I made them each a rag doll with an extra change of clothes. Before long they became friendlier and would bring their dollies and play on the grass.

Mpanzu told me Congolese often told their children white people would eat them. These stories had circulated for years and older kids threatened younger ones with it. Marie's brothers had warned her about coming to my house. One day Mpanzu brought them to work with him and said,

"Last night Marie told her brothers those stories are false, at least about you! She said that anyone who'd make nice things for her and give her cakes wouldn't harm her. She likes coming to your house."

When our MCC director and his wife left at the end of their term, she gave me all her sewing scraps and left over material from three years of making dresses for their children – enough to make countless quilts and sewing projects for several years.

"I sure miscalculated about dresses for myself coming out here," I wrote home. "They literally get washed down the river. Mpanzu pounds our clothes on the rocks and they come back full of little holes. I've made myself several dresses out of African prints and turned collars that had worn through on two of Charles' shirts. They look like new!"

## October 1968

*The women are coming in even greater numbers. They must have talked and invited friends during the summer break. I'm spending most of my Saturday afternoons cutting out projects for them.*

*Yesterday Mayamba, one of the younger women, came with her six-month-old baby boy. The wife of an elementary school teacher, Mayamba already sews quite well She always comes well dressed in a tailor-made matching blouse and long wrap-around skirt. Her hair is immaculate and she has a pretty face. I think some of the women are jealous of her. Today her baby cried and cried. She bounced him on her lap and then tied him on her back, but still he cried.*

*I was busy, but I noticed some unrest among the women, pointing with their chins in Mayamba's direction and snickering. I wondered why she didn't breastfeed her baby like the others. The baby screamed and finally she gathered up her things and left. When I had time I asked Thérèse what the problem was. She turned her face away, fanned, and*

*finally said, "Mayamba's baby was hungry."*
*"Why didn't she feed him?" I asked.*
*Thérèse giggled, "She couldn't; she was wearing a bra!"*

My sewing students wanted to make rag dolls after they saw mine. They embroidered "Je t'aime" or "I love you" over the heart, stuffed them with dried grass, used odds and ends of purple, blue, and green yarn from the sewing cupboard for hair, and scraps for their dresses. Although some of their dollies resembled witches, the girls loved their babies and didn't seem to notice.

Our final project was slightly flared knee-length graduation dresses with collars for the eighth grade girls. They voted for lavender broadcloth. I calculated and bought buttons, zippers, and material in bulk in Kinshasa. We spent half of second semester measuring and cutting and pinning and sewing and fitting and ripping and re-sewing before we finished just in time for the ceremonies. The girls strutted proudly down the aisle in those new dresses to receive their certificates.

"How long did you teach sewing to the Congolese ladies?" Irene asked as we took out pins and began rolling our sampler to the next area to be quilted.

"I can't remember exactly. It must have been close to two years. Until Phyl came out from England. That was her job – women's work. I was just a fill-in."

"Did you miss doing the women's sewing?"

"I did for a while, but I had a full load at school and I got pregnant and had a baby during the last two years we were there and wouldn't have been able to do it then anyway. I still had the girls' sewing classes at school. So it worked out. I was satisfied knowing I'd given the girls and women something they could use throughout their lives."

Ntadingi, an eighth grade student,
hemming a garment in my sewing class.

# A Winter Wedding
# December 25, 1953

**"I**'d like to come visit you," I said to Mary on the phone one hot afternoon last summer.

"And I'd like to see *you*," she said. "I'll be waiting."

I found the condo Mary Stauffer was sharing with her youngest daughter at the end of a private drive, in a cul-de-sac, surrounded by miles and miles of Amish and Mennonite farms in Lancaster County, not far from where we'd attended church together when I was barely a teenager. Mary's black eyes still sparkled and her face still lit up when she smiled. Although she was dressed in a simple cotton off-the-rack dress, her long, now-graying hair was still pulled back in a bun. I recognized her voice, although she'd lost some of her Pennsylvania-Dutch accent, probably from the years she and her husband had lived in Arizona, and from being around her seven well-educated children now spread around the world.

"Come in, come in," Mary laughed, hugging me on her front stoop. She apologized for her small retirement home, but I thought it suited her well and confessed my husband and I were looking for one ourselves. We talked about our children and her grandchildren, about our youth, and about the future.

After an hour I confessed I'd come to ask about her wedding. "I want to write about it," I said, "but I need some details. Would you mind?"

"No, I wouldn't mind at all," she laughed, and I breathed a sigh of relief as we launched into the past – more than 50 years before

"Ben and I were married on my 24th birthday, December 25, 1953," Mary said. "I think it was a Friday."

"Christmas day?" I asked, my eyes widening.

"Yes, it was. I always said I wanted to get married on my birthday, and I did! It was in the morning, about nine-thirty or ten o'clock. We didn't have written invitations. It was announced at church and everybody came."

"After my parents became Mennonites Daddy always wanted to go to church on Christmas morning. He insisted Christmas was the Lord's birthday and we needed to go to church to celebrate it. So it wasn't a Christmas service we went to that year, it was your wedding!" I laughed.

Although Mary Hoover and Ben Stauffer were married in a simple ceremony at North Lebanon Mennonite Church, the issues surrounding their relationship were complicated. Mary had grown up with her nine siblings in a Horning Mennonite church, often called Black Bumpers because they covered the chrome on their cars with black paint to avoid any showy or prideful attitudes. Their proper name was Weaverland Conference; they were an Old Order Mennonite faction that wanted to maintain their ancestors' traditions of community, simplicity, and humility.

"I was happy with my life on the farm and attending weekly services at Springville," she said. "I'd been dating a young man from our congregation for about two years when suddenly our relationship ended and he married my best friend."

"Oh, wow." I said. "That had to be difficult."

"Yes, it was."

"And you saw them every Sunday at church?"

"Yes," she answered quietly. "It was hard. I got depressed and my mother worried about me. When I found a job sewing for Emma Good in nearby Lincoln my mother encouraged me to take it."

Emma, a Lancaster Conference Mennonite, supported herself and her four children by selling piece goods and making cape dresses and coverings for Mennonite women. She was glad to have this capable young seamstress come and live with her to sew and sometimes tend the shop.

"About that time Emma and two of her brothers had become interested in evangelism, which my church did not sanction. They took me to several prayer meetings. Because of my heartache I reached out to the Lord and had a real need in my life fulfilled. When they started a Mennonite mission in North Lebanon, I went with them to Sunday services."

"Your parents must have been distraught to see you leave your traditions and culture," I said.

"But you know, I didn't leave the traditions. I still dressed the same. I'd accepted the Lord and was baptized in the Horning church. The difference was I'd begun studying the Word of God and telling others about it. Emma often prayed with me and encouraged me. About 1951 after I turned 21, I joined the North Lebanon Mennonite Church along with a group of couples who'd also left the Weaverland Conference."

"That's about the same time my parents started attending North Lebanon." I said. "I was eleven and looked up to you. You were my sister Anita's Sunday school teacher."

"Yes, I taught the teenage girls. Sunday school was never allowed in the Horning churches, but I had no qualms about teaching. I searched the Scriptures and even got a Williams New Testament. That's what I used in Sunday school. I found it so much easier to read and understand than the King James version. And that's where I met Ben," she said. "He'd started attending with his mother and sister."

"I remember Ben's uncle Elam Stauffer," I said. "He was a missionary in East Africa for many years."

"That's right. And they were as excited about evangelizing in the city of Lebanon as we were. Ben and I were a few years older than most of the unmarried people at our new church, so we naturally drifted together and became friends. We started dating."

"What did you do when you dated?"

Mary gave me an odd look "We went to church. Sometimes we went to visit someone. Ben would pick me up and take me to prayer meeting. There wasn't anything else. We attended singings for young people held in different Horning homes."

"But the guys were on one side and the girls on the other."

"That's right," she laughed. "Afterwards we'd sit on Emma's front porch or in the living room and talk. We also spent time together at my parents' home; that's how we got to know each other."

"How long were you engaged?" I asked.

"Not long. Once we decided to marry we set a date. Maybe a couple of months later."

"I remember you made your own dress. My mother always talked about your beautiful simple gray dress."

Mary threw back her head and laughed. "She was right. My dress was made over the same cape dress pattern I always wore. A lot of the young brides were leaving the traditional color and using light blue for their wedding dresses. But I felt it was important for me to wear the traditional Horning wedding color. That's why I chose gray – a light gray crepe. I remember it was a fine material, not washable," she smiled.

"I made my own dress. But I remember the day before the wedding I took the skirt apart and replaced the back and front panels because they each had a faded streak down the center!"

"The day before?" I laughed.

"Yes, but I was used to sewing my own dresses, and I wanted the skirt to look right."

"What else do you remember?" I asked.

"After Ben proposed I moved back home with my parents. I thought that was important to them and I had a lot of things to get ready. Ben came and spent the night before the wedding at our house." Her eyes widened, "Oh, it's not what young people today might think. I spent my last night in my parents' home alone in my old bedroom. Ben was in a guest room. I guess it was a tradition, dating back to horse and buggy days, to make sure the groom would be present in case of bad weather."

"Since you were marrying into a different conference, was it a problem with your family?"

"I was the only one (and still am) from our family of ten who left the Horning church. My one brother raised the question, but my mother said she wanted all my siblings and their families to attend. She was a real peacemaker. And to this day I'm grateful for her attitude; they all came and it was a happy day for me.

"Traditionally, Horning weddings take place at the home of the bride's parents. When everyone is seated and ready the girl and her attendants come down the stairs followed by the groom with his attendants. They never carry anything. Carrying flowers or even a Bible is considered prideful."

"I wanted to be married in my new church, but I followed the Horning traditions. The building and the place-ment of the benches were different, but the people looked the same. When it was time and everyone was seated, the congregation sang a couple of hymns and then I walked in from the front anteroom on the women's side with my cousin Anna Mary Hoover at the same time that Ben walked in with his good friend from the men's side."

"That's the part I remember best," I said. "You and your bridesmaid sat on the front bench at the aisle on the women's side, and Ben and his best man sat directly across the aisle from you. You sat there through the whole service."

"That's right. It was a regular church service. We sang some more, a minister read the scripture, someone preached, and then Bishop Homer Bomberger did our wedding vows. Ben and I clasped our right hands and the bishop put his over ours."

"I remember there was no kiss. Just the pronouncement that you were husband and wife."

Mary giggled. "No, there was no kissing in front of the family. Afterwards we stood there at the front and everyone came by and wished us well. I'll never forget a little girl from the city of Lebanon. I can't remember her name, but Ben and I had brought her regularly to Sunday school. She was there that day and came up to us after the service and asked, 'But where's your ring?' I never forgot that."

"I wonder if anyone explained that Mennonites didn't wear jewelry, not even wedding rings."

"I suppose I did briefly tell her that. I don't remember. Afterwards our families went to my parents' home for a reception. My aunt had come the day before to help prepare chicken croquettes and of course all the trimmings like they did for a normal Sunday company dinner."

"I'm sure your mother served the traditional Pennsylvania Dutch seven sweets and seven sours," I laughed.

"I don't remember," Mary said. "It's been so long. Other than the chicken croquettes I do recall my mother saying she wanted to make two kinds of cakes, which she always did when she had company. I told her no, I wanted only one kind. So she made one kind, but I don't know what it was."

"Isn't it odd the things you remember and what you forget?"

"I've had a good life," she said, looking at the photos of her children and their spouses hanging on the living room wall. "They're scattered all around the world. When I heard how they were contacting each other by e-mail I said I wanted to be connected with them. So I got a computer and we e-mail on a regular basis."

"That's exactly what we do in our family," I said.

"After Ben died I lived alone, not far from here. I work as a nursing assistant taking care of elderly people."

"Where's Ben buried?" I asked.

"Well, his death was so sudden I didn't know what to do. My parents had several cemetery plots at Springville and they offered to have him buried there, beside their own. So after the funeral service at my church, we took him there for burial."

I was surprised the Horning church would accept an outsider. "The cemetery plots belonged to them, and we're family," Mary said. "Nobody raised any question about it as far as I know. So in the end I'll be buried next to my parents. Life hasn't always been easy but God is faithful.

North Lebanon Mennonite Church where Mary and Ben Stauffer were married.

# Wedding in a Congolese Village
## May 12, 1968

"**D**o you remember who these people are?" I asked Charles recently, pulling a black and white photo from our Congo album.

"He's the fellow who worked in our school clinic. But I don't remember his name."

"Boti," I said.

"That's it. He was slender and tall, well over six feet. Is that his wife and baby?"

"Sure are. Her name was Jeanne. She came to my women's sewing classes out on the lawn in front of our little brick house and was quite good and quick at sewing straight tight seams by hand. She didn't know any French, so she asked me through a translator if I had any pretty material from America to make her baby girl a dress with a collar. I found a tiny piece of light blue polyester/cotton and cut out the dress their baby's wearing in the picture. Jeanne sewed it up in no time. She was so proud of her baby."

"How'd you get that picture?" Charles asked. "A man and wife were never seen together in public out there in Africa. The women even sat on one side and the men on the other in the Baptist church."

"That's true. The only time you ever saw a couple together was in their own home. I had a terrible time getting to know who belonged to whom. Anyway, Boti came over to our house that day after our sewing class and asked me to take their picture. She looks terribly uncomfortable, standing away from him and twisting her skirt."

"Didn't we go to their wedding?"

"We sure did. Besides our trip down the Congo on the riverboat, I think their wedding was one of our most interesting experiences out in Africa."

We'd been in Africa about five months when one Saturday afternoon Boti knocked on our door. We knew him as the chap who worked in the dispensary. He didn't have much education and spoke little French, but he'd been trained as a clinic aid to recognize intestinal parasites and malaria; he could clean and patch up wounds and dispense simple medications like aspirin. He was the best we had at that time.

We invited him into our living room and I offered him a cup of tea. I could tell he was nervous as he squirmed on a chair near the door. Finally in his halting French, he made us understand that he'd already talked to the director of the school and Ian had agreed to lend him the school's Jeep truck to go to a nearby village if Charles would drive.

"When do you want to go?" Charles asked.

"Tomorrow."

"Why do you need to go?"

"I'm getting married," Boti grinned, as I handed him a cup of tea. "I need the Jeep so I can bring back my wife and her things."

I looked at Charles wide-eyed. He could read my mind. *A village wedding? I can't believe our luck.*

"But we've lots of school work to do with exams coming up," he said to me in English. "Do we have time to take a day off to do this?"

"I've got to go," I said. "We may never have another opportunity to go to a village wedding. Schoolwork can wait until we get back. Tell him you need to take me along."

"All right," Charles told Boti in French, as he stirred sugar into his tea, "I can take you, but may my wife come along?" Boti was surprised I wanted to go, but said he'd be honored to have me attend his wedding.

Boti had no idea how excited I was next morning as I packed my camera in my shoulder bag along with a bottle of boiled filtered water and some tissues. Ever since we'd begun planning our trip to Africa, I'd hoped to see a village wedding, and here was one dropped, just like that, in my lap.

"We'd better eat a big breakfast," I told Charles as we prepared our morning tea. "No telling how long we'll be on the road and when or what we'll have to eat in the village." We scrambled some eggs to go with our usual bread, peanut butter, and marmalade.

"I think I'll eat a banana too," he said. "That should hold us."

Mid-morning we met at the garage where the Jeep was parked. Dressed in a new gray suit, white shirt, and little black bowtie, Boti looked like a bridegroom. Charles had made arrangements with Domingo, an Angolan refugee who worked as our school handyman and mechanic, to drive for us. Ian told us lots of wedding guests would try to hitch rides, overloading our already tired frail Jeep. He asked Charles to take the burden of responsibility and limit to six the number of people riding back with the bride's belongings.

We climbed in the front seat with Domingo while Boti and his friends stood in the back, holding on to the side-boards and leaning over the cab, their usual mode of transportation on huge transport trucks.

I'd never gone north on our road before, but soon realized the scenery was the same as in the other direction:

small mud brick houses clustered in tiny villages in the valleys between rolling hills covered in tall prairie grass and dotted with bush-like trees. As Domingo headed toward the river, dodging ruts and potholes, barely able to maintain a speed of ten to fifteen miles per hour, I asked him if he'd translate for us at the wedding. "It'll be so different for us and I'm afraid we won't understand what's happening."

"Don't worry, Madame. I'll be happy to translate for you." Domingo's native tongues were Kikongo and Lingala, the same ones spoken in this southwestern area of Congo. His third language – in which he'd received his education – was Portuguese. French was his fourth, learned after the war in Angola had forced him and his family across the border into Congo. As bright and quick as he was, I wondered how much English he understood, having been working around the British for several years.

"Ce n'est pas loin, Madame," Domingo said when I asked him how far we had to go. "Not far, maybe 20 kilometers." *That would be about twelve miles*, I quickly calculated. *About an hour's ride.*

When we came in sight of the bride's village, Boti leaned down, yelling into Domingo's window, motioning him to park off to the side under a large mango tree. As Boti and his friends dismounted, we were escorted to the porch of a nearby whitewashed house where we sat and watched the proceedings. A man came out and introduced himself, shaking our hands. "This is the village chief," Domingo translated. "He welcomes you to his village and says it is a great honor to have Americans here today to participate in the marriage of one of their daughters."

"We count it a great privilege to be here and are looking forward to the festivities," Charles said. The chief motioned two little boys forward. They handed us bottles of Fanta, a popular locally produced orange soda. We thanked them as they popped off the metal lids for us.

"Is this the chief's house?" I asked Domingo. He nodded. Charles leaned toward me and whispered, "Look around. I think we're being treated like the guests of honor."

"I'd just come to the same conclusion," I said. "I guess not too many Americans show up back here in these parts. I kind of feel like an intruder."

The whole village seemed to be gathering. Domingo assured me they would all be there, along with many of Boti's relatives and friends from his village. A lively loud man in a bright red shirt and dark pants seemed to be in charge. "He's the bride's mother's brother," Domingo said. "In our culture he's the one who's responsible for her. Her father is responsible for his sister's children. That's just the way we do it here."

Uncle supervised the placing of benches, making a vast rectangle under palms and mango trees in front of the bride's home – a typical structure built with handmade sun-dried bricks.

When everything seemed to be arranged and people were being seated, a man came and escorted us into the rectangle to soft chairs in the shade near the groom. Everyone else sat on backless benches or on the ground, talking and laughing. From time to time several women dressed in their usual attire of homemade blouses, wrap-around cloth skirts reaching to their ankles, and colorful kitambulas (a piece of cloth wrapped to make a beehive style headpiece), slowly walked by the guests handing out shelled peanuts and crispy fried banana chips from small white enamel bowls.

Off to the side a group of men beat out rhythmic African songs, accompanied by whistles that sounded like high-pitched piccolos, music we were accustomed to hearing on Saturdays at our school when our student scouts got together to sing and dance in a circle around the drummers.

"This is when the bargaining begins," Domingo said, pointing toward a line of women, including one who looked to be eight or nine months pregnant, coming from behind a nearby house. Those graceful women, their backs, necks, and heads ramrod straight, arms swaying at their sides, each carried a three or four gallon glass jug of white liquid to the bargaining area. There they bent their knees and someone helped them lift the jugs to the ground.

"What's in the jugs?" I asked.

"Homemade palm and sugar cane liquor. Boti has to pay a dowry to Jeanne's family: money, liquor, and some clothes. Boti's uncle will be his lawyer and argue with her uncle, the one in the red shirt. Finally they'll reach an agreement. It's all done in fun. The families always choose an uncle who's lively and will give a show for the guests."

And argue they did. Jeanne's uncle waved his arms and shouted. He tasted the liquor, passed the cup to his brothers. They shook their heads and asked to taste another. Again they shook their heads. "They say he needs to bring out more liquor," Domingo said, as a woman approached with a crate of orange Fanta. Everyone on Boti's side cheered and clapped. Uncle threw up his hands, got mad, and stomped out.

When he saw more items being brought out he came back to look them over: two nine-yard pieces of new cloth, a pretty head scarf, a raincoat. The uncles continued to argue and confer with their brothers. Two more women approached with jugs and deposited them. After more tasting and more arm waving, suddenly the two uncles clasped hands, clapped each other on the back. The deal was made. The show was over. The crowd roared their approval.

Then Boti's uncle called for the bride to be presented. Several women unfolded and placed a large colorful African cloth in the center of our rectangle. We sat for another half hour before she made her appearance. At first I wasn't sure which one was the bride, since they were all dressed in typical African clothes made from the usual Congolese material.

Domingo leaned over and said, "She's the one that looks sad, the one with the green kitambula on her head."

Jeanne looked as though she'd come to her mother's funeral. Her sisters, singing "Alleluia," escorted her onto the cloth inside the rectangle of guests." I'd never seen anyone look so forlorn and genuinely pitied the girl, finding it hard to believe Domingo's explanation.

"She's leaving her home and family so she's supposed to look sad. It's part of the act," he said. "The crowd will now try to make her smile or laugh. If she does, she'll never live it down."

The bride and groom were seated beside each other on a couch and the uncles took turns counseling them. Domingo said they were giving them good advice about loving and caring for each other, working hard, and remaining faithful. After going through several rituals of drinking some of the liquor, the bride fed her husband some bread she'd baked. And then they were considered married.

But Uncle wanted to torment them more. He linked their arms, took Boti's hat and sunglasses and put them on Jeanne, and placed her headscarf on Boti's head. "Photo, photo," he called as the uncles draped themselves over the newly weds still trying to make Jeanne smile. She never did. Charles snapped the last picture on our film as daylight was fading.

The chief invited Domingo, some teachers from the village elementary school, and us into his home for a special meal: an appetizing stew of boiled chicken combined with palm oil, onions, and hot pili-pili peppers, served with chiquanga. We followed the teachers, tearing off bite-sized pieces of sticky chiquanga from their chunk and then using a spoon dipped it into the chicken and broth. Although Charles enjoyed the sour chiquanga I found it distasteful. Not wanting to offend our host, I smothered tiny bits in the hot spicy chicken as we chatted a little through our interpreter.

As we finished dinner, the chief presented us with a live

rooster, his wings and feet tied. Overwhelmed by his hospitality we thanked him in Kikongo. "Tutondele beni," Charles said, shaking his hand. The chief smiled and thanked us for coming. Carrying our chicken, we followed Domingo to the Jeep where, just as Ian had warned, 25 people were loaded and ready to ride. An argument ensued when Domingo asked them in Kikongo to get off. Finally Charles waved his hands and told them in French that nobody could ride, that Boti had hired the truck to transport Jeanne's things and so it would be. The truck bed was cleared and Jeanne's possessions were loaded. She and Boti and half a dozen of their friends made the return trip with us. Once we left the village Jeanne began laughing and teasing her husband and I realized the sad face really had been a farce.

Since Christian churches in Congo don't accept village rituals as a marriage, the couple still had to come before a minister for the religious ceremony. So when we arrived back at school we deposited Jeanne at the girls' dormitories where she stayed until the pastor married them two days later.

"Do you remember what we gave them for a wedding present?" I asked, scanning our pictures.

"Maybe some kind of food?" Charles suggested.

"I don't know. In a letter I'd written home I said we'd run out of film and never got to take any photos of Jeanne and the two little bridesmaids at the religious ceremony."

"I can't recall that part at all," Charles said. "But I'll never forget those uncles bargaining in the village."

"After 35 years I can see most of that wedding as vividly as the day it took place."

Jeanne's uncle bargaining for her dowry.

# Augsburger Tent Crusade
# July 1957

**"M**om, Anita and I want to go to Myron Augsburger's tent revival down in Lancaster this evening," I said, as we shelled lima beans on the porch one hot afternoon in early August. I was hoping since I'd had my driver's license for several weeks she'd let me take the family car.

"You know your father needs to go to work tonight. Call Peter Smith and see if you can get a ride with him again." Our deacon took people along to church all the time. That's how Mom and Daddy ended up Mennonites in the first place - he'd taken them to a revival service.

"I was just thinking about calling you," Peter said when he answered the phone. "Nancy's not feeling well and I'd be more than happy to take you girls along again. We'll leave a little earlier tonight. Be out at the end of your lane at six o'clock. That way I can park close to the tent. You know how crowded it gets. They said 5,000 people attended yesterday."

When Peter popped over the hill, we were ready and waiting in our long flowered print cotton dresses with pleated skirts and capes, our white coverings fastened to our hair with straight pins, and our usual black nylons and shoes. All the way to Lancaster Peter kept up a running conversation about his farm, Sunday school, people he'd met and invited to church, revival services, occasionally asking a question and giving us a chance to speak.

Three policemen with yellow neon stripes on their shirts were directing traffic off Route 30 into the dirt lane leading to the hay field where the huge six-pole tent had been set up. Peter turned his black '57 Ford Galaxy past the "Revival - All Welcome" sign and got in the line of vehicles bumping along the rutted lane, following the directions of young Mennonite men who'd volunteered to park cars.

"Augsburger's a powerful speaker," Peter said, waving his hand toward the hundreds of parked cars. "He has drawing power."

"I love to hear him preach," Anita said. And she was right. This young preacher mesmerized our whole family. We'd heard him many times when he was invited to come to the Lancaster area to speak at an All Day Meeting or a Weekend Bible Conference.

"This is a huge undertaking," Peter continued. "I came down here two weeks ago and helped the volunteers. They cleared the hayfield and then we helped unload and set up all this equipment - the tent, chairs, lights, everything. And next week they'll come back and take it all down and reload it."

"Sounds like a lot of work," I said.

"But we always have enough help. The Lancaster Mennonites come out when there's a tent campaign." At least ten long rows of black cars were already lined up in the field on each side of the big tent. "This is the most I've seen yet," Peter said, pulling in beside a pickup.

"Where will we meet you?" I asked, as Anita and I picked up our Bibles and purses and slid out of the back seat.

"Take your time," Peter answered, adjusting his black hat. "Find some friends to talk to; we'll leave after the crowd thins out."

Looking at each other, we grinned, knowing how Peter

liked to talk and that suited us just fine. We had lots of Mennonite friends we didn't get to see often and we knew most of them would be here.

Inside the big top, being a deacon, Peter walked down to the front where he always sat with the ordained men, stopping now and then to shake hands and exchange a holy kiss with other men seated along the aisle.

The same bright red, blue, and white banners that had been hung over the platform on the first day of this two-week campaign still proclaimed:

*Christ for the World - the World for Christ*
*Jesus said, "Ye must be born again!"*

Anita and I strolled through the hay stubble down the aisle past women, their uncut hair wound into buns on the backs of their heads and covered with nylon net coverings, seated with their husbands. Little girls in homemade dresses, long braids hanging down their backs, their barefoot brothers in dark pants, white shirts, and suspenders. It was odd to see families sitting together. But separated in such a large crowd, they'd never find each other.

We found seats as the congregation began singing even though it wasn't yet seven-thirty. "That's J. Mark Stauffer on the platform leading again tonight," Anita leaned over and whispered. I nodded. My sister had told me he was Professor of Music at Eastern Mennonite College, her school in Virginia. And how awesome their acappella four-part harmony was in chapel, just like we were hearing tonight. Chills ran down my spine as I joined thousands of voices around and under that tent singing the old church hymns.

Those summer revivals were stirring. Myron Augsburger was a dynamic speaker and put us face to face with God. His articulate sermons showed good solid Bible study as he condemned and named sin. But we thronged back night after night to be cleansed, uplifted, and consecrated. Christ was presented as the only answer for the ills of the world. Myron called us to accept God's atonement for forgiveness of sins.

This evening was no different from the other nights we'd been there. As Myron closed his sermon, he stretched out his left hand toward us, his open Bible on his flat palm, lifted his right hand to God, and extended the invitation to us: "Tonight I ask you to do the wise thing. Come to Calvary, accept God's love, and give your life to Him. God will forgive your sin and give you eternal peace."

With countless others under that big top I bowed my head and vowed once again to be faithful in private devotions, love people, and find a way to be of service to others. J. Mark Stauffer stood, and raising his right arm, began singing softly, "Just As I Am Without One Plea." From all around us deep bass, melodic tenors, mellow altos, and soaring sopranos joined him, blending their voices as one. We sang verse after verse from memory, privately committing our lives again to the Saviour, while countless others made their way down the aisle to meet with counselors at the front.

After the benediction was pronounced, I turned to my sister and said, "Since we have plenty of time, let's go back to the bookstore. I want to buy one of those crusade books they were talking about during the announcements." We made our way through the crowd to the small tent where Mennonite Publishing House had provided a small store of Christian literature and Bibles. Inside I joined the hoards, wandering past the tables, touching shiny new covers of my favorite Christian fiction, admiring the stacks of King James Bibles, and yearning for the latest Mennonite Hour record albums. I used a dollar from my babysitting money and bought a "Crusade for Christ" booklet.

As my sister chatted with friends, I scanned the first pages about the Christian Laymen's Tent Evangelism, a group of about two hundred Mennonites based in Ohio but also some from Virginia and Pennsylvania, whose goal was to provide equipment and facilities for mass evangelism, depending on freewill offerings to meet their expenses. Myron Augsburger, who was pastoring a church in Sarasota, Florida, had become their evangelist in the summer of 1955. Turning over the pages I found a photo of the handsome dark curly-haired evangelist seated with his wife Esther and their two small sons.

"We'd better go look for Peter," my sister said over my shoulder. "The crowd's starting to thin out."

We found him near the platform deep in conversation with fellow-ordained men. "I guess it's time to be going," he said when he saw us.

Peter Smith drove down our bumpy lane and dropped us off at our barn. In the twilight we headed down the walk past the grape arbor to the front porch where our mother had come, hoping for a cool evening breeze. "Mom, you and Daddy just have to go to the tent revival," I said. "Myron Augsburger is the best preacher. Look, I bought their crusade book. They even included two of his sermons."

"Well, I thought maybe we'd go Sunday night when Daddy won't be working," she said, paging through my booklet.

During the sermon at that last Sunday night service, Myron stressed the importance of doing something practical to serve the Lord. After an extended invitation calling sinners to repentance, a member of the Mission Board stepped up to the pulpit and made an impassioned plea for volunteers to come forward and dedicate two weeks of their time in service to the Lord, teaching Vacation Bible School in a new housing project in upstate New York. "This is the kind of practical service Brother Myron was talking about tonight," he said. "We know that in this large congregation the Lord is speaking to hearts. Will you say yes to God? All you have to do is get up out of your seat, come down to the platform, and sign up to go and teach these children."

I looked wide-eyed at my sister Anita and she nodded. We both enjoyed children and had had several years experience teaching Bible School, so we turned to our parents. In the heat of the moment they agreed. We came out of our seats and headed down the aisle.

Peter Smith saw us coming and met us there at the front, elated with our decision. While he introduced us to the chairman of the Mission Board, the congregation stood and sang, waiting at their seats as men and teenage boys started at the back folding the metal chairs and carrying them to a central point. In a matter of minutes the rows were gone. The chairs were stacked and ready for the vans. Volunteers would come early the next morning, tear down the tent, and load everything.

Someone took our phone number, telling us to go home and pack; they would call us with details of where and when to meet the other four volunteers later in the week. The tent crusade with its wonderful sermons and awesome singing had ended, but my sister and I were anticipating an exciting new adventure.

Augsburger Tent Crusade under the big top in 1957 near
Lancaster, Pennsylvania.

# Matondo, A Baptist Association Meeting February 1968

Two months after we arrived in Congo Ian made an announcement in French one Monday at morning prayers: Wednesday afternoon our students would help the Congolese teachers build an enclosure for Matondo. Everyone seemed to know what he meant, so during a break between classes I asked Lesley if she'd explain.

"Matondo means thanksgiving in Kikongo," she said. "Twice a year – in February and September – we have Association Meetings here on our mission post for Baptists who live within a fifty-mile radius."

"Oh, I get it," I said, tapping my forehead. "That sounds like our Mennonite Conference meetings, or tent campaigns. They actually come that far to attend?" I asked, thinking about the muddy roads at that time of year.

"Oh, yes. They come from poor outlying villages, so most walk. If they've saved up enough, or their local church pays, they ride on transport trucks."

"What's the enclosure Ian mentioned?"

"The church is too small, so we build an enclosure."

"Do you have a schedule of events?"

"It's always the same. Everyone knows, but announcements will be made."

"I'd find it helpful if you could give me a run down of the activities," I said, pulling out my notebook and jotting down the schedule as she reeled off times and activities.

### *Matondo, February 1968*

*All Day Thurs. and Fri.: Meetings for Pastors, Deacons, and members*

| | | |
|---|---|---|
| *Friday Morning* | *9:00:* | *Interview Candidates for Baptism as Scheduled* |
| *Saturday Morning* | *9:00:* | *Grand Entrance of Villages; Introductions* |
| | *10:00:* | *Preaching by Charlie Harvey, Canadian missionary* |
| | *11:00:* | *Baptism in the River* |
| | *12:00:* | *Dinner* |
| | *3:00:* | *Separate Meetings for Men, Women, Youth* |
| | *7:00:* | *Storytelling by villagers and students* |
| *Sunday Morning* | *9:00:* | *Choirs, Preaching, Baptism in the River* |
| | *12:00:* | *Dinner* |
| | *3:00:* | *Sermon, Membership Cards to New Members, Communion* |

Wednesday after lunch I walked over to the primary school to watch and take pictures. There, under a grove of mango trees, Congolese secondary instructors, elementary teachers, and our students were pushing tall stakes into the ground at four-or five-foot intervals to build a fence about forty feet across and thirty feet deep. They intertwined the posts with thin green saplings the whole way around, one row about two feet off the ground and another three feet above it.

Vadia in tattered brown shorts and ragged shirt climbed palm trees and cut long green branches for building the enclosure. I was terrified he'd fall, towering thirty feet above us at times. But he laughed and said, "Oh, non, non, je ne vais pas tomber, Madame," pointing to the leather belt securely fastened around the tree. He'd slipped it over his head and leaned into it with his back, keeping it taut as he shinnied up the trunk using his feet and hands.

The children giggled and laughed when they saw I my anxious look. A cheer went up when Vadia started cutting. They ran backwards as a branch fell, then rushed forward to grab it up and search for palm tree larvae – fat squirming white worms, like the cutworms we fed to our chickens back in Pennsylvania. Finding one, they'd wrap and tie it securely in a leaf before dragging the branch to the fence. Those larvae, boiled with tomato paste and onions, would make a tasty high protein soup for their supper.

Désiré supervised the students poking palm branches between horizontal saplings that held them upright, forming a tight enclosure about eight to ten feet high. He'd been doing this for years, from the time he first came here to school as a child, then as a teen, and now as a teacher in our elementary school. The children respected Désiré; he spoke French quite well and had a manner of authority about him in his freshly creased seams and white shirt.

My students wanted to pose for pictures. "Venez ici, Madame," they'd shout, gesturing with their hands. When I explained I wanted photos of them working, showing what they were doing, they went back to pounding, pushing, cutting, stuffing.

"Why are you building this enclosure?" I asked Désiré in French. "I know the church is too small for these meetings, but why not just have the services out here on the grass without a fence?"

"Everybody's distracted by people walking along the paths, and it helps keep out chickens and dogs," he said, pushing another palm branch in place. I knew what he meant. Just last Sunday a dog had slept through the sermon, lying on the platform, and two chickens had strolled down the center aisle looking for cockroaches.

Students carried all the straight-backed benches from the church to the enclosure and placed them in rows, three sections across. More seating was needed for the crowds that would attend, so deacons rounded up boards kept in storage to make additional benches. Several of our biggest soccer players carried the podium and communion table from the church and placed them at the front. Since we were at the beginning of the wet season, I wondered what would happen if it rained. But nobody seemed concerned.

Lesley told me most deacons from the surrounding villages had arrived by Wednesday evening. Some stayed with friends or relatives, but many more bedded down in primary classrooms on bedrolls. My houseboy, Mpanzu, a deacon in the church, took Thursday and Friday off. When he came by in the afternoon to do a few chores and carry several buckets of cistern water into the kitchen for me, I asked him what they'd debated. But he said he couldn't express it in French; he didn't know the vocabulary.

I knew one of the major points was the lives of the candidates for baptism, whether they acted like Christians and were ready to be baptized. "It sounds more like a Mennonite than a Baptist custom," I said when Lesley told me.

By the time Saturday morning classes ended at nine o'clock so our students could attend the meetings, I'd already taught my seven-thirty freshman Geography of Africa and my eight-fifteen History of Congo. I raced home on my bike, dumped my books on the kitchen table, and got a quick snack before walking to the enclosure with Charles, camera in tow. Our whole school was required to attend. I think the students would have preferred to have the day off, but I was most interested in the proceedings.

Being newcomers, and Americans at that, Charles and I were invited by Pastor Kwama to come and sit up front with the honored guests on chairs he'd had carried from his house. We declined, saying we needed to be near our students. Lesley had saved me a seat beside her behind the eighth grade girls, where I could observe and take photos without disrupting the proceedings. She translated the services for me since they were all in Kikongo, the women and many village men not understanding French.

This opening service began with a welcoming ceremony for the people from surrounding villages. Our students, faculty, and the locals were seated inside the enclosure, men on one side, women on the other. A traditional African band of eight teachers and students stood outside the fence in white shirts and their best trousers creased as though for army inspection, beating drums, playing flutes, and blowing whistles.

The visitors gathered further away, near the primary school, until the parade began. They came, one village at a time, singing a hymn, banner held high, marching across campus and into the enclosure. Once inside and standing at the front, the congregation greeted them with applause and a traditional welcoming song. And then the next group trudged down the path and up the aisle to be greeted.

After all had finally entered the enclosure, singing had ceased, and the banners were leaning against the front "wall," the pastor introduced visiting dignitaries: Charlie and Fran Harvey, Canadians who'd served Angolan refugees for years, first in Angola and now in Congo, he as a missionary pastor, she as a nurse. Dora and Lily Jenks, sisters who'd worked in Congo for 29 years. Lesley told me Dora was a secretary at their British mission headquarters in Kinshasa. That she'd worked as a translator for Dag Hammarskjold when the Secretary-General of the United Nations had visited Congo four times trying to resolve the civil war in the aftermath of independence. Dora had traveled with him when he came to Congo, but fortunately she wasn't with him on his last visit, just four years earlier, when he was killed in a plane crash.

Then Pastor Kwama introduced Charles and me. We heard our names and the word Americani. Knowing we didn't understand Kikongo, he repeated it in French, asking us to stand. Everyone turned around smiling and staring at the first Americans ever to work on this mission post and probably the first most of them had ever seen. As he continued talking, the women all nodded and hummed. Some giggled out loud. The schoolgirls turned and smiled, proud to be students of these newly arrived Americans.

"What did he say?" I whispered to Lesley as I sat down.

"That you're just a young girl and that's why you don't have any children yet." I rolled my eyes. I knew Congolese feel sorry for anyone who's childless. I knew they'd be watching and listening for any rumor of a baby.

On Saturday afternoon men, women, and youth met in separate meetings. I followed Lesley to the women's meeting inside the enclosure; the men carried several benches back to the church; the youth sat on the grass in the distance and before long we heard them singing to the beat of their drums and whistles.

The lady deacons from our post were in charge of our

service. Someone read a passage in Kikongo, another prayed. A ladies' choir performed for us. They were dressed identically in blouses and traditional wrap-around skirts made from light brown cloth covered with large yellow and blue sunbursts. Some carried babies tied on their backs. "They're from Kinshasa," Lesley whispered as they assembled at the front.

I recognized most of the old church hymns they harmonized with an African flair, a lead singer beginning, the others singing underneath her or coming in on the chorus. Several women accompanied them with percussion instruments and whistles; one lady beat a handmade skin-covered drum tied in front of her with a matching cloth. Another held a five-foot-long notched hollow log about four inches in diameter. With her right hand she rubbed a little six-inch round stick up and down the notches in rhythm to the music, making a clicking sound. The most fascinating instrument was a rattle made from two tin cans, shaped and soldered together into a cylinder with a point on one end and a handle on the other. Tiny stones inside made a tinkling sound as it was shaken. They sang from the heart, their voices blending in praise to their Lord.

Lily Jenks spoke to the women in Kikongo. I admired this seasoned missionary who'd given most of her life to work in tropical Africa, spreading God's love and training women how to teach other women. Lesley translated for me, writing as I read over her shoulder. Lily, in her sweet grandmotherly voice, encouraged these hard-working women not to neglect their own spiritual lives, to read their Kikongo Bibles, to teach their children, to love their husbands. To be Godly women.

The girls thought Lesley and I were passing notes during the service. They asked me about it later. When I told them she was translating for me, they seemed surprised. I guess since they understand and speak several languages it hadn't occurred to them their teacher might not.

When the church bell rang that evening we got our flashlights and climbed the hill to a bonfire so huge we wondered where they could have found that much wood. Amid drums and whistles, our students led us to ringside benches reserved for special guests. Our whole student body and many Matondo participants were seated on the grass, talking, animated, anxious for the stories to begin.

Sabakinu and Lufimpadio, two of our middle school teachers sat beside us to summarize the stories. "The best storytellers from the villages will be telling African fables tonight," Sabakinu said.

"Dramatic stories with animals as characters," Lufimpadio added. Watching them perform these ad-libbed plays was entertaining in itself, but with the added interpretation, the stories came alive for us.

"This one will be in French," Lufimpadio said. We listened as several of our seniors dramatized the story of a man who swaggered into a village, asking for a teaching position in their primary school.

"You'll have to teach French, you know," the chief said, sitting tall in his chair.

The man nodded.

"How's your French?" the chief asked, thumping his ornately carved cane, a symbol of his position and authority.

"I talk French real good," the man said, shifting from one foot to the other.

"Conjugate the verb être."

"Nous suis, j'a, vous est," (we am, I has, you is) the man stammered as the audience guffawed and howled, slapping their legs, remembering their own experiences with such primary school teachers.

"Get out!" shouted the chief. "You can't teach at our school." The man begged and pleaded for a job until he was run out of town, the audience applauding and hooting as he ran away.

"Next is a fable about Mr. Rat and Mr. Tricky Lion," Sabakinu said as two men stirred up the bonfire and others threw on more wood. "This'll be in Kikongo. We'll tell you what's being said, although you'll understand a lot from the actions."

Two villagers came into the area serving as a stage in front of the bonfire, each wearing a long fabric tail, one with yarn resembling a mane. "That's Mr. Lion," Sabakinu said. "The other one is his wife." The crowd fell silent as the two lions began an animated conversation. "He's telling her to send word to his friend Mr. Rat that he's very ill. Even though Rat has always treated him kindly, Lion wants to kill him."

A messenger ran to the side of the bonfire near a tree, waving his arms and talking to Mr. Rat in the shadows, gesturing for him to follow. But Rat, paper ears sticking up and whiskers painted across his cheeks, ignored the invitation.

Mr. Lion pounded the ground with his front paws, yelling and screaming at his wife, crackling wood accentuating his words. "He's saying he'll catch Rat and eat him up. He's telling his wife to send word that he died." When Lion brandished his machete, lay down on his mat, and hid his knife beside him, the audience hissed and booed. His wife covered him with a blanket.

The messenger again ran around the bonfire to the tree, and found Mr. Rat in the dim shadows. For a second time he talked and gestured back toward the Lions. "Mr. Rat is telling himself he doesn't want to offend his friend, but finds it hard to believe Lion's really dead. He's decided to go and test him." Rat put on a big hat with several tall rooster feathers waving on top, picked up his walking stick, and stepped out of the darkness into the searing heat and bright flames of the roaring fire. As he approached Lion's house he began to wail and sob. Mrs. Lion came out to meet him. By now the audience had become more animated, laughing and gesturing in anticipation.

"She's saying, 'Why didn't you come before he died?' He answers, 'I was busy, but I'm here now.' Mrs. Lion tells him to come and sit in the chief mourner's chair close to her husband's head. 'Before I mourn I'll call the jungle animals to bury him,' Rat answers," Sabakinu translated.

Lufimpadio took up the story. "Rat says he must make sure Mr. Lion is dead before they bury him. Only then will he be able to properly mourn his friend." Mr. Rat shuffled around, keeping his distance, but Lion never moved. Finally Rat stood in front of him and shouted. Lion's front paw shot high up in the air, red and yellow flames dancing behind him. The crowd erupted in laughter.

"He said, 'If you're really dead, raise your right paw,'" Sabakinu chuckled. Rat grinned, rolled his eyes to the audience, and moved to Lion's back side. "He's placing himself between the Lion and an opening to a tunnel that leads to his home." Rat again shouted and Lion began shaking.

"He told Lion to shake all over if he's really dead." The crowd went wild as Lion, realizing he'd been duped, jumped to his feet, grabbed his machete, and lunged toward Mr. Rat. But Rat was too quick and disappeared into his tunnel behind the tree, although we could still see his long tail. In an instant Lion pounced, holding it down with his paw. Rat called out, Lion lifted his paw and the tail disappeared and the crowd again went wild, kids jumping up and down, dancing round and round.

"What did he say?" I asked.

"He said, "Why are you trying to hold onto that little old tree root?' He tricked him again," Sabakinu laughed. The actors bowed as everybody cheered and whistled and drums rolled.

Then a man stood and quieted the audience. Lufimpadio

translated. "Be careful. Satan is wandering around like a roaring lion, waiting to deceive, to destroy, causing us to do wrong. Never make friends with the devil. Be alert. Don't let him trick you. Give your heart to Jesus and try to please God."

"He's a pastor in a village about five miles from here," Sabakinu said. "Their congregation is growing and they're building a new church."

"His members certainly did a good job illustrating an important truth," I said. "Their acting was great." We stayed through several more little plays, but when the singing began we decided to head on home.

"Do you know what's happening at this afternoon's meeting?" Charles asked as we finished our Sunday dinner of leftover saka-saka and rice.

"For one thing they're going to give certificates of membership to the ones who were baptized this morning and welcome them into church fellowship," I said, clearing the table.

"And communion?"

"After a long sermon, I'm sure."

"I hope they don't get too long. You know it always rains by three or four o'clock."

"I'm sure Tata Kwama'll move things along," I said, spreading on the dining room table the white cloth and matching napkins I'd recently finished cross-stitching.

"I hope so, or we'll get soaked."

I arranged my nicest cups, saucers, small plates, and my little English teapot so the embroidery showed. "Don't worry about it. He won't want the pulpit and communion table getting wet. You do know Dora and Lily are coming by for tea after the service?"

"I remember," he said, staring out the window at the clouds. "You have everything ready, don't you?"

"Now I do. The teakettle's filled on the stove. I just have to light the burner. When they get here I'll set out some of my cookies. I don't want them out of the tin yet. They'll get droopy in this humidity."

Just then the church bell rang. "I thought they said the service would begin at three," Charles said, looking at his watch. "It's only two o'clock.

"They probably hurried their meal along so they can start earlier to avoid the rains," I said, gathering up my purse and French Bible.

We walked up the path past the primary school buildings where several women were cleaning huge pots they'd used to cook dried beans for lunch. When we waved and I called out to them, "Kiambote, Mamas," they bent over laughing, slapping their knees.

They waved back, calling out, "Ah, kiambote, Madame. Kiambote, Monsieur," laughing at their pronunciation of these French words, but using them as a sign of respect for foreigners. I knew these simple village women were delighted I had greeted them, yet hesitant to speak. I knew they found it amusing to see me walking openly with my husband, something they would never dare to do.

We cut across the grass to the enclosure where many of our students, smartly dressed in their freshly pressed school uniforms, were already seated. I helped Lesley check the girls' roll. They were all present, anxious to share this first communion with their classmates who'd just been baptized.

As a village pastor handed out membership cards and gave advice to the new followers on how to remain faithful to God and the church, fluffy white clouds were building up in the gray sky, pushing in closer and closer, beginning to hide the sun.

When a few drops of rain fell, Tata Kwama stood and said the communion service would start immediately to ensure the newly baptized members would participate in this ritual. Lady deacons dressed in white hurried to the front and uncovered plates holding squares of cut up bread on the communion table.

Charlie Harvey prayed in Kikongo, asking God's blessing on the new members, and on those partaking of the communion, that their hearts and lives would be pure and they would remain faithful. The first round of deaconesses quickly carried the bread to the congregation. Others followed with trays of individual communion cups, each containing several drops of grenadine. These too were distributed down the rows.

The clouds were turning black and the wind was picking up as Pastor Kwama pronounced the benediction. Several strong men picked up the pulpit and communion table and hurried to the church. Others grabbed their village banners and everyone scattered. Charles grabbed my hand and we ran down the path and onto our porch just as the rain fell in sheets.

Sitting on our veranda watching torrents of rain gush from black clouds, thunder roaring and rumbling around us, I recalled those long communion services back in Pennsylvania when I was a child. I wondered how my Mennonite bishop would have reacted to barefoot women scurrying around serving communion in individual cups instead of the traditional plain pewter mug. And using grenadine instead of grape juice. And allowing people who aren't members to participate. And what would he think if he knew that I had taken communion today with Baptists?

Building the Matondo enclosure for the Baptist Association
weekend meetings.

Kinshasa women's choir performing at Matondo.

# Vacation Bible School in New York August 1957

Bath, New York
Sunday evening, August 18, 1957

Dear Mom and Daddy,

I know you're anxious to hear from us so I decided to write and let you know what's happening up here in New York. Lloyd was a good driver, but we thought the trip would never end. The six of us arrived at the Weaver's farm last evening just as they were finishing the milking. Levi's wife had supper ready for us at their house. She has a darling little dark-haired baby, Carol Sue, and some other kids but I don't know their names yet. Lloyd will be sleeping at Levi's. Ethel, Dorothy, and Lorraine, the three girls who rode up with us from Lancaster County, are staying with Levi's brother Irvin's family in their huge farmhouse.

After supper, Levi drove Anita and me to Mr. and Mrs. Olin Morrow's house at 5 Elm Street in town, which is where we'll be staying for the next two weeks. The Morrows are a conservative Mennonite couple in their sixties. When they go out he puts on a plain coat and she wears a big covering with white strings and a cape dress. But around the house she wears fancy aprons. He likes to crochet and she does woodworking in her little shop in the garage. They both said they're going to make us a gift while we're here. I guess hers is something to do with sewing because she asked us if we sew and was happy to hear we do.

Anita and I are sharing a front guestroom upstairs with a colorful chenille spread on the bed and lacy Priscilla curtains at double windows that overlook a quiet residential street. I think it was her daughter Catherine's room. We hung our dresses in the large wardrobe and each of us has a drawer for our other things in an oak dresser. But we can hardly find space to put our coverings and hairpins at night. Every square inch on the dresser tops is covered with picture frames holding photos of guess who: Catherine. She was a cute kid with curly hair and a happy smile. Her parents talk about her all the time.

This morning we attended services at the only church in this farming community: West Union Mennonite, a former community church that Levi and Irvin opened last year when they moved their families up here from Pennsylvania. It's a white frame building, but it doesn't look anything like our Mennonite churches at home with its big bell tower over the main entrance. At least the tall narrow windows with the arched tops aren't stained glass.

The members want to build up attendance, which is the main reason why they're having this Bible School. After the morning service we all went to Levi and Irvin's farm and had a picnic dinner. They and their wives work hard to make a living, but seem to have easy-going personalities and get along well. Irvin's wife, who's expecting a baby, already has several children including Timmy and David. They'll both be in my kindergarten class.

In the afternoon we piled into cars and drove to nearby

Beaver Valley, the large new community where we'll be teaching. We spent two hours going door-to-door delivering gospel tracts and flyers inviting the children to vacation Bible school.

Afterwards we all met back at the big round brown tent, which the men had set up on Saturday, to see where our classes will be held and to get our "rooms" ready. My kindergarten children will sit on a long bench on each side of a piece of plywood laid on two sawhorses, our table, behind a curtain at the back edge. Levi gave us supplies and I had fun setting up my classroom: Bible school books and packets, lesson pictures, stars, scissors, glue, and crayons. I hung my attendance chart on one of the tent poles.

Anita and I spent most of the evening cutting out tomorrow morning's craft and reviewing our lessons. This is the third time I've taught Herald Press' kindergarten Bible school lessons this summer, so I feel quite comfortable with the material.

I'll write more later and let you know how many children show up. Anita says hello and to tell you she doesn't have time to write, but she will later. (She's reading Mrs. Morrow's books)! Your loving daughter, Janet

Bath, New York
Wednesday, August 21, 1957

Dear Mom and Daddy,

I'm so glad you decided to let Anita and me come up here for two weeks to teach even though it's a hardship for you. As Brother Myron Augsburger said at his tent meeting, we need to do what we say. We can dedicate our life to God, but if we aren't willing to go and serve, our words are vain and profit nothing.

Bible School was a great success the first three mornings. On the first day Levi and Irvin had the kids all line up at a table under an oak tree to register as they arrived. The children looked different from the Mennonite ones we teach at home. Here we don't see waist-length pigtails or plain long-sleeved dresses. Most of the girls have short hair with bangs and wear anklets and patent leather shoes. A lot of the older ones wear full skirts over wide crinolines with white bobby socks and saddle shoes. But they're interested in our lessons and we're glad they come.

Sixteen darling little four and five-year-olds showed up for my class. These people don't have lots of religious activities like we do with all our churches down in Lancaster County, so they're happy to send their children to our Bible school.

Levi and Irvin want us to get our students ready to participate in a program for parents next Friday. We'll have our last regular morning session and then come back that evening for the program. They're hoping for a big turnout of adults. So every day I need to practice our verses with my students.

Mrs. Morrow fixes us a big breakfast every morning before we leave for Bible school. She seems overjoyed to have us here since her daughter has moved to Florida. Pictures of Catherine hang on the walls and cover every table in the living room as well as the dressers in our bedroom. I think they must be kind of lonely without her. They both talk and bombard us with questions the minute we walk in the house. They want to know about our family and, as I said, they talk incessantly about Catherine.

Mr. Morrow is crocheting a pretty little purple and white doily for each of us. He has one almost finished. Mrs. Morrow showed us her workshop this afternoon. She cut out two roosters for us with her band saw and fastened them to a base. I don't know what she's going to do with them. Anita says hello and to tell you she'll write soon. (She's still reading). Love, Janet

Bath, New York
Tuesday, August 27, 1957

Dear Mom and Daddy,

Thank you for your letter, which Mrs. Morrow gave us when we got back from Bible School at noon. We're sorry we can't be there to help you can tomatoes and shell limas. No, don't send our mail. It probably won't arrive in time if you forward it to us here.

I want to tell you about our trip to Niagara Falls. When we arrived last week the Weavers said we should plan to visit the falls on the weekend. So that's what we did on Saturday. We five girls, Dorothy, Lorraine, Ethel, Anita, and I piled into Lloyd's car at five o'clock in the morning so we'd have plenty of time at the falls. Levi's wife packed us a huge lunch in a cardboard box: sandwiches, cookies, carrots and celery, apples, and a gallon thermos of cool aid.

When we got there Lloyd found a parking space on the hill across from the American Falls. We crawled out of his car and stood there, hanging on the fence for a long time, just staring at what has to be one of the most spectacular sights in the world - foaming, churning, steaming water pouring itself out over the edge of a cliff. Lloyd said we should climb over the wire, scramble down the bank, and have a picnic on the little beach at the bottom, directly across the river from the American falls. We didn't see any signs and nobody seemed to mind, but Anita and I worried about what it looked like for Mennonite girls to do that, wearing our coverings and all. It's a wonder we didn't tear our dresses and nylons or sprain our ankles on the way down, but the view was worth that chance.

We spread Mrs. Weaver's tablecloth on a large flat rock and sat around it facing that foaming wall. After lunch we stayed for the longest time soaking up the atmosphere, watching the never ending roaring water plunging to the rocks below, its rumbling resounding through the valley, it's fine mist reaching us even there, on the other side.

As we walked around I remembered your stories about coming here with Daddy on your honeymoon and wondered if we were walking and standing on the same spots where you and Daddy stood. The Canadian Horseshoe Falls are incredibly large; we couldn't get enough of watching them either. We saw the cable car across the whirlpool that you always talked about. There's no way I'd ever be persuaded to get in it either!

We got home about midnight, tired and ready to sleep. That's what I need to do now. Anita's already snoozing. Love, Janet

Bath, New York
Friday, August 29, 1957

Dear Mom and Daddy,

You probably won't get this letter until after we get home, but I just had to write. We finished our tenth day of Vacation Bible School this morning. I had all my students line up at the fence and had Levi take a class picture. All sixteen of them held up their little Bible verse paper cutouts from today's lesson. They're such cute children; I'll miss them.

Last evening Mr. and Mrs. Morrow took us to a Gideon picnic. He's a Gideon. You know, the group that hands out Bibles. He talks a lot about their work, putting Bibles in hotels, hospitals, and doctors' offices. He said they even gave out New Testaments to the local school children. Mrs. Morrow insisted we go with them. They've been so nice to us, so we decided we should. They're the only Mennonites in the group but the others didn't seem to mind that we're plain; they just want to get Bibles handed out. We sat at long tables covered with white sheets under the trees in someone's backyard. They cooked chicken on a barbecue grill and the ladies brought wonderful salads and desserts.

I'll wait until we get home to tell you about the other two places we visited this week: the Corning Glass factory on Monday afternoon, and Watkins Glen on Tuesday. Watkins Glen is an area in the mountains near here that's been eroded by a small stream until it became a deep ravine, like a mini-Grand Canyon. They've reinforced the sides with rocks and cement, and made paths with stairs so you can walk the length of it. At times the mountain was split in two by the stream that had torn the surface away exposing the edges of layers and layers of shale. And then again evergreens towered over us. I doubt I'll ever see a more gorgeous sight. I hope my pictures come out.

Well, tonight's our Bible School program at Beaver Valley. The men are tearing down the tables in the tent this afternoon and rearranging the benches church style. We're expecting lots of parents because they want to see their children perform in the program. Irvin will preach a short sermon at the end. I can't believe this is the last day. It's been a great two weeks. We're so glad you let us come. See you Sunday night. Love, Janet

P. S. The Morrows gave us our gifts this afternoon: the purple and white doily that he's been crocheting, and from her, a white wood rooster with pin cushion wings made from black and white material filled with sawdust. Around the base there's room for bobbins and spools of thread, and on top a little hole for scissors. She painted our names on one side and "Jesus Saves" in gold on the other. It really was nice of them to do that for us. I'll always treasure these gifts as a memory of the two wonderful weeks we spent here in New York.

A Mennonite church with a bell tower, formerly a
community church at West Union, New York.

# Serving in Yakusu
# Summer 1969

"**D**o you have plans for the summer?" Peter Sawatsky, our MCC director in Kinshasa, asked us over dinner at his home during one of our infrequent visits to the capital.

"We'd like to fly to Kisangani and teach at Yakusu in a five-week refresher course for elementary teachers," Charles said.

"You're free to do what you want after school's out: rest, vacation, travel," he said, looking us both in the eye. "Don't feel obligated to work."

"But we want to, Peter," I said, leaning forward in my chair. I'd grown up joining Mennonite short-term voluntary units. And this one seemed like an ideal situation for us – helping a needy group while getting to travel.

"Several weeks ago we met Doreen West – a British nurse at the Yakusu hospital," I continued, feeling I needed to convince him. "She said Monsieur Polidor, their Superintendent of Schools, is setting it up and recruiting teachers."

"Those guys missed so much of their own education during the rebellions out in the northeast," Charles said, laying down his fork. "The idea is for us to go and give them a little booster shot."

"Winnie Hadden, a British teacher in their Bible Training School, wants us to house-sit for her," I said, looking from Peter to his wife. I couldn't read their faces. "So we'd have free housing. And then last week we met Mike Krivo, a Harvard grad who just completed a term with the Peace Corps in Kenya. He traveled to Kisangani by train and then came down the Congo River."

"We could fly to Kisangani and return on the river boat!" Charles said, more enthusiastic than I'd expected him to be.

"Sounds like a good project if it's what you want. You put it together, we'll pay your travel and food," Peter smiled.

"If the rest of the summer turns out to be a flop, that flight alone will make it all worthwhile," Charles said as we walked across the tarmac at the Kisangani airport one week after exams had ended our second year of teaching at Ngombe Lutete.

Flying over a thousand miles from southwest Congo to the far northeast, we'd had a smooth flight and a clear view hour after hour of the vast green tropical forest covering most of the interior. Occasionally we saw a dirt road, a landing strip, or a stream of shimmering water, but for the most part, the forest was so thick it hid whole villages. As we headed north we watched the mighty Congo, at times roaring down deep narrow gorges, at other times spilling out over ten miles, looking more like an ocean than a river.

"I'm not worried," I said. "Whatever happens, we'll have a lot of stories to tell."

Monsieur Polidor, looking professional in his dark suit and tie, met us at the airport and drove us in his baby blue pickup to the guesthouse at the Congo Free University where several of our former students were enrolled. Over the next few days they took us to see the hydroelectric plant on the Tschopo River and to the famous Stanley Falls. There we saw Wagenia fishermen who'd lashed tall poles together and suspended baskets from them to catch fish that catapulted over the rapids into these wide-mouthed traps. We watched them mending nets and flinging them over the bubbling water. Scars from the recent civil war were evident everywhere – bullet-pocked walls at the university, cracked and taped plate glass windows along main street, deserted homes.

Monday morning Monsieur Polidor came by, his pickup loaded with people, barrels of diesel fuel, sacks of rice, bags of beans, and boxes of school supplies. They rearranged and squeezed in our piece of luggage and two book bags. "The road to Yakusu isn't paved," he said, "but being flat here we don't have pot holes like you do down south. So we can make good time, unless we have a problem at the ferry."

"We have to cross the river by ferry?" I asked.

"The Lindi River," he said, shifting into high gear and racing along the stoned road. And, as he'd feared, there was a problem. We sat and waited on the landing dock while the ferry operator finished his lunch on the other side. He sent word across with a young man in a canoe saying he had no fuel. After speaking rapidly in the local dialect and waving their arms for a few minutes, they made a deal. We handed over fuel and he took us across.

"Come in, come in." Mary and Doreen, the two British nurses who ran the Yakusu hospital welcomed us when Monsieur Polidor dropped us at their bungalow. "We'll get them settled in," they said, waving him off to unload supplies at the school.

"Won't you have a cup of tea before we take you next door to Winnie's house?" Mary said, picking up her teapot.

"We're so sorry to have to tell you," Doreen said, nervously arranging spoons and napkins on the table.

"Winnie's house was burglarized three nights ago. She lost most of her kitchen utensils, a kerosene burner, and quite a bit of canned food. But we've taken over some of our towels, a set of sheets, and some pots and pans we can get along without."

After we'd finished our tea Mary said she wanted to introduce us to Baelo, Winnie's houseboy. "He's at your disposal for the summer. He'll cook for you, shop for food, wash dishes, clean house, launder and iron clothes, carry in buckets of water from the cistern. Most afternoons he works in Winnie's garden. She has some nice pineapple plants, and I think he's trying to raise corn and beans this summer. He's being paid, so let him do his work."

I was delighted with Miss Hadden's quaint three-roomed wood-shingled cottage overlooking the river. A canopy of trees kept it relatively cool even though we were sitting on top of the equator. The living room reminded me of my great-grandmother's house: sparse plain furniture, a rocker, a tiny ancient pump-organ in one corner, but wonderful built-in shelves filled with English books that I couldn't wait to read, even by candle or kerosene lantern.

"Winnie says you should help yourself to anything you need," Mary said as she showed us around the kitchen. In the corner stood a tin tub where we'd get our evening baths after dipping water from the buckets Baelo carried in and heating it in a large iron teakettle on the propane stove.

"It's like our house at Ngombe Lutete," Charles said. "We have the same system for bathing and cooking."

"Only this little cottage is old-world, picturesque," I said. "I'm going to enjoy my summer here."

Monsieur Polidor called a staff meeting at the nearby freshly painted primary school in classrooms we'd be using for our refresher course. He began by introducing us to our Congolese colleagues, all teachers from Kisangani. Some of us would be teaching five days a week; others could come for only one or two days.

"We have 225 elementary teachers enrolled in our program," Monsieur Polidor said, looking at us, one after the other. "They'll attend classes every morning from 7:30 until 12:45, Monday through Saturday – six days a week. We divided them into five groups based on how much education they've had. Two groups have finished primary school; two have completed middle school; and the other has had at least one year of high school."

I looked at our colleagues, men our director had hand-picked; we all understood he wanted the best for these teacher-students. "You need to remember as you teach subjects you think they should already know," Monsieur Polidor continued, still looking us in the eye, a broad smile on his dark face. "They don't. They're here to learn. So start at the beginning. Teach them subject matter, but also teach them *how* to teach. Most of you will teach five classes each day, five days a week, but for only *five fleeting weeks*. So make every minute count."

As we left to find our classrooms, I said to Charles, "That means 45 to a class."

"Being teachers themselves, they should be well-disciplined," he said, scanning the purple ditto lists of names of men who'd grown up and lived their entire lives in a primitive tropical forest.

Looking at our schedules we discovered that besides Sunday we both had Tuesday off - a day to catch up with lesson plans, read, explore the mission post, or take a trip into Kisangani or the surrounding area.

On school mornings Baelo arrived just after we'd eaten our peanut butter and jelly sandwiches and had had a cup of tea in our little kitchen. He always asked what we wanted for lunch. And our answer was usually the same. "Fresh fish." In the local markets he bought chunks of mild Capitain, a huge fish that grows to six or eight feet long, that he'd prepare with a white sauce.

"Make some soup," I'd say. "We love your pureed soups." Baelo bought onions, leeks, carrots, cabbage, green beans, and spinach from the villagers who traveled up and down the river by pirogue, a type of canoe made of a hollowed-out tree trunk, selling whatever they had. And when we came home at one o'clock after teaching five classes, our lunch was ready and waiting on the stove, Baelo already gone for his noonday break.

"How'd your classes go this morning?" I'd ask as we enjoyed our rice and fish and vegetables.

"We're plugging along. They know so little French," Charles would say. "But I feel like I'm making some progress teaching basic grammar and phonetics, which is exactly what they need."

I taught the same geography lesson each day to five different classes. So I had only one preparation, based on the texts and curriculum I used in my yearlong high school classes. Since we'd received our subject assignments ahead of time, and knowing that children in Congolese primary schools learned African geography, I'd decided to concentrate on Egypt, Nigeria, and Congo. I'd brought my text, my atlas, and lots of notes and maps for them to copy and learn and in turn teach to their students.

"I think their biggest problem is poor French language skills," I agreed. "They often don't understand me but pretend they do because they're ashamed to admit it. Being forced to listen and respond in French for five hours every morning, six days a week, they're improving."

"But it's slow and they get discouraged," Charles said, taking another helping of fish in Baelo's tasty white sauce. "They need several years of education, not just this little refresher course."

We visited Doreen and Mary sometimes in the evenings. "Do you realize some of the men you're teaching came up river a hundred miles or more to attend this summer session?" Mary asked one evening as we drank tea around their dining room table.

"I know some of them had never seen electric lighting," Charles said. "It's only since arriving here that they've been able to comprehend that electricity's transported by means of metal wire." Of course our lights functioned off a generator on the station, and we had electricity for only several hours each evening. But it was still electricity.

"Most live in the forest, depending on the river for their livelihood. Some had never seen a white person before," Doreen added.

"Monsieur Polidor told us to stay away from the men's camp," I said. "I'm not sure why."

"They're living in our school dormitories," Mary explained. "Nothing was in them when they arrived. They brought their own mattress bags, which they stuffed with dried grass for their beds. The education department of the province is supposed to be feeding them, but food's expensive, so they only receive two meals a day."

"Two?"

"They have sweetened tea with a piece of bread for breakfast, and manioc and dried beans in the afternoon. A few have a little money to supplement this meager fare with a bit of fish or vegetables. But most are so poor their boat fare took all they had. We understand there's some unrest in the camp. And don't forget, these men have recently been through a civil war. Both sides are represented. So listen to Monsieur Polidor. He knows them better than we do."

We taught our classes, ate our lunch, and rested during the heat of the day until the talking drum hammered out its afternoon message. I found Baelo in the garden one afternoon and asked him what it said.

"Did you eat well? Have you had a nice rest?" he said. "And the children always shout, 'Yes.' Do you hear them?"

"Oh, yes, we hear them. We just didn't understand what they were saying."

Baelo explained the drum is made from a piece of hollowed-out log laid on its side. The top is carved to look like a giant rectangle piggy bank slot. One side of the slot is shaved quite thin and the other rather thick. When the drumstick, which is wrapped in rubber to give the appearance of a small mallet, hits the thin side, a high tone is heard. The other side produces a lower tone. Since these people speak Lokele, a tonal language, they can understand what the village drummer says. He drums to get them off to work in the morning, to stop at noon, to go back to work at two o'clock, and again to stop at five. This amazing invention has been in use for hundreds of years.

We spent our afternoons reading, grading papers, and preparing the next day's lessons. Toward evening when a small breeze came up we'd stroll through the station: along the river, around the two-story hospital, by the old brick Baptist church with its tall bell tower, and past the talking drum. But we always made sure we were back at our cottage before six. Living on the equator we'd been startled to experience daylight suddenly breaking at six o'clock in the morning and then disappearing just as quickly twelve hours later, with no lingering twilight.

One hot evening as we lay on our bed, reading by the open window, hoping for a small breeze, someone from the school came shouting up the walk to our house. Speaking in French he identified himself and said, "Don't open your doors. Keep everything locked, even the windows! Thieves are out tonight. Have you heard the drums?" We'd heard the drums but hadn't understood.

"Thieves have burglarized houses quite far away," he continued, "and then again in a village closer to us. As soon as it was discovered, the drummers began relaying the message up the river so that everyone would be warned." We thanked him and he hurried away, not wanting to dawdle in the dark.

"Drums work well in place of telephones," I said.

"Maybe better," Charles laughed. "The burglars can hear the message too!"

On Thursday afternoons when we heard the toot of the weekly riverboat's horn, we would run to the banks of the Congo and watch it glide by on its descent to Kinshasa. This boat actually consists of two barges and the riverboat all fastened together. Third class on a flat open-to-the-stars barge passes first, followed by the brown second-class covered two-story barge, and pushing them both is the first class white riverboat, which reminded me of the Mississippi steamboats Mark Twain immortalized. We stood with the village children and waved and thought about what an exhilarating experience it would be to ride home on that boat.

On a trip to Kisangani with Monsieur Polidor one Tuesday we stopped by the riverboat office, booked and paid for a cabin in first class – the only private rooms with linens, a semi-private bath, and meals in the dining room.

Our summer course was coming to a close. I'd taught over a hundred hours of African geography to my respectful, hardworking teacher-students. We prepared and administered exams, typical European style essay questions written on the chalkboard. Our students were expected to rewrite word for word the notes they'd taken in class and memorized. Being teachers themselves, they were under a lot of pressure to do well. Their hard work was apparent as we corrected and graded compositions. We were pleased to have contributed new materials and more knowledge for them to take back into the bush to their own students.

The last several days in Yakusu were bittersweet. We had come to love the area and the people we'd worked with for almost six weeks, and now it was time to face reality: we'd never see them again. We walked around the station saying goodbye to the drummer and the village children, and snapping photos of what we wanted most to remember: our students in group pictures, the colorful open primary school buildings where classes had met, the two-story brick hospital on the riverbank, Mary and Doreen in their nurses' uniforms, the riverboat, Baelo working in Winnie's garden, the pastor, the market, our little house.

A week later we got off the riverboat in Kinshasa and caught one of Mobutu's Mercedes taxis to Mr. and Mrs. Sawatsky's house. "Well, the long lost travelers! Welcome home," Peter called out when we knocked on their door. "Come in, come in. How was your trip?"

"The best," we both said, setting our suitcase and book bags inside the door.

"Sit down and tell us," his wife said, offering large glasses of iced tea.

"I don't know where to begin," I said. "We've just spent five days gliding down the second largest river in the world, through a primeval forest, watching boat people emerge from dense jungle to swarm us with wares."

"We saw and heard talking drums," Charles added.

"Once we accompanied a British nurse on her weekly trek out into villages to hold baby clinics."

"Our houseboy and his friends rowed us across the Congo River in a dugout canoe."

"That's where we visited the leprosarium village where Audrey Hepburn starred in 'The Nun's Story' about twelve years ago," I finished.

"We met officials from Kisangani and Orientale Province."

"We learned first hand about the rebellions – from British nurses who lived through them and returned to continue their work."

"And the school," Peter said. "Was it a success?"

"Can you imagine watching the faces of men who'd never experienced electric lighting, seeing for the first time how it works?" Charles asked.

"Or teaching 225 teachers with only a few years of education themselves, who'd come from jungle villages and had never seen an American?" I added.

"They studied and worked hard; but I'm sure we learned far more than they did."

"We can never thank you enough for allowing us to go."

"It's my pleasure to watch good things work out," Peter smiled. "And in this case your enthusiasm and preparation paid off for everyone."

A talking drum, used as a means of communication in northeastern Congo.

# Reading *Martyrs Mirror*
# 1950 - 1965

July 6, 1965, my mother had written on the flyleaf. I was getting married and moving to California. Mom was worried about me, and not just because I was moving so far from home. I was marrying outside our denomination and she feared I'd leave my faith. She gave me an English edition of Van Braught's 1660 *Martyrs Mirror* and told me to read it and not forget.

Mom had always kept her *Martyrs Mirror* on a little end table by the sofa. She spent many of her spare minutes pouring over that book, reading the summaries of martyrs beginning with Jesus and ending in the seventeenth century. Growing up, I'd drag that bulky 1,157-page book down onto the living room floor. Too small to hold such a big book on my lap, I'd sit over it, reading scraps here and there, mostly looking at the gruesome lithographs. Nasty men nailing Jesus Christ our Redeemer to a cross, hammers pounding huge spikes into his feet and hands. Disciples who'd been willing to die for their Lord: Peter crucified upside down because he didn't think he was worthy to hang as his Savior had; Thomas being cast into a fiery oven; Luke hanging from an olive tree branch.

But the pictures that petrified me most were those of early Christians: Antipas, lying on his back inside a red-hot brass ox. A little door on the side was open and I could see his hands folded in prayer as fire raged beneath. I knew I would have recanted. How could I have been strong enough to bear the pain and agony of that scorching metal and smoke choking my lungs? Vitalus was buried alive in a pit, three men throwing shovelfuls of rock and dirt on his head. He would eventually suffocate.

From time to time I'd jump up and run to the kitchen. "How could they be so cruel?" I asked my mother. "How could they stomach making people suffer like that?"

"Because they didn't love Jesus," my mother said, sitting me down at the kitchen table. "They were still following the Old Testament teaching of an eye for an eye and a tooth for a tooth. Jesus said we must love our enemies."

"Why didn't they just believe in their hearts and not say anything if everyone was going to be so mean to them?"

"We have to declare our faith and do something or it's meaningless," Mom said.

Phocas was thrown into a burning limekiln; Ignatius stood in the center of a deep arena, two lions racing toward him, soldiers and civilians observing and waiting on the wall above.

"How could they bear to watch someone get eaten by lions?" I asked.

"Because they didn't love Jesus, their hearts were hardened," Mom said, pushing a stick of wood in the cookstove.

Horrible as his execution seemed, Paul got off pretty easy compared to the other apostles, I thought. He knelt in prayer and someone from behind whacked off his head. I couldn't endure the thought of the pain Mark and Barnabas must have suffered. Both were shown being dragged along on the ground, a rope around their necks, sharp metal crooks digging into their thighs. And then they were burned at the stake.

"I can understand that right after Jesus died his enemies hated him and they didn't want anyone following Him," I told my mother as I read further into her *Martyrs Mirror*. "But why would people, 1,000 years later, still torture and kill others, saying their kind of Christianity wasn't the right way?"

"Because they didn't truly love Jesus," she'd say, looking up from sewing a dress or rolling out pie dough.

As I paged through Mom's book, I came across a picture of a giant bonfire, soldiers and nobles standing back from the heat. The accompanying text was ghastly. Fourteen Anabaptists were being burned together in Orleans, France, accused of having spoken evil against God and holy baptism. At their interrogation they admitted they'd been baptized as adults. The king thought they'd quickly change their minds if he ordered them burned alive. But they refused to recant. Later, the rest of their group was found and executed in the same way.

I found story after story through 16 centuries, names of people who, after reading the New Testament, believed they needed to be baptized on confession of faith. And they were slaughtered.

"Mom, you'll never believe what I found out," I shouted one afternoon, running out to the clothesline where my mother was hanging up socks. "A man told on them!"

"Told on who?" my mother asked, pulling clothespins from her mouth.

"They called him a Judas. He went to the priests and said if they'd pay him he'd find the new believers and tell on them. He went around crying and acting like he wanted to get converted. So finally a member took him to an Anabaptist secret gathering. They prayed with him and he pretended to repent. Then he told them to wait there and he'd go get his wife and child like the jailor did when Paul was in prison. But instead, this Judas went to the judge. He sent magistrates and soldiers with sticks and swords and they arrested the whole group. Isn't that dreadful? How could he do it?" I asked, throwing my hands out in despair.

"The Bible says that kind of person's punishment in hell will be even worse," Mom tried to console me.

During our six-week Winter Bible School sessions I learned more about the Anabaptists, the founders of our Mennonite church. Our teacher asked us each to report on a different martyr from the 1500s. I found them in *Martyrs Mirror*, pages and pages of interrogations and biographies. I wanted to write about a woman.

"Don't you fear dying?" the interrogators asked a Dutch woman named Wenyken. She said Christ had promised anyone who followed Him would never see death, like the rich man in hell. So no, she was not afraid. I admired her bravery, but knew I'd have dissolved in tears.

I found it difficult to choose just one of those courageous women: Anna of Freiburg, Christina Tolinger, Barbara of Thiers, Agatha Kampner and her sister Elizabeth. George Blaurock, who himself was later drowned, had secretly baptized most of them.

In the end I chose Elizabeth, a single lady. When the authorities came to take her away they found her Latin Testament and accused her of being a teacher. Tears streamed down my cheeks as I read their accusatory questions and this gentle woman's answers. Torturers applied screws to her thumbs and shins, telling her to confess who'd baptized her and who the other believers were. When she prayed aloud for God to take away the pain, she fainted. In 1549 she was drowned, never having recanted her confession of faith or revealed any other believers' names.

I rested in the thought that children didn't undergo torture, until I came upon a drawing of two young girls being led to their execution. Reading the text I learned they'd been baptized and faithfully followed Christ's teachings. Girls my age! Thrown in prison, severely tortured, and eventually, because they refused to renounce their faith, put to death.

I read pages and pages of letters from imprisoned believers to their church families, defending their faith to the end. One 53-year-old lady, who couldn't read or write, was imprisoned when a neighbor turned her in. She was charged with taking up with Mennonists, followers of Menno Simons, the founder of our own denomination! She praised her Lord to her bitter death.

Believers' poems, hymns, and prayers written from prison, so filled with encouragement and hope, unsettled me. I prayed that persecution wouldn't come to America in my lifetime, cringing at the thought of heartless guards and interrogators watching me writhe in pain beside them.

I worried when we heard about Christians being persecuted in communist Russia and China. "Do you think they'll ever do that here in our country?" I asked my parents.

"You never know," Daddy said. "We need to thank God every day that we live in a free country." I often heard him pray that we'd be found faithful.

"Guess what," my sister said one Sunday morning on the way home from church. "Christmas Carol Kauffman wrote a new book." We'd already read two, *Light From Heaven* and *Unspoken Love*, serialized in our "Youths' Christian Companion." Anita and I saved our Sunday school papers in boxes in the attic, stacked in order by date for rereading.

"What's the name of it?" I asked, hoping for a story about another Mennonite family.

"*Not Regina.*"

"Regina?" I asked, knitting my eyebrows. "What's it about?"

"A 17-year-old girl who lived in Switzerland in 1525. You know, when the Anabaptists were being persecuted."

"Is it a fiction story?"

"Yes, about Regina, her boyfriend, and her family, but set in the time of religious persecutions."

"What happens to them?"

"We'll have to read the book; that's all my teacher told us."

And read we did. With the first installment we began devouring it chapter by chapter, Sunday after Sunday. Thirty-five weeks later, after working as a maid in a Christian pastor's household, watching Anabaptists being herded to prison, and worrying about her two brothers, tender-hearted Regina was finally reunited with her family as they made their way to safety in Austria. I was relieved to learn Regina hadn't been executed like so many Anabaptists of her day.

My mother shouldn't have worried about me. I knew I wouldn't leave my faith. As I moved on I reevaluated what I'd been taught growing up. Like the martyrs, reading and studying the Bible became more important to me than the church's Confession of Faith. I'd never forget their struggle for religious freedom and would continue to the end, studying, growing, and evolving spiritually.

Ignatius Devoured by Wild Beasts

One of the drawings I scrutinized as a child in Van Braght's *Martyrs Mirror.* Used by permission from Herald Press, Scottdale, PA 15683.

# Learning to Cope
# 1969-1972

Dear Mom and Daddy,

Our summer vacation has come to a close and we're back at Ngombe Lutete getting ready for a new school term, which begins next week. It's hard to believe just two weeks ago we were about 1,000 miles from here in the northeastern jungles at Yakusu. That was a great vacation even though I taught five hours of geography, five days a week. We're both glad we had the chance to help in that project.

I still find it hard to visualize rebels coming out of their jungle villages into that peaceful spot terrorizing, maiming, and killing. But they did – twice. After independence from the Belgians in 1960 the entire country suffered several years of political chaos, each tribal group wanting its own leader to be president. But the northeast with its Simba rebels was particularly hard hit.

Doreen West, a kind soft-spoken British nurse at Yakusu, bears the scars of those wars. As an angry young Simba raised his machete to strike, Doreen threw up her arms to protect her head, breaking the blow with her forearm. The cut was horrific, completely severing both bones.

She fell and lay still; he didn't hit her again.

"I often wondered why I was spared when so many others died," she said softly as we chatted one evening. "The Yakusu people say they know who struck me, and that he's been here to the hospital for treatment. But I don't want to know who he is."

It took a year of surgery, treatments, and therapy in England for her to heal. She has the use of her arm, but the disfigurement is a daily reminder of those ugly times. The rebellious youths were flushed out of the jungles and assimilated back into society, and Mulele, their leader, was executed. I don't think I could have come back, but Doreen says you can't let a few wicked people destroy the church's work.

Do you remember hearing about Dr. Paul Carlson? While we were living at Yakusu I found a book in our living room library about him: *Doctor among Congo Rebels* by Dr. Helen Roseavere. Carlson was a well-paid medical doctor from Los Angeles who gave up his practice and brought his wife and two children to Congo in the fall of 1963. He worked in Wasolo, about 200 miles north of where we were in Yakusu, serving 100,000 people in an 80-bed hospital.

Like us, he and his wife struggled with poor vehicles and primitive living conditions. Their house roof poured their drinking water into barrels when it rained, and in the dry season they brought it from the river in their truck. He was a kind gentle man, greatly loved by the Congolese he served. They called him "Monganga Paul." That's Swahili for "my Dr. Paul." When the Simbas threatened the staff at their hospital he sent his wife and children across the border into Central African Republic, but he stayed on in Wasolo caring for his patients.

Several weeks later the rebels brought him to Kisangani and threatened him with death, singling him out as an American spy after they found his radio. That November day in 1964, he and other foreign hostages were herded into the streets. Ironically, out of a group of more than 150, Dr. Carlson and the 30 others who died had not been targeted; they were shot by chance. We saw the wall he was trying to scale in Lumumba Square when a bullet hit him. Dr. Carlson willingly gave his life. He said more people have died for Christ in this century than in those we think of as the days of martyrs. I admire him, but I don't think I could stay if trouble like that came to our area of Congo. Love, Janet

April 16, 1970

Dear Mom and Daddy,

We've been enjoying huge yellow grapefruit from the orchard in Ian's back garden. They make the most luscious juice and I don't seem to be allergic to them, not like the abundant sweet mangoes that cause my face to swell. My eyes were almost closed one morning when I woke up. Irene, a British pharmacist living here on our mission post with her teacher husband, immediately asked if I'd eaten a mango. She said an allergic reaction to the mango skin isn't unusual for foreigners. After a round of Benadryl I was fine. On her advice I've been having my houseboy peel and boil mangos while I'm at school. Mashed and sugared, they're better than applesauce!

Charles' worst problem has been with malaria. I haven't written much about it because I didn't want to worry you. We have screens and pink house lizards scouring them as well as the walls and ceilings for mosquitoes. But those aggressive pests are waiting, ready to attack whenever we step out the door. We've both faithfully taken our weekly 500 milligrams of Nivaquine, a prophylaxis that prevents malaria.

The medication works wonders for me. But Charles, now that's another story. Even though he'd started taking 700 milligrams, every few weeks he'd be down in bed with backache, headache, and violent shaking chills followed by raging fever and sweats until the bed was drenched. One weekend it was so bad I had to hang sheets over dining room chairs to dry so I could put them back on the bed or I'd have run out! He took the extra-prescribed dosage whenever he felt an attack coming on, but then he'd get nauseous and vomit. The worst part was the exasperating hiccoughs, often lasting two days.

During our last Christmas holiday a British nurse was visiting some missionaries on our post when a malaria spell hit Charles. She came over and I explained his problem. Her answer was that with his "cure" – an extra high dosage of Nivaquine – he should always take a sedative. She found a tranquilizer in our local dispensary and it worked! No nausea, no hiccoughs! She also suggested he switch to Chloraquine, a different prophylaxis that's readily available in pharmacies here. And he's experienced no malaria for the past four months. We're keeping our fingers crossed.
Love, Janet

April 22, 1971

Dear Mom and Daddy,

When we corrected state exams two years ago we got to know some of the Belgian teachers at the Catholic school at Ngombe Matadi, about four miles away. The majority of their teachers are priests and the rest are all single guys, except for one family, Mr. and Mrs. Haveaux and their four children. Mr. Haveaux told us he gets double pay from the Belgian government for coming out here and teaching, and that he couldn't afford to go home just yet. They invited us to their house once for supper. The children were all in bed and we had an enjoyable evening, chatting and eating cheese fondue.

Mrs. Haveaux became quite depressed after their fourth child was born. One afternoon her husband came to our house and told me he needed to take her to Kinshasa for a break from the children, to get some rest. He had sitters for the two older boys, but would I keep Benoît and the five-month-old baby girl on the upcoming long holiday weekend? Thursday he brought them to me with bottles, formula, clothes, and diapers he'd dumped in a bag. The baby cooed in her folding bed and 18-month-old Benoît watched wide-eyed as their dad drove away.

What a weekend! It was like running a French nursery, having twins in diapers! But they were surprisingly good. Charles held one while I changed the other. He read to Benoît, and we took them for walks. I thought the village women would faint when they saw us pushing two babies around the post in a stroller. We had fun playing nursery and Madame came back from Kinshasa refreshed, able to cope again. Being out here with no extended family is difficult, but I can't imagine it with four children. The foreigners in our missions help each other, but it's still not like real family.

A couple of months ago we stopped by the Haveaux's house. In the course of our conversation the subject of malaria came up. Charles told them about his struggle and that Chloraquine was no longer helping. "Oh, I wish I'd known," Mr. Haveaux said. "I had the same problem. I tried everything. But since I started using Resochine several years ago I've never had another attack."

"What's the difference?" Charles asked.

"They're all the same, but people react differently to them. Doctors don't understand it when I tell them, but I know it works for me." He gave us several packets to get started and Charles is now hooked. He's not had one malaria spell since November! Love, Janet

May 10, 1972

Dear Mom and Daddy,

Last Monday, Ron showed up on our doorstep just about

lunchtime. Ron teaches in the Kimbanguist secondary school at Nkamba about 20 miles up the road from us. We seldom see him or their other MCC teacher because they get rides to Kinshasa on a transport truck that goes straight through. So I was surprised when he appeared. He stumbled through our back yard and fell into a chair on the porch.

"I'm sick," Ron said. "I have fever and I ache all over."

"Classic symptoms of hepatitis," I told him. "It's currently ravaging the missionary community down in Kinshasa. But I'm five months pregnant and can't risk bringing you in the house. We'll work out something if you can just sit tight for a bit." Charles raced off on his bike to see if Ron could get a ride on our school truck, which just happened to be leaving for town in a few minutes.

Mpanzu brought him a glass of cool water and a stool to prop his feet. I knew Ron might have a bad case of malaria. That I could deal with, but not the dreaded hepatitis. We made arrangements to have him taken the 75 miles to IME. In the end it turned out he had cerebral malaria, so it's good he went straight to the hospital because they were able to treat him and he's now on the mend.

Charles and I've talked a lot about the British missionaries lying in their graves halfway down the hill to the Tombe River. They sailed out here in the 1800s knowing they'd probably die. But they came anyway, many bringing their food and equipment in a coffin. When they got malaria they used quinine, which wasn't always effective. Lesley told me Sidney Comber, a medical doctor, was the younger brother of Henry who traveled, well into his old age, up and down the Congo River on a boat called "Peace." I guess Sidney had planned to heal the people his brother evangelized but he died before he had a chance.

Charles and I probably wouldn't have had the courage to remain in Africa if it hadn't been for modern medications, the nearby hospital with an international staff, and the airport within a few hours' drive. Nowadays it's not usually foreigners who succumb. Congolese have a life span of slightly over 40 because of the high infant mortality rate and the many deaths among children and adults who don't have access to proper medical care.

I want to tell you about Tata Levi. I can't get him out of my mind. This clever kind old man lived in a neighboring village, about a 30-minute walk from our station. Whenever we sent for him he'd come and paint at our school – classrooms or faculty housing. I helped him several times during the summer when we were getting duplexes ready for new teachers. He understood very little French so we didn't talk much.

But Tata Levi could sing. He would start a hymn in Kikongo and I'd sing alto in English. Or sometimes I'd begin in English and he'd recognize the song and harmonize using Kikongo words. Tata Levi came down with dysentery, a common ailment caused by contaminated water or food. After several days when he'd become so weak he couldn't walk his son-in-law contacted us. Domingo fetched him in the truck, but it was too late. He died in our dispensary six days after he fell ill. I'll miss this gentle Christian man and his wonderful singing voice.

Whenever Charles and I go down the hill past the cemetery we stop for a few minutes. I mourn mothers who didn't live to see their child, toddlers who missed the chance to grow up, and young people like Kalu who died of meningitis before they could finish their education.

When we gaze at the ten marked graves of missionaries in that barren clay, Charles always shakes his head and says, "So young and forgotten." I've taken photos of their cross-shaped iron monuments. I need to remember the sacrifices they made helping others in the name of Christ. Love, Janet

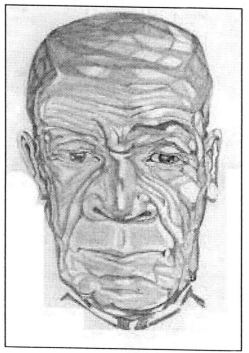

Tata Levi, my singing and painting partner,
drawn in Congo in 1972.

An iron cross marker, reminding us of a life given in
service to God.

## Ten Graves

Ten graves lie forsaken in red clay
outlined with river rocks
lugged up the hill.

Ten graves hold crumbling bones
representing dreams renounced
at fiery revivals in England.

Sidney Alfred Comber, age 27,
tore himself from his mother's embrace
left the comforts of England,
sailed across stormy seas
certain he'd never return
from a land ridden with
parasites, vipers, scorpions,
foul water, and famine.
On December 24, 1884,
Sidney returned his spirit to God.

Andrew H. Cruickshank, age 25,
struggled to learn Kikongo,
suffered malaria and dysentery,
eluded cobras and mambas,
walked for days on end
through torrential rains or burning sun
preaching Christ's power over fear,
evangelizing villages.
On March 27, 1885,
Andrew relinquished his life to God.

Ten graves testify of faith
buried beneath rusting iron monuments
still standing strong
shouting across a century the
assurance of salvation in Jesus.

# Epilogue

Nowadays in most Lancaster Mennonite Conference churches few besides the elderly wear coverings, capes, or plain suits, but enthusiasm for being a doer in the name of Christ goes on. Mennonite Central Committee still relies on Christian volunteers to work overseas. Today not only Mennonites but other peace-loving people as well support MCC's varied programs of providing food, water, shelter, medical care, education, job training, and peace-makers to needy people around the world. MCC maintains an office in Kinshasa and, now in its 43$^{rd}$ year in Congo, continues focusing on women and youth with self-help programs, school kits for children, peacemaking training, and medical school scholarships.

About a year after Kutubila was incarcerated for helping Ntadingi get an abortion, we visited him in the Matadi prison. Broken and contrite, he was trying to get through endless weeks, just sitting day after day in a cell. He was eventually released and returned to his country across the river. Kutubila graduated from Marien Ngouabi University in Brazzaville and has taught on staff. Nobody has been able to give me news of Ntadingi.

I've often been asked why, after teaching in Congo for

six years, we suddenly pulled up stakes and came home. During the last two years we were there, Mobutu, the country's self-proclaimed president for life, a non-practicing Roman Catholic, tightened his grip on the government. Using the country's finances for his own gain, he intruded on his people's everyday lives in the name of African authenticity. Religious holidays such as Easter and Christmas were outlawed, women were forbidden to wear western dress, Congolese were forced to give up their Christian names and adopt African ones. Even the name of the country was changed to Zaïre. Indian, Portuguese, and Greek businessmen lost their shops to nationalization; anti-foreigner sentiment was not discouraged.

During the last few months of our 1973 school year a Belgian priest at the Catholic institute four miles from us was wounded in a shooting, and a Belgian couple was murdered in Mbanza-Ngungu just 35 miles down the road. Our post was placed under a dusk to dawn curfew with several soldiers constantly patrolling the campus. Charles and I felt an urgency to take our tiny son home to America.

But we never lost our affection for the villagers, the staff, and our students. Over the past 30 years I have kept in contact with many of our ex-colleagues through emails and exchanging letters at Christmas. In 1992 Charles and I spent a super day with ten of those former missionaries in London when we took a group of high school students to Europe. Margot and her husband Augustin Bafende came to the States in 2000 and stopped at our home in Virginia for a wonderful reunion.

From time to time I receive messages from former students who need money for worthy projects. Due to unrest and prolonged civil war in Congo, hardly any schools are presently operating. Some children whose parents band together and hire teachers are getting an education. Few foreigners are willing to work or invest in this devastated country today. The former British Baptist post at Ngombe Lutete has gone back to the bush, the houses and other buildings are falling into ruin.

In spite of these reports I do not feel we wasted our time in Congo. During those six years we touched many lives and believe we made a difference. But what we ourselves learned and the love we received from our Congolese friends far outweighs anything we ever gave.

# Author's Notes and Acknowledgments

In the late 1980s, my mother-in-law Rosemary Patton gave me a scrapbook containing the weekly aerogrammes I'd written to her from Africa, all arranged in chronological order. Even though she'd campaigned vigorously to persuade us first not to go and later to bring us home, she preserved my letters. After retiring from teaching in 1998 I began reading them. The details in those almost three hundred letters stirred in me a desire to share my stories. While reviewing our sizable slide and photo collections, Charles and I agreed to collaborate on this memoir. We are grateful to the many people who helped.

Charlotte Morgan, my gentle yet challenging creative writing teacher at Dabney S. Lancaster Community College, gave me the guidance and confidence I needed to begin, continue, and finally complete the project. I am indebted to her for her insightful critiquing.

Two colleagues from our African school, Margot Stockwell Bafende, still living in Congo, and Lesley Fuller, who makes periodic trips back to help with women's work, gave me practical assistance with Kikongo words, identified people and places in photos I sent them, and provided important details I'd forgotten.

During trips to Pennsylvania I interviewed pastors, teachers, friends, and family members; I visited churches and schools. At the Mennonite Historical Society in Lancaster, Pennsylvania, and the Menno Simons Historical Library at Eastern Mennonite University I uncovered a storehouse of minutiae in magazines, old diaries, clippings, photos, and memorabilia. I searched the attic of our family's old home place and discovered letters, pictures, records, and mementos from my Mennonite past, which I used to refresh my childhood and teen memories.

Before her death in 2001 I was fortunate to be able to reminisce with my mother Mildred Runion and ask her many questions about our early years as Mennonites. Her excitement about this project and the details she supplied were invaluable.

I owe special thanks to my aunt Charlotte Rissler and my older sister Anita Ovalle who listened, suggested, and jogged my memory, bringing back details of stories stored in far corners of my brain. I am particularly grateful to my sister Ruth Runion Slear, a research librarian at Penn State University, who answered my endless questions. She supplied me with data and facts whenever I asked, or steered me in the right direction for needed information.

I'm indebted to Sara Gehman and her niece Evelyn Hinkle who filled in details about the funeral at Fairview Mennonite Church. Without Mary Stauffer's help, I would not have been able to write Ben's and her story. Ruth Frey and Alma Snavely provided photos and facts about years of sewing circles. Charles and Etta Brubaker answered questions about Stauffers church. Kathie Clarke, Ellen Cox, Dorcas Williams, Suzanne Stratmann, and my sister Anita proofread and critiqued my work. Earlene Horn advised me and helped with computer problems. To them all I owe a debt of gratitude.

And last but not least, I want to thank my dear husband Charles, not only for his drawings, but also for listening to me read my essays aloud, making helpful suggestions, encouraging me when I faltered, and for his truly amazing patience with me.

Printed in the United States
18236LVS00003B/43-255

## About The Author

Janet Runion Patton, a retired French and Spanish teacher, holds a B.A. from Eastern Mennonite University. She has worked on the staff of *LUMINA*, the literary magazine of Dabney S. Lancaster Community College, in which her poetry and creative non-fiction have been published. Her essay "Ordination by Lot, J. Frank Zeager, Wednesday, July 28, 1954" appeared in the July 2001 issue of *Pennsylvania Mennonite Heritage*. For the past five years she has been writing a bi-monthly column, "Retirement Trails," for the *Virginian Review*, a daily newspaper serving three counties. In 2002 she published 19 of her essays in a collection about her travels, *Retirement Trails, Southwest Virginia*. Her most recent writings include memoirs about teaching English at a Bible institute in Korea. Patton and her husband have lived in the Alleghany Highlands of southwest Virginia for 30 years.

## About The Artist

Charles A. Patton, a retired elementary school principal, holds an Ed. M. from the University of Virginia. A self-taught artist, he began drawing pencil portraits while teaching in Congo in the early 1970s. After his retirement in 1998 he subscribed to several art magazines, studied art books, and began drawing in pen and ink. He studied briefly under Jeanne Shepherd in Clifton Forge and since then has produced numerous watercolors, preferring to paint flowers, old buildings, and trees. Patton has won first-place and best-in-show awards for his pencil drawings in Virginia regional art exhibits.